This is His House and These are His Rules

Third Edition

Nicholas M. Cuono Sr.

Copyright 2024, Nicholas M. Cuono Sr.
Cover by Al Esper Graphic Design
Interior layout by The Persnickety Proofreader

Scripture quotes from the *New American Bible, Saint Joseph Edition* and the *King James Bible*.

For information regarding reprint permission, contact the author at: muchoboozo@aol.com.

Cuono, Nicholas M. Sr.
This is His House and These Are His Rules

Print ISBN: 979-8-9901449-0-3
Ebook ISBN: 979-8-9901449-1-0
Library of Congress Control Number: 2017937679

Printed in the U.S.A.
Third American Edition, February 2024

Dedication

For my entire life, sinful as it has been, I've tried to dedicate most of what I do to the repentance of my sinful ways. I often fail and sin again, but never intentionally. I have experienced the wonders, beauties, and miracles in this life; and I have always known that these treasures were not without cost.

I prayed with all my heart and soul for the strength to get this entire message right because this message is His will.

I dedicate this book to all of humanity. My prayers are for my neighbors so that you, too, may find the path to God's deepest love, as I have in my life.

This is
His House
and These are
His Rules

Introduction

In June of '98, I had my second major back operation. The complications that resulted from this procedure were life-threatening: colon infection, intestinal tract infection, bowel infection, and a major blood clot. I was truly at death's door.

I was prepared to pass, and as I was about to pass into the next life, I prayed to an archangel of God by the name Raphael. I simply asked Him to heal me or to assist me in my passing. Raphael granted me healing though the grace of God because God wasn't ready for me to enter those doors that would lead to my physical death just yet...

Soon after that event, I had the strongest desire... a message... to me to complete the mission He had previously assigned me. The mission was to write the book that I had started several years before.

I did, but apparently not to His satisfaction. So, on Ash Wednesday in 2004, I got a second "request" while attending Mass in the Church of Our Lady of Mt. Carmel to rewrite this book because it was not accurate. Write what He tells **you** to write and do what he tells **you** to do concerning this work, for God is our Master, and sharing this message with humanity is one of your missions. Be cautious, be aware, and pray for guidance. Everything you need will come to you when the time is right.

Again in 2009, God... through His messenger instructed me to redo this book. I finished that manuscript on Good Friday, 2009. I believed the writing was complete.

But after five more years of prayer and three more attempts to get this right, God, through His messengers has again delivered instruction me to edit this book in this fashion. This is the seventh and final draft of this book; this is the one I wrote for you.

Today is November 22, 2014, and I know that I was trying too hard, but that is not the mission behind this writing. This writing is from my soul through the grace and power of the Almighty. It is one of the things I have been sent here to do.

God chooses the sinner to accomplish his work, and I am indeed qualified to write this manual since I am one of His greatest accomplishments when it comes to that category.

I have prayed fervently and asked God Almighty to guide my hands through this final edit. I also wanted to fulfill this burning desire to do what God and His friends have been whispering in my ear to do for so many years.

The concept of this book first started in the early nineties as an instructional tool for me and close friend. We were both young and a bit uncertain of the reason, the purpose, and the actuality of our existence. At that time in my life, I thought I had an intimate relationship with God… as I do today; however, I believe since I was much younger, I had a great deal of lack of control over outside influences and messages delivered to my mind. In other words, the devil seemed to have a greater hold on my soul than I could control and was whispering in my ears.

The original manuscript was perhaps 25 pages and was penned in a collaborated effort. It provided insight—some good, some not so good, but the first attempt did accomplish the intended end, which was to strengthen our faith. It also convinced me that I had to write a book on this topic… the rules.

My second attempt which was about five years later and was good, but I tried to make the book an "interesting" read. It was a decent read, but it wasn't right—too much fluff… and way too long.

On the third attempt, I removed some of the "fluff," but I still was attempting to "fill" the book. My vanity, I suppose, caused me to think I had to impress someone with a 500+ page book.

The fourth was also a decent manuscript but wasn't quite right, so the fifth and sixth were focused on getting this easier to read. While doing the sixth, some other messages were delivered. I asked God to let me finish that edit and I would make the changes on the seventh. He must have heard that request and granted it without question.

That said, this may not be as long as most books, but, I am hopeful it will be enough to accomplish His work.

But before we start, I want to tell you about the very first time…

Before I tell you this, let us be very clear on one thing: There is a God. I know Him intimately and without a doubt, He has spoken to me directly but only on just a few occasions. I'm going to tell you about the very first time I heard Him speak directly to me. This is the day when I lost any doubt whatsoever that there is a God.

At the time in my life, I was working for a general contractor as a "steel guy." I did fabrication of structural steel and other tasks related to metal repair. I was pretty decent at my trade, so one day, one of the owners named John asked me to fabricate railings for the local parish church, a church where I was a member and had attended when I actually decided to attend Mass. I was baptized, confirmed, and married in this church. I also attended the Catholic school within its authority from kindergarten until graduation of high school.

I agreed to do the job because I really didn't think I had a choice. I can tell you with certainty I didn't know how to do this nor did I want to do this incorrectly for fear of my job. I was young, married with two children, my wife didn't work, and I was the sole source of support of our household — what pressure!

The morning I was to start, I walked into back of the church. I'm sure I never said a prayer that was so genuine to that point in my life. I stood at the back entrance, simply bowed my head, and said something like this: "Lord, I have no clue how to do this. I need your help. I don't know what you want, and I don't know how to do this. Please help me."

The moment I walked out of the church, I knew exactly what to do and how to do it; it was such an overpowering feeling, and at that moment in time, I knew without any doubt that God Almighty existed. I knew without any doubt He heard me and was going to guide me while fabricating these rails.

When they were complete, they were perfect. They are still there to this day. I paint them once a year, just before the yearly celebration to honor Our Lady of Mt. Carmel, and they are still perfect.

I hope you enjoy…

Chapter 1

Let's Start at the Beginning…

There are two basic theories of how this universe and this planet, as we know it, started. The first of which is the biblical version. The second is the theory of the "big bang."

There are many documents that assert the correct era of the creation. Some early historians made educated guesses, which included 3761, 3928, and 4456 BCE. In fact, an actual date was set for this event. It is October 22, 4004, BCE. This date is attributed to a Christian scientist and researcher named Bishop Ussher. This date was the generally accepted actual creation date until the early eighteenth century.

Then it finally became obvious to most researchers that geological processes were excessively slow, and it was not possible for the Earth to be only around six thousand years old, new theories began to be formulated. Scientists of the day were becoming more and more fascinated with this research. In the year 1859, Darwin published *The Origin of Species by Means of Natural Selection*, and in 1871, he published *The Descent of Man, and Selection in Relation to Sex*.

Prior to these released publications, many philosophers and early scientists had speculated on the formation of the "heavens." Aristotle, Copernicus, Johannes Kepler, and Sir Isaac Newton—all had theories and writings on the subject, but none had been so bold to question the creation of man as presented in biblical text. However, two publications by Darwin were released and they were so compelling that the scientific community then began its quest and commitment to explore the heavens.

Edwin Hubble and Vesto Slipher began using the world's largest known telescope that they had designed in the early 1900s to search space and find its limits. With this, the most powerful telescope then known to mankind in that era, they could peer deeper into the heavens and into the vastness of the universe. Using other research results and mathematics, their initial research results lead to the conclusion that the universe was about two billion years old.

There was another pair of scientists in that era. Their names were George Lemaitre and George Gamow. These two scientists are credited with the big bang theory. They released the completed research in 1948. When the theory was first introduced, it was called "hypothesis of the primeval atom." However, it was given the accepted name by a radio show host after a snide comment intended to be derogatory. Thus, the universe is two billion years old.

Let's take a look at what the first big bang theory said. Two billion years ago, in the vastness, the void, there was a mind-bogglingly dense atom, and it contained the entire universe. This atom was given a name by the two renowned scientists. They called this dense sphere the "ylem" or, as it was also known to the lesser intelligent, the "cosmic egg."

The age-old question is, what came first, the chicken or the egg? To this point, no one is exactly sure. So far, no one has spotted the "cosmic chicken."

Needless to say, this ylem at some point in time, reached its minimum contraction at a temperature of a "decillion" degrees Celsius, that's a 1 with thirty-three zeros, then suddenly and violently expanded. Within just a few hours of this event, nucleosynthesis, a scientific term referring to the changing of the center of the atom began to occur. When this happened, the lighter atoms, today known as hydrogen, helium, and lithium, were manufactured in this intense heat. So as the universe expanded and cooled, the atoms began to clump (another less scientific term, meaning "gather together"), and within a few hundred million years, stars and galaxies began to form. The other heavier elements are assumed to have formed later due to a remarkable effect known as nuclear fusion.

But alas, research from the Hubble telescope again changed the time line on this spectacular, stellar hatching of the egg. In 1973, another scientist by the name of Harwit set the age of the universe at nine billion years. Then in 1992, Pasachoff set it at eighteen billion. Then in 1993, a man named Gribbin said twenty-five billion. In 1994, Freed said eight to twelve billion, Hawking said fifteen billion, Kuhn said twelve billion, Mathews said eight billion, Ross said seventeen billion, Schmidt said ten to twelve billion, and Wolff said thirteen billion.

The newest theory of creation accepted by many cosmologists is now called the plasma theory, and if this new theory prevails, we might see the universe declared to be somewhere in the middle of the previous ranges. The most recent time line was in 2003, by a scientist/cosmologist by the name of MacRobert. He gives an age to the universe of 13.7 billion years, which is now the accepted age of the universe by the scientific community.

Seconds tick into minutes then hours, then days, days into years, years into centuries, but has anyone really identified what time is? Time on the planet is measured by one revolution around our sun. This is called by our terms of today, the year and was established some five thousand of our years ago, then they were divided into smaller segments known as days, one complete revolution of the Earth... well, they didn't know about complete revolutions of the earth yet... day-night-then the new day.

Months, hours, minutes and seconds didn't find their way into the standard until around the fourth century AD, but those standards were limited to specific cultures. Through the next fifteen centuries, mankind has further refined the established measurement of time has made this globally accepted measuring standard.

Time is an invention of man to accurately determine a set period and/or more commonly the existence of an individual, an event, or whatever man has the need to measure for his records. Time, as we know it, reflects a finite and determined period. But the unknown, the infinite, most of us just cannot comprehend what that means.

Did you ever hear the term "seemed like an eternity"? Of course, you have. But what is eternity? The best explanation of eternity I ever heard was on a television show. It was on a show that had an actor posing as a minister. We all knew that he wasn't

3

a minister and the description he used was written by the writers of the show, but oh, how accurate the analogy. Let me share it with you.

Imagine there was a two-hundred-foot round brass ball. Once a year, a dove flew past this ball and brushed its wing on the ball. By the time that this ball would be ground into dust, this would only have been the beginning of eternity. How profound!

Could you even imagine how long that would be? No, you cannot imagine that because the human mind is not capable of having any understanding of the length of time this could or would take.

Science is the analysis of information that can be explained in terms that the human mind might interpret. So far, the scientific explanation of the creation has fallen short in a lot of respects. No one can accurately tell us when this incredible event did take place.

I could go on for volumes and cite argument after argument on the correct and most accurate scientific documentation of the time line of creation. But that would be a waste of our time. It would take an "eternity," and we would never have all completely convinced that the reference materials are 100 percent true and accurate.

So, what is truth? What is accuracy?

The truth is that man's creator gave him the option of which path to follow. When this present-day man was formed, and brought into existence, he was formed to the image and likeness of the Supreme Being who men call by many names. Most often, I like to call Him God, which is His universally accepted name. Sometimes I actually use His name Adonai — great name; look it up sometime. However, I will refer to Him by many names in this manuscript. God created everyone and everything, and all He created is good.

Why don't we take a step back and take a look at the beginning of this universe and the Earth? Scientific evidence claims that this planet is somewhere between four and five billion years old. Why not check within the Bible and see if it can find some answers? The Bible has withstood the test of time but its accuracy has not been proven to everyone's satisfaction. It has been questioned time and time again, but this is the document that I've put my full faith and trust in to be the truth.

Contained within this holy and sacred text are all the truths. But this present-day man has ignored this fact simply because he cannot interpret its contents. Nor does he have the understanding of the true meaning of life because he lives in his present existence.

Man, throughout his history has questioned the meaning of life. This age-old question is limited solely to our lack of faith and understanding. We all know that seeing is believing; however, in this state of being, there is no way that we can actually accomplish seeing all there is to see. Hence, because of man limitations in the physical being, he has had the need for some directions.

Of course, every individual being that receives direction will never understand it the same way. This is caused by our lack of exposure to the factual truth, our limitation to a perceived truth, and our personal interpretation of the accepted truth. Within the sacred words are all the factual and exact truth of any question that can be asked.

However, the question is, because this text has been translated and open to the translator interpretation so many times, can it, in fact, be totally accurate?

The Bible has survived in its present-day format for a little over 425 years. Prior to that, the text was written in the Latin language, which happened around the 4th century. This is when the Old Testament and the New Testament were translated from the Hebrew and Greek languages into a complete manuscript of the history of God and Man in the Latin language. This is also when the punctuation, chapters, and verses were introduced. Around the early fifteenth century is when the translation from the Latin occurred.

Prior to the fifteenth century, the Bible was not the Bible as we know it. It was the "Torah," which was written by thirty-one prophets and holy men between the years of 2300 BCE and 425 BCE and in the traditional Hebrew and Aramaic language. A collection of letters and gospels written by the founders of the Christian church was then introduced in and around the end of the first century. These were written in the Greek and Hebrew language. Around the second century, this collection was added to the Torah, forming a writing, which would eventually become today's Bible.

There were more letters and gospels in this original version of the New Testament, fourteen to be exact; however, they are not included in the final and accepted version of today.

The "lost" doctrines have been excluded because they are not and were not the actual word of God. They were written by what you might call "want to be" prophets. There is no historical evidence to verify the facts or events contained within those writings. Whereas, the remaining text in the New Testament are verifiable historically and deemed to be authentic by the past- and present-day leaders of the Catholic Church, the popes, as the true word of God.

Our present-day version is the combination of works by the truly inspired prophets of God and apostles of the Jesus for the past 4,200 years, give or take a few. One other thing about this book of history is that this book was written in such a way that it can be interpreted in a countless number of ways which confuses most.

With that bit of information, how is it possible to even consider this text as the factual truth? Well, here's where an individual's faith comes into the picture. I believe that the Bible contains all the secrets of life. It contains the answers to all the questions that we, simple-minded humans, have not been able to answer in all of our existence.

It was purposely handed down to us in the format of "parables" for a reason. The reason is not so obvious. But we, by nature, design, and intent, were created for one specific goal. Our goal was and is to find our way back to our God and to "heaven." If it was that easy and the "instructions" were crystal clear, how could we be judged worthy of the eternal life and happiness promised? How could we learn without looking inside ourselves for some of the answers? How could we pass this "test" on our own merit?

Once we look inside the Bible, we will discover that the mystery of this universe is not such a mystery if you just have some faith in its creator. We will see together that it is possible to understand the instructions, to read between the lines, to interpret the enigma, to understand this puzzling text filled with our perceived and imagined contradiction that this limited human mind can't fully grasp.

Before we go any further, let's learn one simple truth. I assure you that once you grasp this simple truth, conceivably, you may then understand the how, the who, and the why our universe was created.

Peter was one of the apostles of Jesus. He was also one of the men of this world that received the unabridged truth by Jesus. Peter was enlightened in the secrets of God and man and entrusted not to reveal these truths to man. But Peter, being the simple creature that he was, couldn't keep these truths to himself.

Thank God, thank Jesus, and thank the Holy Spirit for Simon Peter!

In this verse, Peter wrote this, which is one of the most basic truths contained within the New Testament:

"But do not ignore this one fact, beloved, that with the Lord a day is like a thousand years, and a thousand years is like a day." (2 Peter 3:8)

The truth is that man invented time. God has no time, because God is time. He is the alpha and the omega, the beginning and the end. A thousand years is like a day. Perhaps a million or even a billion years is like a day as well. Keep in mind, the author of this text was using terms of his day and era. "Like a thousand" was interpreted as eternity, which we still cannot fully understand.

Additionally, the people that he was talking to thought that the beginning of the Earth was a mere four thousand years earlier. Peter, being one of the "enlightened," was composing a letter that was, first, a well-written letter and, secondly, in this letter, gave the people of the time a tangible explanation of the incomprehensible infiniteness if the Supreme Eternal Being known as God.

Throughout the entire text of this book called the Bible is the same theme: literary disguise. Not only is this text the greatest source of the "His rules" of life, but it is also considered one of the greatest literary works known to mankind. In my opinion, it is the greatest.

However, before man added the readability of today's version in the form of punctuation, chapter, and verse, it was simply a collection of sacred documents that the forefathers of this evolving religion kept as a historical record.

But, hidden within the words of this sacred text are also all the truths of this physical life. When man can accept this fact, then, and only then, will he become that which the Almighty intended.

Just to clarify the fact that the words of God are contained within this text, we will look at two verses before we investigate the beginning of the world as recorded in the Bible.

About 1002 BCE, David, slayer of Goliath, prophet of God, wrote this psalm as well as many of the other 150 psalms. In these two lines are contained another important truth.

"The words of the Lord are pure words; as silver tried in a furnace of earth, purified seven times. Thou shall keep them O Lord, thou shall preserve them from this generation forever." (Psalm 12:6, 7, King James Version)

I gave you some of the history of the Bible earlier. I said that it is not the same now as it was when the "original" documents were written. I also told you that it had been modified and punctuated, chapter and verse added, and literary value added throughout its content. However, in my adult lifetime, the Catholic version has again been changed from the long-accepted King James Version to the New American Bible. The change was intended and designed to assist in the language barrier of the commonly understood terms of today's people and an attempt to accurately translate the oldest original texts using the knowledge of ancient languages by the more educated scholars of translation in today's society.

This new Papal Authorized Version is the seventh version of the words of God. We have seen the final purification of this word.

Let me give you as close to an accurate summary and true time line on the "seven" purifications of the "words" of God. I say this because the first and second are estimated date which cannot be 100 percent verified historically.

First purification: circa 1000 BCE; collection of writings, poems, and sacred text, the first official gathering of Job's and Moses's *"words"* of God.

Second purification: circa 425 BCE; formation of the Torah, the first official gathering of formal Jewish law.

Third purification: 90 AD; the entire collection of the Old Testament is put into place to solidify the Jewish law. This is the time that the New Testament was being written, but not all of the wittings were combined into one text.

Fourth purification: 210 AD; the combination of the Old and New Testaments into one Book, the birth of the complete Bible. This text is a combination of all the writings pertaining to the law of the one true God in three persons — the Father, the Son, and the Holy Spirit.

Fifth purification: 405 AD; formatting of these ancient writings into one common language and standardized into a readable format containing punctuation, chapter, verse, and a standard language of the times, Latin.

Sixth purification: 1518 AD; translated from a "dead" language into a new and Papal Authorized Version of the text that applied to the times. Bear in mind, the actual Words of God, were not changed, but rather refined for the understanding of the people of the times.

Seventh purification: 1970 AD; the final change — purified seven times, the accepted Catholic version of the entire collection of actual "Words" of the one true, living, and ever-present God in three persons.

Now let's read the verse noted above from the newest version of the text, the New American Version.

"Because they rob the weak, and the needy groan, I will now arise," says the Lord; "I will grant safety to whoever longs for it." The promises of the Lord are sure, silver refined in a crucible, silver purified seven times." (Psalm 12:6, 7, New American Version)

The promises of the Lord are sure, silver refined in a crucible, silver purified seven times.

At first glance there seems to be a notable difference in the two texts. This newest version titles this psalm "Prayer against Evil Tongues." In fact, this version's translation was started to carry out the directive of Pope Pius XII in 1943, in his famous *Encyclical Divino Afflante Spiritu* and the decree of the Second Vatican Council. The Council prescribed that an "up to date and appropriate translation be made in the various languages."

With the approval of the Church authority, these translations may be produced in cooperation with our "separate brethren" so that "all Christians may be able to use them." The translation was taken from the oldest extant forms in which the texts exist.

But does this newest translation really and significantly change the meaning of the two verses? I say no; I say that it makes the meaning of the two verses even clearer. The most obvious is that the purification was to happen seven times. Every word that comes from God is truth; His words are a promise, and His words are sure.

Crucible and furnace do have a similar meaning. The difference is a crucible, is a furnace within the ground or Earth, and a furnace is typically a melting device on top or supported by the ground.

The more times something is "melted," the purer of a material it will become. The melt process removes the impurities from the "ore" and refines it into a purer form. Languages are ever changing, so the fact is Almighty God knew that the text would have to be interpreted into a language of each and every era.

The meanings of the two verses, even though they don't read the same, are the same. These two verses are of separate eras and may seem to have different translations, but both say, without doubt, that the words of God are forever. They also say very clearly that if man has faith and trust in the Words of God, God's Word and support will be with him throughout his generations.

Let's go to the Creation…

Chapter 2

The Creation: Genesis 1:1–31, Genesis 2:1–4

What a beautiful story, and for many centuries, most believers in our one true God took this, the first chapter and four verses of the second chapter, as the literal truth. When the scientific community introduced numerous and plausible theories to the contrary that seemingly disproved the creation story in the Bible, doubt resulted. How could all this evidence be disputed? Well, it can't be, because it is based on science.

I am not going to type out this entire text of the passages at this point because I type rather slowly, and everyone should know the essence of the story. God created the heavens and the Earth and all the creatures in six days. On the seventh day, He was bushed, so He rested. That's it, the whole truth... just kidding.

Okay, let's refer back to this truth. The concept of time is not the same with God. He does not exist in hours and/or days. He has no need to measure intervals of the passage of events like this finite creature known as man. So, let's think outside the box and roll back the hands of time a few billion years or so.

The most current information from the scientific community indicates that this universe has been in existence for a little over 13.7 billion years, give or take, but they're not really 100 percent sure. Most claim that this rock we live on is 4.5 billion years old, plus or minus a half billion, so let's go with that...

Well, who's to say for sure — other than God Himself...

Science calls this era the Hadean Era. During this era, this Earth was a barren rock. So about 4,500,000,000 BCE, there was this potential planet floating somewhere in space along with countless other celestial bodies, all of which were on a course for destinations somewhere in this vast universe.

This Earth was on course for a place in this vastness that would and could ultimately support physical life in all its forms. It was floating in space for some ten billion years or so and finally guided by the hand of the Almighty was perfectly placed into position by His all-knowing wisdom. It was placed in a gravitational rotation around this sun and in this solar system. But why? Let's look at his passage to get part of that answer.

"Moreover, between us and you a great chasm is established to prevent anyone from crossing who might wish to go from your side to ours." (Luke16:26)

These are recorded words of the Apostle Luke. Luke was one of the chosen apostles. He was privy to the truth about heaven, hell, and Earth. This passage is contained in the parable of the Rich Man and Lazarus. It, in fact, claims that there are three separate planes of existence.

They are the physical plane that we live in, the spiritual plane of "heaven," and the spiritual plane of "hell." What is revealed in this passage is that there are at least three different dimensions or planes that exist within this vast universe. There is more than we can see, feel, hear, smell, or taste. There is more to this universe than our physical senses can fathom. However, many members of the scientific community continue to lean towards the belief that this universal is all-physical universe.

Look at this passage:

"In my father's house there are many dwelling places. If there were not, would I have told you that I am going to prepare a place for you? And if I go and prepare a place for you, I will come back again and take you to myself, so that where I am, you may be." (John 14:2, 3)

Please keep these two passages in mind as we go on…

"In the beginning, when God created the heavens and the earth, the earth was a formless wasteland, and darkness covered the abyss, while a mighty wind swept over the waters. Then God said, "let there be light," and there was light. God saw how good the light was. God then separated the light from the darkness. God call the light "day" and the darkness He called "night." Thus, evening came, and morning followed — the first day." (Genesis 1:1, 5)

Okay, now I'll address the "day" question. No, this did not happen all in one day, a twenty-four-hour period as we know it; it happened in a day, as God knows it. Our standards of time, man's standards, do not apply to the Almighty.

This passage uses an unusual word in the first sentence; it is the word *abyss*. *Abyss* means an immeasurable deep gulf or great space, or it can also mean an intellectual or moral depth. So, when God created this universe and in particular, this planet, He was setting the stage for, as I like to call it, "the test." He needed to create a place in time and space that was separate from the place in which he normally resides. It had to be a new place yet it had to be just another room in our Father's house.

I also believe that the word abyss and how it is placed in the seventh purification of the text is more accurately used then we can grasp. It specifically states that the Earth was a formless wasteland, and darkness covered the abyss, while a mighty wind swept over the waters.

This also can be interpreted from this passage…

God, with all His might and power, with one single breath sent this new "testing field," planet Earth into place. And from His existence, He guided this new and separate plane into the vastness of this new physical universe. The entirety of physical life was on track for this predetermined location in this new and changing universe. From His intellectual and moral depth, this wasteland covered in darkness was about to begin. It was complete with the most important element of life to those yet to come. Then God said, "Let there be light," and there was light. God saw how good the light was; God then separated the light from the darkness.

This should be interpreted as this truth contained within this single and very important passage below… the darkness is the sin of one of His angelic creatures which questioned His sole authority in His House.… let's take a look at this passage.

"And the Lord said to Satan, "Whence do you come?" Then Satan answered the Lord and said, "from roaming the earth and patrolling it." (Job 1:7)

What is revealed in this verse from Job is that the new Earth was set into place so that the testing of the physical/spiritual human could occur. This is very important because before any recorded history, a great disturbance happened. Now there is no actual scientific proof of this, but religious teachings tell us that God has always existed. These teachings state that He created angels for His companionship.

Some angels felt they were greater than the creator. However, one by the name of Lucifer who was then known as the Angel of Light took the lead. He was and still is the most arrogant and proud of the angels. The teachings claim that at the time of this occurrence, Lucifer gathered those angels and raged a war against God.

God's devoted angels fought the fight, but ultimately, God had to step in and expelled Lucifer and his demons from heaven. God then created a second plane of existence, the dark and dismal plane of hell, setting the chasm or abyss between the two planes.

God saw how good the light was and separated the light from the darkness. He kicked Lucifer and the bunch to the curb so to speak, right into the plane named hell because He saw how good, good really was and this group was not. However, the darkness in this plane was and still is part of His plan.

Back to my thoughts about the purpose of this... God is very mysterious and more times than not will deliver hidden messages within His words. Even though Moses is responsible for the writing of the first five books of the Bible, Moses was not there at the time of creation. He simply wrote the words that were delivered via God's methods. Our minds, hearts, and souls must look within the penned words for the hidden truths.

We're going to look at "day" 2 and see what happened next.

FYI, the power of God is so great; it really could have taken him six days to do this. But understand the truth, and the truth is that the literal translations we interpret may not always be the actual truth because we can only see the truths as interpreted by our minds.

The power of the Almighty is so great that if He wanted, He could have done all this in six of our days as we perceive time. But if He would have, then man would not have had the opportunity to explore this planet and beyond. There wouldn't have been enough contradiction for this curious animal known as man. There would have been no doubt. Here's another factual truth: this dimension of our reality was set up with that factor in mind, the doubt, which is the essence of this test. Without the doubt, this would have been clear-cut, and this testing field could not have accomplished God's purpose and will.

What we have here is a failure to communicate—no, that's from something else, but it applies. We have a failure to communicate with the Almighty. We are so limited in our understanding that we just don't get it. We can't see certain things so we can't believe in their existence.

The scientific community would have you believe that God didn't create man; man, created God. They would have you believe that this started with an unexplainable explosion from an intense heat and gathering of cosmic material, a giant "cosmic egg," without origin. Well, I'm gonna tell you that the chicken did come before the egg and that "cosmic chicken" was indeed the Almighty—our God—please pardon me, God, for referring to you as a chicken, and please pardon the grammar.

When we look at "day" 2, we will find the evidence of science states that this happened circa 3,800,000,000 BCE and is called the Archaean Era by the scientific community.

Let's read about this day in Genesis 1:6, 8…

"Then God said, "Let there be a dome in the middle of the waters, to separate one body of water from the other." And so, it happened; God made the dome, and it separated the water above the dome from the water below it. God called the dome "the sky," Evening came and morning followed-the second day."

The interesting thing about the biblical description of creation is these passages contained in Genesis closely mirror and confirm the scientific evidence of the evolution of this planet.

In fact, the entire Bible mirrors what happened throughout history. The Bible originated as a historical document and was provided to us for our guidance and understanding of events, which lead us to this exact "time" in history. It is actually an instruction manual, but as all of us know, a man, a real man, doesn't read the instructions.

Perhaps it should be pretty clear to everyone what happened on the "second day"? If it's not, well, obviously, our new planet was undergoing changes and was now developing a basic atmosphere to support the life forms that were about to be introduced, over the next few "days."

Also, bear in mind that there is no rush in God's plan for how long this or any event should take. Throughout the natural course of the plan, and the infiniteness of the Creator, what's a few hundred million years anyway? Do you think He had a boss to answer to? Do you think there was a deadline to meet? Because God has no beginning and no end, time doesn't matter now, does it?

He was preparing the stage. He was putting things in motion. This third plane of existence had to be perfect in every way.

Let me clarify what I mean by perfect in every way. This planet at this point in history was perfect, developing in such a way that it was ready to support what's going to happen next. Not only next, but for duration of this test, which would be defined as the time necessary to fulfill God's ultimate plan. Perfection was needed to support all the life forms that have existed and will exist on the "picture perfect" Earth that we, mankind, continually destroy due to the turmoil, grief, strife, greed, and desire to be equivalent to the Almighty. These are all influences of Satan who has been rooming and patrolling this Earth.

And here's another factual truth we can learn at this point in time; mankind is the spiritual / physical being who has used and abused the natural resources put here by the Almighty. Mankind doesn't have a true respect for all life forms. Man, has begun to consider himself equal to the Creator, just like Satan did and does. If we could just see the perfection created here on Earth, it would be the paradise He created.

Well, at this point it "time," the planet wasn't really perfect by our standards. All the bodies of water and land masses haven't been formed, the air wasn't breathable, there are no plants, no animals, and man wasn't here yet. The factual truth I'm telling you is that when the "six" days of creation were completed, this Earth was a paradise, a most perfect environment to support the "animal" known as man... but not yet.

I must digress for a moment. In this verse of the text of Genesis 1:1, a mighty wind swept over the waters and the dome was separating the waters, so what does this word *waters* mean? Again, we must look past the word itself and interpret the essence of the text.

Water is the key element on this planet. All living creatures, whether they be plant or animal, cannot exist without this precious substance. It is the main ingredient to the whole existence on this planet. It is the "essence of life." Perhaps we should consider the "essence of life" as the interpretation for this word in this text. It would clarify a great deal of the uncertainty and perhaps allow for the acceptance of the "creation story's" accuracy.

Basically, the first two days of creation were needed to establish an inhabitable physical plane of existence for this new human who was about to be part of God's plan.

The first two days were a preparation for an environment suitable to support these "temples" of the Spirit of the one Living and True God.

Let's look at the basics of chemistry for a moment since the scientific community tells us our universe is a result of this, shall we?

The atom is most basic of the elements. Atoms are the building blocks of everything we know. They are the essential materials that make everything in this universe, no matter the size or shape. All in agreement? Good!

Here's how atoms work. There is a proton that carries a positive charge. There is a neutron that has no charge; it is neutral. Together they form the nucleus of any atom, the center. The third component is called an electron. Electrons have a negative charge and create balance. Based on their nature, electrons will cling to the proton and neutron and attempt to make it balanced, creating a complete atom.

Okay, great, what's that got to do with anything? Come on now, just stop and think a little while… I have to refill my coffee anyway… be right back.

Well, here's my point…

Scientists think that a giant atom was the foundation of this entire universe. This one gigantic atom containing everything needed to create this vast universe, complete enough for an infinite number of planets, stars, moons, and all contain on this global sphere we inhabit. This atom was large enough to support all life forms here and in the unknown regions of this vast universe and they called it a "cosmic egg." And they are right.

Typically, an atom will rarely combine to a point where it does not achieve balance and it will almost always combine to achieve as close to balance as possible—that's basic chemistry… that's science… proton (God)… neutron (us)… electron (Satan).

My two questions about the theory of one gigantic atom are these:

How could this be remotely possible without a Creator?

Where did the raw material that formed this "cosmic egg" originate?

I'll answer those two questions... Before creation the of this universe, the 3-dimensional universe, two other universes existed... heaven and hell... God made the "cosmic egg" appear, which was the essence of the third universe yet to be created to balance the existence and the completion of God's plan... God's competition of this atom... this universe.

This would be the "testing" ground for the souls that had not committed one way or the other during that great disturbance in heaven. The remaining souls are the "neutron souls" that have already undergone the test and are the souls still in heaven awaiting their test. These "neutron" souls were and are the souls that the Creator was setting the stage for, the ones who would achieve balance here, and then decide here if they wanted to take on a positive or negative "charge" while in this dimension... God was the first chemist.

Somewhere in "time" Satan got all uppity, just like he was supposed to, causing the great battle in heaven for the reign of the first singular universe. Some of the other angels followed him and some stayed loyal to God. Also, there were the souls that couldn't choose a side when this great disturbance broke out in heaven... that would be us... the "neutron" souls.

Next came the chasm. The second spiritual plane of existence was created from within this once singular universe, which caused the separation of the good and evil; positive and negative split, which caused an imbalance in this bi-dimensional atom. In order for the atom to again be balanced, a third universal plane of existence had to be established — the neutral component, which is this physical universe containing planet earth.

Get it? Basic chemistry... I'll explain...

Because we can't accept the fact that God is everything, including the first scientist, is the reason we can't with certainty come to a factual conclusion on the origin, age, or formation of this universe. And even though there is an instruction manual, we cannot follow the text. This information, I assure you, is in the Bible. It's written between the lines. It's hidden from us because we can't handle the truth.

Perhaps, the first man with a soul was actually named Adam. But, could the word that was given to Moses through the passing down of the written and verbal history been atom? Could it have been changed to Adam by Moses? Perhaps…

This God, who I love with all my being and have true faith in, is truly a mysterious God.

Day 3, which is called the Proterozoic Era, circa 2,000,000,000 BCE.

"Then God said, "Let the water under the sky be gathered into a single basin, so that dry land may appear." And so, it happened; the water under the sky was gathered into its basin, and dry land appeared. God called the dry land "the earth" and the basin of water he called "the sea." God saw how good it was. Then God said, "Let the earth bring forth vegetation; every kind of plant that bears seed and every kind of fruit tree on earth that bears fruit with its seed in it." And so, it happened; the earth brought forth every kind of plant that bears seed and every kind of fruit tree on earth that bears fruit with its seed in it. God saw how good it was. Evening came, and the morning followed—the third day." (Genesis 1:9, 13)

It looks like God was pretty busy on day 3 as well. He now has created the sea and dry earth and has filled the planet with plants.

This past spring, we worked around the house, and it took two days just to mow the grass, trim some trees, and clean up the dirt from the winter. How could God have done all this in one day?

But the evidence shows it was a very long time, as we see time, which is indisputable; however, with God, all things are possible.

Perhaps by now, we fully understand that the term "day" is simply a figurative translation. These "days" are actually eras of the Earth's development, and quite accurate, in fact.

Before any living creature could inhabit this planet, there had to be land, water, and food. The ecosystems had to be established. The basic atmosphere was just formed the day before and separation of land and sea, along with the new vegetation had to be the next step.

"Let the waters be gathered into a single basin so that dry land may appear." There are a number of oceans and seas on this planet, but they are all connected and are all one sea. Even though man has named them for identification purposes, they are all still one body of water. Now that portion of the sentence, gathered into a single basin, is really kind of ironic, don't you think? This text has been questioned for its accuracy, and so far, it's been right on track. We know that water was on the Earth on day 2, but it was separated on day 3 so that the formation of the ecosystems could continue for the next day or era, as the case may be.

On the third day, when our waters were called to separation, the process of purification of the two different types of water on this planet began. Only about 3 percent of the water on this Earth is what we would call freshwater, which is suitable for drinking by most living, air-breathing mammals. The balance of the water on this planet is in the "sea," which is rich in minerals, particularly salt; hence, it's called saltwater.

Salt is a mineral that is found in the ground and in the rocks of this planet. It is contained in the sea simply because the rivers carry it there. However, this process, according to scientific research, took millions upon millions of years to fulfill. It's a fascinating bit of research, and if you have the opportunity to read material on the subject, please do, it is very educational and entertaining.

God's purpose at that time in our history was solidification of the land into landmasses, which would shape the things to come.

This new Earth, at this point, had no breathable oxygen to support living creatures. However, the trees and plants were now placed here to purify and in fact, manufacture breathable oxygen for the future living creatures of this planet. And of course, research indicates that this process also took millions upon millions of years to unfold, which is indisputable.

There are other extremely educational and entertaining items of research, and if you have time, I suggest you read the material on the different types of plants and trees that were then on the earth. In fact, they have evolved into the present day's vegetation. But the vegetation introduced on day 2 and present here on day 3 was intended to serve another purpose.

The vegetation that had evolved on day 3, which was placed here on day 2, was certainly different. This vegetation had to serve a dual purpose. It was specifically placed on this Earth to support the new life forms that were about to come into existence in a day or two and to purify the air.

Let me ask you something, when you start a project, you have a plan, right? You typically don't just start something without having some idea or direction to follow. Sure, sometimes the end result is not what you expected, and the procedures you follow may be modified during the entire process... but you have a plan!

God also had a plan then, as well as now. God put this new creation into action. He guided it and touched it as needed to get to the result he wanted. Every time he made a piece of the puzzle, he had to make it fit. When it fit correctly, then and only then was that day completed. He "stepped" back to admire His work, and each and every time, God saw how good it was...

In order for this era or any of the six main stages of development, to be complete, He had to take a good look at the progress of the project and see that the work to that point was "good" and complete to His specifications. This great endeavor of the Lord, His little science project, is the most outstanding endeavor of all — the next day, day 4 is called the Paleozoic Era, circa 540,000,000 BCE.

Keep in mind, this one may sound a little out of place, but once I explain what this story really tells us, you'll see that again, this account of creation is extremely accurate and it cannot be viewed as anything but a historical recount of how God created the physical state of being, we are in.

"Then God said, "Let there be lights in the dome of the sky, to separate day from night. Let them mark and fix times, the days and the years, and serve as luminaries in the dome of the sky, to shed light upon the earth." And so it happened: God made the two great lights, the greater one to govern the day, and the lesser one to govern the night: and he made the stars. God set them in the dome of the sky, to shed light upon the earth, to govern the day and the night, and to separate the light from the darkness. God saw how good it was. Evening came, and morning followed — the fourth day." Genesis 1:14, 19

Now how could this be? Were the sun, moon, and stars just now created? How could plants grow without sunlight? Is this when the Earth became part of the solar system?

This doesn't say what you think it says. It was at this stage of the evolution of this great plan of creation that the atmosphere had changed. The ozone layer was now being formed, allowing the full and clear penetration of the light of the stars, sun, and moon.

There already were heavenly bodies in place, but this is the era when God had commanded the refinement of the conditions of the atmosphere for the new life about to be placed on this now almost-perfect ecosystem.

Take a really good look at paradise. That's what we're seeing here on day 4. A perfect and complete new planet, ready to support the new life forms about to be placed. Complete with fresh, breathable oxygen... no holes in the ozone, no smog, just pure clean air. All the gases had been eliminated and now the "luminaries" would shine through this absolutely clear sky. This project was almost complete. The only things left were what was to occur through the next two days. But these next two days were going to be long ones.

Still don't get it? Let's go a little slower... let there be lights in the *dome* of the sky. This is the first line and also the key line. What this is indicating if you read on just a bit further is that the lights were already there: "God made the two great lights, the greater one to govern the day, and the lesser one to govern the night: and he made the stars" — they were already there. He was now allowing them to clearly shine through to serve as luminaries in the *dome* of the sky, to shed light upon the Earth and let them mark and fix times, the days and the years. *The dome is the ozone layer*. This was a necessity for the future days to come.

First, the vegetation that was growing prior to the event was not the same as it is today. It was the simplest form, which would develop into the food supply for the upcoming creatures that were going to inhabit the Earth prior to man and the current day animals. This vegetation was put in place on day 3 for a certain purpose, which was to clean up the atmosphere. These plants grew and flourished in the dimness of the day; they did not need a strong sunlight to develop. Secondly, as man was to evolve, he would need these luminaries for many purposes: navigation, time data, his curiosity to reach them, false gods, and so on.

It took many of our measurable years for day 4 to be completed. This fourth day was as we measure time, about seven hundred million years. But without the finger of God, this day 4 absolutely would not or could not have happened. Let's see "day" five...

Chapter 3

It's Alive

Before we move on and see what happened on day 5, I'd just like to again review this typically unrecognized fact. The first five books of the Bible are accredited to Moses; however, the oldest text in the Bible is the Book of Job. Some biblical experts say that this text was written somewhere around 2300 to 2000 BCE, while others say that it was written between 700 and 500 BCE.

The truth is Job's text was in existence when Moses lived on this Earth, and Moses had access to this information. It was later refined to be included in the Torah around that second timeline of 700 to 500 BCE. The book of Job is the oldest writings contained in the Bible. I believe that contained within the book of Job are many of the answers the skeptics are looking for.

The contents of Job's book, along with its artistic structure and style, have placed it among the literary masterpieces of all time. But more then that, it is a truly historical masterpiece. It's basically a story about this man named Job who has every earthly treasure that any man could want. Satan made a claim to God that the only reason that Job was faithful to Him was for that reason. God disagreed and took everything away from Job to prove his faith to the demon. Long story short, Job was faithful through the most terrible time any man could experience. God restored all and then some to Job, because he "passed" his test of faith.

But more than that, it has historical accounts of "prehistoric" creatures, animals, and events; and we will look at some of passages so that clarifications may be made. Okay, let's look at day 5 called the Mesozoic Era by the scientific community, circa 245,000,000 BCE in Genesis 1:20, 23.

"Then God said, "Let the water teem with an abundance of living creatures, and on the earth let birds fly beneath the dome of the sky." And so it happened: God created the great sea monsters and all kinds of swimming creatures with which the waters teems, and all kinds of winged birds. God saw how good it was, and God blessed then, saying, "Be fertile, multiply, and fill the waters of the sea: and let birds multiply on the earth." Evening came, and morning followed — the fifth day."

Because of the punctuation, the interpretation of the content of this passage is in question. However, the first ten words state that all the living creatures on the earth originated from the waters, which is the baseline of the evolutionary theory. It is the one arguable fact by which the scientific community can show the progression of life on this planet. So, we should consider the words written and not the punctuation pauses. Then God said, "Let the water teem with an abundance of living creatures and on the earth let birds fly beneath the dome of the sky."

God willed the Earth to produce life from the waters. All the material was there for Him to work with; it was just as simple as Him applying His will. He then ordered two separate life forms: one that could fly and one that could not, to come from the water.

These life forms started as primitive life forms, taking millions upon millions of years to develop into the life forms of the current day. In fact, this day was going to take about a 180 million of our years to come to a close.

From the water came many countless types of life that can fly. Too many birds and insects for us to number in the world today, and it all started on that day. The day that God said, "Be fertile, multiply, and fill the waters of the sea: and let birds multiply on the earth." And so, it did. It had to happen like that, it was His will. He was preparing the stage for us. He willed all of this to happen just as it did.

I truly wish that the two communities could agree on this one simple fact: God willed evolution. He needed evolution. He had to have evolution. All the creatures that came from that one simple order to be fertile, multiply, and fill the waters of the sea and let birds multiply on the Earth.

They were all necessary to support the present-day man. We needed those prehistoric creatures to develop, live, multiply, and to die, so that we ourselves could flourish. Without many of those prehistoric creatures, there would be no fossil fuel sources for this present-day man.

This Earth currently supports more human life than any time in God's plan. It is capable of this because man has developed into the limited technologically advanced creature of right here and now. He will advance further hopefully if he finally comes to grip with the one true fact, and that is that God is really in charge, not man. God set this in motion, not some imaginary cosmic chicken. God delivered this new physical universe, guided it, shaped it, and provided for it the necessities of all generation of creatures that were to inhabit this planet within this universe. He was the designer and builder of this "testing" ground.

God ordered the single-cell organisms to come into existence. He ordered the rise of the multicellular organisms to evolve from those single-cell organisms. He willed all to follow. This was and still is part of the plan. Just as today, people change simply because of the breeding processes, being fertile and multiplying. And during that fifth day, God ordered the process of evolution and those changes to occur. Nothing or no one was every intended to be exactly the same. But why, you might ask.

I will be glad to tell you…

God is everything; He is the beginning; He is the end. He is in everything and everyone at any and all times of eternity. He is the source of all life, physical and spiritual, that ever has or will exist.

The fulfillment of His plan required the "planting" of the seeds of physical life on that fifth day. There would be no question of His existence if the Bible stated that He created this world through the evolution process. However, His whole plan is wrapped around the question of His existence. This "test" could and would not work if we already knew the answers. Everything and everyone you will see or have ever seen, or has or will exist, is an extension of the Almighty, all different in so many ways. The Almighty is infinity, thus there is no limit to the variation of life in this plan. Let's take a look at this passage really quick: Job 40:2.

"Will we have arguing with the Almighty by the critics? Let him who would correct God give answer."

This is the answer God gave Job when he asked about the variation and questioned how all the creatures came into existence. Job was asking for answers about how and why certain animals and birds were made and became the way they were.

God's plan is His plan, and we should not question it unless we have the answer. Truthfully, we will never have those answers unless we pass this test. Our whole reason in life is to try our best, study for the test, and ultimately get a passing grade on this intense test — the hardest test we will ever be asked to take.

But it's not so difficult, if you read the book the "teacher" has put in front of you. This is His house, and there are some rules — His Rules. Following the rules guarantees success and will ensure your success passing the exam.

With that said, let's go back to Genesis and day 5.

The life forms that God willed to evolve on day 5 were intended to serve man in the future. These life forms were the most primitive of all the life forms but were a speculator work of God's creation. The true essence of life, the building blocks for all future generations, and all future inhabitants of this new paradise, in His physical universe.

He had to start out with the simplest cells and let "nature" take its course. Nature was and still is guided by the hand of the God. For His plan to work there had to be order and balance; like the atom, always looking for true balance and completion.

First and foremost, all life has a purpose and a reason. It has to serve to the Master's plan and has to follow His intellectual and moral depths... the "abyss."

Secondly, His plan was, is, and always will be to separate the "questionable" souls identified in the heavenly rebellion. By placing their spiritual being within a physical human being would allow them to use free will to decide which side they would follow. In order to accomplish such an enormous task and to have the man creature survive on this planet, provisions had to be made.

Not to belabor the point... people tell me I have that flaw... this day was simply the beginning of our evolutionary process; it was intended so that life could continue to the fulfillment of God's plan. Take a moment and read chapter 40 in the book of Job. God tells us that He made the "behemoth," which translates to dinosaur, and He covered them with dust for us. Still not convinced? Look at John 1:3, 5:

"All things came to be through Him, and without Him nothing came to be. What came to be through Him was life, and this life was the light of the human race."

Now this passage is considered by most to be referring to the Lord Jesus Christ. But most authorities of the Bible also agree that this text is highly literary and symbolic. I agree with these experts. The word in the second sentence that is highly symbolic is the word *light*. Jesus is the light of the world, but could the word *light* in this sentence be also referring to yet another type of light? Let's read the next verse:

"The light shines in the darkness, and the darkness has not overcome it."

Here the light is Jesus, and the darkness is Satan. Does it also say that this light is everlasting and will not be exhausted as long as the human race exists? Can this be interpreted as this?

God made life and all provisions for the human race throughout his existence, which included the most basic needs of man... light. A light, which will be available to him until the end of the testing period and until all the questionable souls were run through this gambit.

Here's a "did you know." Every bit of man-made light from primitive times, until now, requires some sort of fossil fuel. Sure, the new technology of today offer us power from nuclear power plants and solar sources, but fossil fuels are required to be used to deliver the equipment that supplies this energy to the home. These fossils fuels are a result of the fifth day; talk about a long day at the office...

Anyway, let's just go a little further in this chapter. John said that he came to testify and give testimony to the light so that all might believe through Him. Here, John is without any doubt speaking of Jesus. John claims that he (John) is not the light, but only was testifying to the light... the very next verse, John 1:9, "The true light, which enlightens everyone, was coming into the world."

One has to wonder, what other light can there be, and which light was not the true light? Was it the light that the human race was using for illumination?

Unlike many of God's creatures, man needs light to see. His senses are not developed to the point that he can function properly in the dark. Necessity is the mother of invention, and man is an inventor, but not the Creator. The Creator supplied us with all that we would need, including the intellect to invent whatever we wanted or we needed to flourish.

At this point in "time," God was sending us replacement lighting. The true light of the world, His Son, because man had gone far too long without His direct presence. Man, was getting to a point that he assumed he was equal to the Creator. Look at the history that we know up to this point in time. The Egyptians, the Greeks, the Romans, and many more, all had leaders who assumed the role of living gods.

But so much for this right now; we might come back to this extremely interesting topic in a little while, but for now, we're going to look at day 6. But first...

Here's a summary and the real skinny on day 5: all the creatures that preceded mankind were a necessary part of the plan. The evolution, the life, and the existence of these creatures served God purpose to provide for things to come. We could not exist if they did not exist... fact.

Circa 65,000,000 BCE, called the Cenozoic Era by the scientific community...

"Then God said, "Let the earth bring forth all kinds of living creatures; cattle, creeping things, and wild animals of all kinds." And so it happened: God made all kinds of wild animals, all kinds of cattle, all kinds of creeping things of the earth. God saw how good it was. Then God said: "Let us make man in our image, after our likeness. Let them have dominion over the fish of the sea, the birds of the air, and the cattle, and over all wild animals and all the creatures that crawl on the ground." God created man in His image, in the divine image He created him; male and female He created them. God blessed them, saying: "Be fertile and multiply; fill the earth and subdue it. Have dominion over the fish of the sea, the birds in the air, and all living creatures that move on the earth." God also said: "See, I gave you every seed-bearing plant all over the earth and every tree that has seed-bearing on it for your food; and all the animals of the land, all the birds of the air, and all living creatures that crawl on the ground, I give you all the green plants for food." And so, it happened. God looked at everything He made, and He found it very good. Evening came, and the morning followed — the sixth day." Genesis 1:24, 31

Again, if you take a really good look at the evolutionist theories of the creation and development of the human and animal populations of this Earth, this is right on the mark. A new "generation" of living creatures had been ordered by the Almighty, and His plan was progressing nicely, so now was the time for the "man creature" to be introduced to the planet.

Now this "man creature" was not the man that was going to have the precious gift of His "breath of life." That man was yet to come, but first the prototype had to be done. That prototype man was not ready, nor would be ready for some time. Many developmental changes had to occur. That prehistoric man was not mentally capable to take the "test."

Also, the Earth had to bring forth a new breed of creatures... cattle, creeping things, and wild animals of all kinds. These new creatures were the replacement creatures for all those scary prehistoric beasts. Those beasts had served their purpose and would not fit into the plan in the day to come. And so, all the threatening beasts from the day before were going to become extinct. This new breed, a breed of creatures evolved that this present-day man could and would have dominion over was ordered on day 6.

Now no one really knows for sure what cause the extinction of the dinosaur. Some say it was an asteroid that hit the planet and caused all the plants to die. This left those creatures without an abundant food source, causing their extinction. Some say that the last "ice age" was responsible for the extinction of the creatures. Both of these theories are plausible, I would suppose, but how then could this new line of replacement creatures be evolved so quickly if the evolutionist theory was indeed accurate?

How about this? God said that this should happen on the sixth day, and so it did. This is the only sensible and or plausible answer. This happened through God's divine intervention. One of man's biggest pitfalls is that he always complicates the situation. He looks too deeply into everything for the answers. He rarely is satisfied with a simple explanation or the simple truth.

Mankind was at this point to evolve into that creature. Yes, I said evolve. God ordered everything for this man's future existence on that day. "See, I gave you every seed-bearing plant all over the Earth and every tree that has seed-bearing on it for your food; and all the animals of the land, all the birds of the air, and all living creatures that crawl on the ground, I give you all the green plants for food," but this man had to develop into the creature that could bear the responsibility of possessing the "breath of life." At this point in "time," man was merely an animal without a soul. Here's yet another fact: man, is still an animal, which is one of the complications of this test.

To get back to what I was talking about, if man was an animal without a soul at this point, how could this make any sense? And if man evolved from the monkeys as most evolutionists believe, then this really is out of place. It throws the whole creation scenario out of kilter.

Then God said, "Let us make man in our image, after our likeness. Let them have dominion over the fish of the sea, the birds of the air, and the cattle, and over all wild animals and all the creatures that crawl on the ground."

God created man in His image, in the divine image He created him; male and female He created them.

Okay, line by line: "Let us make man in our image, after our likeness." "Let us" — us being the three persons of God, the Father, the Son, and the Holy Spirit. God's plan from the beginning of any existence included all that was to happen throughout eternity. God knew before any other universe, spiritual or physical, was created, how this whole saga was to unfold. His entirety was part of the plan from the start. These simple two words, "Let us," confirms this.

God the Father was going to be in "charge" of everything. He's the boss. He has no limitations and is everywhere at all times. God the Son, the Lord and Savior Jesus Christ, was to be, and is the king of this universe, the physical universe. God the Holy Spirit is the protector and guardian of all three universes, the physical and two spiritual universes. He protects us from being swallowed up by Satan. His job is simple yet complicated. Keep the abyss, the chasm, secure so that this plan that He, God, has devised can come to pass. As we move on through this book, we'll look at some places within the Bible and talk about this a little further. But for right now, let's look at man in our image, after our likeness.

Man, in our image, after our likeness... no, this doesn't mean a fat, Italian, middle-aged, man sitting at his computer at four o'clock in the morning, smoking cigarettes and drinking coffee, trying to write a book. Nor does it have any association whatsoever with what we look like. It is all about the essence of God in all His divinity.

We were created in the image of immortality. We were created to have all knowledge, all power and infinite existence, provided we fulfilled the task given us. Scary that God would create a being that has all of His divinity, but this fact is absolutely true.

Power and knowledge are funny things if you have no idea of how to handle them. But God gives every man, woman, and child the opportunity to share in His divine nature and to live for an eternity. We are part of the infinite wonders of His inconceivable love for us, and we will share in His total power and knowledge if we pass this test.

Look at the next sentence: "Let them have dominion over the fish of the sea, the birds of the air, and the cattle, and over all wild animals and all the creatures that crawl on the ground."

God has now charged us with the responsibility of caring for all the creatures put here for us. He made us "gods" over all His creation. He has entrusted us to watch over all the living creatures on this planet. We are to care for them and make sure we do not destroy His miracles of creation.

The next line simply reinforces the previous: "God created man in His image, in the divine image He created him; male and female He created them."

God is neither male nor female. He is the divine essence of life, the new-age believers call this energy, but they are a little confused. They just don't get it. We are not "cosmic" energy; we are of God's divine existence. We didn't get to this place by some freak chance. This was all part of God's plan and is His will.

I don't really want to elaborate on the feelings that I have for this new-age cult, but the new-age religion is nothing more than Satan's work. The people who believe in the basis of this religion are simply misinformed and have fallen into the lies, traps, and snares of the prince of sin. The prince's power over the meek is getting stronger and stronger because this present-day man has gotten further and further away from God Almighty, but that's an entirely different subject and maybe the theme of my next book... I want to now show you something in Psalms 8:4, 9 — it's right on the mark...

"When I see your heavens, the works of your fingers, the moon and stars that you set in place; what are humans that you are mindful of them, mere mortals that you care for them? You have made them little less that a god, crowned them with glory and honor. You have given them rule over the works of your hands; put all things at their feet: all sheep and oxen, even the beasts of the field, the birds of the air, the fish of the sea, and whatever swims the paths of the seas."

So, on the sixth day, God was preparing the human race to be the temple of His Divine Majesty, but this man was the base product and is not the same man of today. He was the prototype man; he was the primitive man, the cave man, the man that would evolve from a breed of monkeys or apes into the refined species that had the mental capability to handle the awesome responsibility that was yet to come. This man did not have the soul at this point in time. He was truly an animal... an intelligent animal nonetheless, but still an animal. He was the animal that would eventually take charge of the planet and care for it and all the creatures on it.

That's what happened on the sixth day.

Coincidentally, the scientific community has unknowingly confirmed the distinct eras and time lines and has, to the best of their ability, confirmed that the development of this Earth happened based on the biblical text... imagine that!

The funny thing is that the evidence of evolution is really in sync with the biblical rendition as it is presented in the creation story, but the experts have refused to confirm that God is... and I have to call You this again... the cosmic chicken.

Chapter 4

Rest and a Day in the Garden

Well, after a week of work like that, you just need some rest and relaxation.

And so, Genesis 2:1, 4:

"Thus, the heavens and the Earth and all their array were completed. Since on the seventh day God was finished with the work He had been doing, He rested on the seventh day from all the work He had undertaken. So, God blessed the seventh day and made it holy, because on it He rested from all the work He had done in creation. Such is the story of the heavens and the earth at their creation."

Some say that we are still in the seventh day, and God is still resting. They are somewhat accurate, but not completely. This is the seventh day; however, God never really rests. He's God, He really can't afford to take the vacation. First of all, He's got no money, and secondly, he's everywhere at all times, so where could he really go? He's got such an awesome responsibility, so how could He really get away from it all? Sip a margarita on the beach, catch a little sun, read a book, fall asleep on the hammock, or maybe take a cruise? That's just not in the cards for the chief.

What this passage says is all the creation that was indeed going to occur was now complete... except for one little detail: the man creature was not in possession of a soul. The man had no direction or rules to follow. God created all things for a specific purpose. Man's purpose was simple. This creation of flesh and blood was a finite being. It was designed to last just a moment or two in God's perspective of this yet-to-be-invented time, but long enough to be the image and likeness of God and complete the "test."

Man's destiny was and is to be the temple of this precious, infinite, and heavenly being called a soul. But this man was not put here without being told that this is the test. Nor will he ever be left to fend for himself.

Sure, most of us go to work to make money so we can eat, support our families, and pay our bills, but that's part of this physical universe, not of the spiritual universe. It's one of the two major questions in this "test" we are taking. Think about that for a moment or two.

Here's the first of the two questions: Are we a physical or spiritual being in nature?

Here's the second question: If every human was made to the image and likeness of God, then why don't we treat all humans as if we were in the presence of God?

These are the major questions in the test and are the heaviest weighted. These two are worth more "points" than the other question you may be asked on this test. If we could just get these two questions right, we would in fact pass this test on these two questions alone.

In fact, all of God's rules were all based on these two questions. And sure, there are a few bonus questions on this test, but not many of us get the bonus questions correct either. The way to get the first two questions correct is to live this momentary existence following the rules that have been established by God.

So how many of you out there can say that they never broke the rules? No human that I have ever met on this earth and no human that you've ever met either... I'm sure. There has only been two people who ever lived this human existence that fall into that category, and we are neither of them. Here's a bonus question: who were they? I'll put the answer on the last page if you don't already know. Anyway, let's not stray too far off the path. Let see how God started His "vacation."

"At the time when the Lord God made the earth and the heavens, while as yet there was no field shrub on the earth and no grass of the field had sprouted, for the Lord God had sent no rain upon the earth and there was no man to till the soil, but a stream was welling up out of the earth and was watering all the surface of the ground. The Lord God formed man out of the clay of the ground and blew into his nostrils the breath of life, and so man became a living being. Then the Lord God planted a garden in Eden, in the east, and He placed there the man whom He had formed. Out of the ground the Lord God made various trees grow that were delightful to look at and good for food, with the tree of life in the middle of the garden and the tree of the knowledge of good and bad." (Genesis 2:4, 9)

"The Lord God then took the man and settled him in the Garden of Eden, to cultivate and care for it. The Lord God gave the man this order: "You are free to eat from any of the trees in the garden except the tree of knowledge of good and bad. From this tree, you shall not eat; the moment you eat from it you are surely doomed to die." (Genesis 2:15, 17)

Here he is, this present-day man who God named Adam through the pen of Moses. The man was a complete and finished product. They call this section of the Bible "The Second Creation." They call it this for a very good reason. This is when the Lord God Almighty was looking at the work he had done and knew that His plan was in place. He did this when He was done and "resting." But I know that God never rests. He can't, too much work around the house. But just like you and me, the work around the house is a labor of love. We work all week at our jobs, but on the weekend, we maintain all that we've been working for…

We mow our grass, weed our gardens, and paint our decks or anything else that needs to be done to make our homes look good. Needs to be done… well, all these things we do out of pride of our accomplishments. Sure, these things are sometimes hard work; sometimes I can't wait to go back to the job on Monday… just to rest from all the work I did on the weekend, but the reality of the work that we do on the weekends is that it really doesn't have to be done. It does not have any effect on our survival. It's not necessary to earn our living… it's simply a pride issue. We're going to get to pride in a little while, it's good, it's bad, and sometimes we make it ugly — we're getting there soon.

The Lord God formed man out of the clay of the ground and blew into his nostrils the breath of life and so man became a living being. Here's the problem for all who disagree on the subject at hand: who made man appear on this earth? I didn't see here how some creatures from a distant galaxy landed on earth and started a new race of beings because their planet had been exhausted of the resources that maintained their lives. Nor do I see that an ape magically evolved into a human being with a soul. Man did evolve from some species of monkeys… but not this man.

Did evolution allow this to happen? No, this isn't a bonus question; it's simply a flaw in the evolutionist theory regarding man. They seem to be fascinated in answering this question in a plausible manner, leaving God out of the picture. Evolution did not breathe the soul into this evolved man; God Himself did.

I seem to remember that God created the man creature on the sixth day, but today, the seventh day, is the day he would become a "living being." Today as God was simply "tinkering" in His garden, He set His plan into action by giving the evolved man a soul. The test is about to begin. That bit of clay… one of evolution's results.

Let's just back up for a moment: while as yet there was no field shrub on the earth and no grass of the field had sprouted, for the Lord God had sent no rain upon the earth and there was no man to till the soil, but a stream was welling up out of the earth and was watering all the surface of the ground.

Here's that water issue again. No rain had fallen on the ground is merely symbolic. There was no life in the image and likeness of God is more like it, no living soul. But on this earth, was a stream welling up out of the ground. More symbolism, the earth was fertile and multiplying yielding the pre-soul creature man from the evolution specific breads of apes. Man, was still just an ape, a monkey trying to survive like all the time. True that he was a creature with a higher intellectual level than all other apes or monkeys of the earth, one that had dominion over all, but not in possession of the infinite soul. Hence this man could not till the soil... more symbolism. Here's a question: What's tilling the soil got to do with anything?

The symbolism here is that God planted a garden and placed man in the garden to care for it... The Lord God then took the man and settled him in the Garden of Eden to cultivate and care for it, and of course, man was set here to be fertile and multiply, so caring for the garden means watching over this planet earth and tilling the ground represents the instruction of God's children regarding the rules of this new man creature who bears this soul.

Now here's the kicker: When God placed, or blew, the breath of life into this man... free will became part of the equation. The Lord God gave the man this order: "You are free to eat from any of the trees in the garden except the tree of knowledge of good and bad. From this tree you shall not eat; the moment you eat from it you are surely doomed to die."

The man was now going to have to use his free will so he could decide whether or not to obey this first rule. However, this first "rule" was given to this man with consequences... break the rule and you will surely die, but die a physical or an eternal death.

This might get a little deep... and no, you don't need boots.

When this whole thing started, God knew that this was all going to happen. He knew when He first created all the heavenly beings that there was going to be a rebellion. He gave every being all the same power and glory as He Himself had because God is not afraid to share. Naturally, the bully named Lucifer stepped up and made the challenge and some... well, a lot of the others followed along with this challenge of God's authority. But Satan wanted to be in charge of the "toys."

So as part of the plan, God had to establish the test and the rules governing this exam, a "time-out" so to speak. After the first rebellion of Satan and his colleagues, God had to create a separate universal plane known as hell, a penalty box. But not all the heavenly beings supported both of the two forces… let's call the forces what they are, good and evil. And so, the third field of play… planet Earth and this universe we live in was created… the "time-out."

Now not to spill the beans, but let's say for now that when this is all said and done, there will only be one universe left in His great plan and that's why if you break the "rules," you will surely die. You will not be part of that universal plane of heaven nor will you be reunited to the presence of the Almighty; you will not be one with Him and He will not be one with you.

All humans die; you, me, and everyone in this physical plane is going to die a physical death, but the breath of life allows the righteous soul to live forever. The choice is simply this: Obey the rules and you will live forever; break the rules, and you are banished from the game; not too deep that you needed boots.

Now before we move on, I want to answer a question: What year was this?

According to biblical scholars, this occurred around 4000 BCE, and according to evolutionist, it's happened around 1,600,000 BCE; but I'm positive this was in the year 13,671 BCE. Pretty bold statement you say… well, let me give you the reason this is so.

First, some evolutionists claim that the first man… the early "hominids" were on this planet six to eight million years ago; they base this on carbon dating of fossil remains. That is possible, I suppose. Carbon dating shows that the earth is 4.5 billion years old. But is carbon dating accurate? I believe that it's not accurate enough, and I also believe that the scientific community puts too much faith in this procedure. Most carbon dating is considered to have a margin of error of 15 percent. If this statistic is correct, then the oldest that these "hominid" could be is seven to ten million years old. But these "hominids were not the man of today, day 7… not even close. Most scientists agree these "hominids" were of the ape family… perhaps.

Then the next man, the *Australopithecus afarensis*, "southern ape from afar," evolved from the early hominids. They base this on the discovery of "Lucy" in Ethiopia. "Lucy's" carbon dating results make her about three million years old. Nature took its course and the early species of the Homo group evolved from a specific group of apes. *Australopithecus robustus* and *Australopithecus boisei* were also evolving which gave us the ape and chimp families, so they say. Then, around 1.6 million BCE the Homo Sapiens evolved from the Australopithecus Afarensis. Now there is very little evidence to support any of this, but it's their theory. Read it sometime when you really want to be confused; you will be.

The biblical scholars, on the other hand, have use simple math to extract the date of this event for the text in Genesis. You try it. I did; it works out to 4004 BCE, just like the Christian scientist, Bishop Ussher, had calculated so long ago. This is why this date was accepted by most for such a long time; the math works out.

Now then, do you want to know why the year was 13,671 BCE and why I am so certain of that date? Of course, you do; you're sitting on the edge of those seats…

All right, I was just trying to build up the moment. God's word in this text is clear to all those who believe in it to be true. I believe it with all my heart and soul. I believe that if you ask the Lord God Almighty for the answer to any question like a child would, He will give it to you without hesitation.

"Ask and you shall receive, seek and you shall find" … never were any truer words spoken.

I prayed to the Lord God Almighty and said simply this, "God, how can I write this book without your help? I am a simple man, a sinner, and I don't know everything that I'll need to know to tackle such a task. I don't know this truth on this date."

And then God's answer came to me through a messenger. The answer was "I will guide your heart, your soul, and your mind."

And I said, "Lord, how?"

This is the answer I received, and I was assured that these words are as true as any words ever spoken.

He is the One True God: 1.

He is God in Three Persons: 3.

He created all in six days: 6.

He rested and made man on the seventh day: 7.

He breathed the life into one man: 1 (it was 13,671 BCE).

The year 13,671 BCE is the date that God's messenger told me via His favorite method, which is by delivering clear thoughts to my mind. This actually happened in my kitchen while I was pouring a cup of coffee and His message was pretty clear about this date. Now not to question the Almighty, for I have all faith in what he tells me in this manner, but I simply thought this: *You know I believe what You're telling me to be the truth… but how are the people reading this book going to buy into that date based on this?*

Before I went to bed that night, I prayed this: "God, I need clarity. Can You please give me a lead on this? I did the math and it works out to 4004 BCE. How can I assure them that this date is Your word?"

The next morning, this message came to me in the same fashion as the day before, by the same messenger. This message was one of the clearest messages that I had ever received. Over and over, this is what I was "hearing" in my mind: "Look where I show you and you will see."

Okay, great, so I opened the Bible to this!

"Then the Lord said, "My spirit shall not remain in man forever, since he is but flesh. His days shall comprise one hundred and twenty years." (Genesis 6:3)

I'm reading His words and wondering where God's taking me, and of course, nothing is hidden from the Lord. I look to the page to the left and see chapter 5, Generations: Adam to Noah. So, I start to read this passage yet again. Funny thing, all these men lived up to eight hundred... almost a thousand years, and Methuselah, 969. Then I got a calculator. I didn't want to make a mistake, and I added the "whole lifetimes" of the men listed... 7625. I subtracted that sum from 13671, and it was at 6046 BCE as a date that Noah lived.

Then I was again directed to read these passages in The New American and The King James Versions of the Bible.

"This is the record of the descendants of Adam. When God created man, He made him in the likeness of God; He created them male and female. When they were created, He blessed them and named them "Man." (Genesis 5:1, 2, New American Version)

"This is the generations of Adam. In the day that God created man, in the likeness of God made he; Male and Female created them, and called their name Adam, in the day when they were all created. "(Genesis 5 1, 2, King James Version)

In both, there were twelve names that followed Adam's name. They are the following: Seth, Enosh, Kenan, Mahalalel, Jared, Enoch, Methuselah, Lamech, Noah, Shem, Ham, and Japheth.

I was then "informed" these names were not only individuals; they were the twelve tribes of Israel's foundation. These "whole lifetimes" were the years needed to purify the race of those people. The names given are also the tribes of His people. God made he; male and female created them and called their name Adam. Adam was the name of His tribe, and from that tribe, the twelve tribes of Israel were born. Only one soul had been placed in the first man and then his mate. The rest of the "primitive men" living on this planet were without souls. The 7,625 years were necessary for the purification of this new species.

He must have heard my mind again because His next words were to read a few pages further in the New American Version. I did and found the next "historical" time line. It is located in chapter 11 of Genesis. Starts at verse 10 and is titled "The Line from Shem to Abraham." Now here I encounter twelve new names of twelve entirely new tribes of Israel, but to get to Abraham himself, you must read until you get to chapter 17.

I then thought that men are still not living the normal time line of man's presence on this earth… his numbered years. His days shall comprise 120 years. So, I factored this in while doing the math. I then decided to look at the King James Version chapters 10 through 17 and compare the two texts. When I did this, I prayed for guidance so that God would show me the way.

I did as I was instructed, and guess what? I was delivered right to the place where Abram became Abraham on 2453 BCE through the use simple of math.

Abram was an actual man, but he was the man who "fathered" the Abraham tribe of men, women and children who lived during this time period according to historical records available, which is documented factually. But the man "Abraham" was not just Abram; Abraham was the entire Abram tribe. You will see this in the next chapter or so the two years of 6046 BCE and 2453 BCE as well.

But we really must get back on track and finish what happened on the seventh day, which occurred in the year 13,671 BCE. I assure you that this is the year I was told, and it came directly to me from one of the "chief's" messengers.

Read the texts, do the math, judge for yourself; use your free will and make the choice… or just trust.

You might be thinking that I'm a real freak at this point, but I assure you, I am not.

Everyone in this world can hear God's words; I'm just one of the ones who listen. God might talk to anyone at any time, typically through one of His trusted servants and, more often than not, information delivered to your mind of things you just didn't know with extreme clarity. Ask and you shall receive, seek and you shall find. Pray like a child, ask for the simple things; you'll be amazed what the Good Lord will convey to your mind.

"The Lord God said: "It is not good for man to be alone. I will make a suitable partner for him." So, the Lord God formed out of the ground various wild animals and various birds of the air, and brought them to the man to see what he would call them; whatever the man called each would be its name. The man gave names to all the cattle, all the birds of the air, and all the wild animals; but none proved to be the suitable partner for the man.

So, the Lord God cast a deep sleep on the man, and while he was asleep, he took out one of his ribs and closed it up with flesh. The Lord God then built up into a woman the rib that He had taken from the man. When He brought her to the man, the man said:

"This one, at last, is bone of my bones and flesh of my flesh; This one shall be called woman, for out of her man this one has been taken." That is why a man leaves his father and mother and clings to his wife, and the two become one body. The man and his wife were both naked, yet they felt no shame." (Genesis 2:18, 25)

This is taking place in the Garden of Eden. Now, the "Chief" knew that man had to have a mate to join in on the plan and to breed with to produce a pure species of this new generation of mankind with a soul, and so, "It is not good for man to be alone. I will make a suitable partner for him."

God bought forth all living animals from the ground (earth) and was giving this man the first opportunity to use his newly found free will to find a mate from the existing female population.

And of course, if he was to have dominion over all the animals on the earth, it just makes sense that he had to have another female with a soul, don't you agree?

The soul that God had placed in this man made all the difference in his judgment. Mankind had been on this planet for millions of years at this point in time; he was being evolved into the correct format of man that the Lord needed for the soul.

When the first man received this soul, he was completely different from every other man that was on earth at that time. That's the reason that God separated this man from the rest of the men and placed him in the Garden of Eden for this initial test. The Garden of Eden was God's personal fenced-in yard that no other human animals were allowed to enter. God wanted no outside interference from any of the other "man creatures" in this little test of the first man of this kind. And now the "operation."

So, the Lord God cast a deep sleep on the man, and while he was asleep, he took out one of his ribs and closed it up with flesh.

Did you know that up until the early 1900s, the human race actually believed the man had one less rib than a woman? And did you know that until autopsies were common and scientists were looking at skeletal remains from an information-gathering position, most people assumed that this rib statement was factual? But it's not; men and women have the same number of ribs.

The real truth that has not been interpreted through the ages is that our God temporality released Adam's soul from his body so that he could retrieve his "soul mate," which was in heaven at that time.

The deep sleep that Adam experienced, in my opinion, was mortal death. This is the only way that any soul can be released from the body. But not to fear! God raised this first man from the dead, too, because this "Son of God" had not yet completed the mission he was asked to undertake here on earth.

This first couple, Adam and Eve, "bone of my bones and flesh of my flesh," were this because of this "operation." They were a completely united couple because Adam himself selected Eve's soul as all of us are supposed to do when selecting our mate.

Completion: Now they were truly made in God's image and likeness—male and female He made them…

This one shall be called woman, for out of her man this one has been taken. That is why a man leaves his father and mother and clings to his wife, and the two become one body.

I have been married to my wife since October 16, 1976, and I will be married to her until physical death separates us. I'm sure my wife feels the same way that I do about our marriage. When we took our marriage vows so many years ago, we swore in the presence of the community and in the presence of God Almighty that we would remain together 'til death do us part… we meant it.

We have become one flesh, one soul: a complete being in the truest sense of the word.

Now don't get this wrong, we are still individuals, but when it comes down to it, every decision that either of us makes, which would have an effect on the other, is made with that consideration in our hearts, our minds, and our souls. Neither of us would ever do anything intentionally that would cause the other harm or pain of any kind.

This passage does not say man has one less rib than a woman. It doesn't say that some surgery of some sort took place. It doesn't say to keep looking for our mate until we find the right one, no matter how many it might take.

But what it does say is that God united this woman to this man from the essence of this man. He formed her in the same fashion but allowed Adam to have a say in the matter of selection. Eve was going to be her name. Her original name as written in Hebrew was Hawwāh, and translated as "living one" or "source of life."

When we finally find the mate that we are going to marry and take that mate, that mate becomes bone of our bones and flesh of our flesh forever in our existence on this earth. It not a trial marriage that we can just say we had enough of and try a new one; "it just didn't work out."

In today's society, it's almost fashionable to be married more than one time. It seems to me that many people today don't have the moral fiber to make the commitment to this lifetime vow and union. It also seems to me that today's society suffers from the strongest influence of the devil and his evil in our history.

We are neglecting the rule given on day 7. The first and most important rule, to preserve the sanctity of marriage, the bonding of two souls into one... bone of my bones and flesh of my flesh.

In fact, many of the variations of the Christian faiths were formed because of this single principle: divorce and the ability to remarry. Even the Catholic Church is now granting annulments with a freer hand than ever before.

Up to about 1970s or so, annulments were only granted under the most extreme circumstances. These potential annulments were highly scrutinized before any action was taken. It sometimes took years of scrutiny and counseling of the couple, which often resulted in the annulment not being granted.

But nowadays, annulments are done on a local level. The parish pastor first recommends this annulment to the diocese. The local bishop will either approve or disapprove of the dissolving of the marriage. The new procedure is swift and requires very little to accomplish in comparison.

You'll have to trust me on this next statement. God is very angry about this new development. He is not a happy camper because again, we as humans have assumed the role of a god. We totally ignore the first and most basic of God's rules which is this: When we marry, we are one, three-in-one in actuality, just like God... man, woman, and God. Only the physical death of the man or the woman should dissolve this bond... period.

Chapter 5

Sin, and So the Test Begins...

I'm sorry that it's taking me a bit little longer than I expected to get to the rules, but it is necessary for you to be able to understand how the evolution of this planet and man fits the creation story in the Bible and why rules are an absolute must for us to survive this journey that we must undertake.

So long ago, man was given the opportunity to "live the life of Riley," and man could have lived a carefree life, free from all worries if he would have just followed one simple rule. It wasn't that difficult a rule to adhere to, don't eat the fruit from the tree in the middle of the garden; everything else was okay... well, let's see what happened in God's Garden...

"Now the serpent was the most cunning of all the animals that the Lord God had made. The serpent asked the woman, "Did God really tell you not to eat from any of the trees of the garden?" The woman answered the serpent: "We may eat of the fruit of the trees in the garden; it is only about the fruit of the tree in the middle of the garden that God said, 'You shall not eat or even touch of it, lest you die.'" But the serpent said to the woman, "You certainly will not die! No, God knows well that the moment you eat of it your eyes will be opened and you will be like gods who know what is good and what is bad." (Genesis 3:1, 5)

One has to wonder why Satan appeared to Eve in the form of a snake... a talking snake no less. I don't know about you, but that would have freaked me out. You'd think Eve would have been a little suspicious when the snake started chatting with her.

Now, the serpent was the most cunning of all the animals that the Lord God had made; I think a snake was chosen for the following reasons:

All snakes or serpents have several distinct characteristics that are associated with this creature. A snake doesn't have eyelids. Clear scales instead of moveable eyelids cover the eyes, and as a result, the eyes are always open. Additionally, this particular snake, like all snakes, had a narrow, forked tongue, which repeatedly flicks out; that's where the term forked tongue, which is associated to a liar, originally came from.

The choice of animals to identify Satan is appropriate using this creature because the most cunning creature that God created was Satan, and so the story goes. The serpent asked the woman, "Did God really tell you not to eat from any of the trees of the garden?"

Now Satan knew that God told them that they weren't allowed to eat from the tree. So, this cunning serpent was now putting doubt in this innocent woman's mind. He didn't tell you, did he? Opened eyes: always seeing everything; forked tongue: always speaking mistruths. Satan knew what God told them.

Eve knew that the fruit from the tree in the middle of the garden was forbidden; however, this cunning creature convinced her that this rule wasn't put in place for any other reason than to keep God in the "driver's seat." The serpent was speaking the lies that only this being could speak, questioning the authority of the Lord God Almighty.

"Did God really tell you not to eat from any of the trees of the garden?" The woman answered the serpent, "We may eat of the fruit of the trees in the garden. It is only about the fruit of the tree in the middle of the garden that God said, 'You shall not eat or even touch of it, lest you die.'"

This is what the text says; however, I imagine that it could have gone something like this... let's have a little fun:

Snake: Hi there, little girl, what up?

Eve: Just taking a walk in the garden looking for some lunch.

Snake: How about one of those nice juicy apples hanging on that tree in the middle of the garden?

Eve: Oh no, God told me never to eat from that tree.

Snake: And you listen to him? You're a free woman!

Eve: Well, yes, I am, but God told us that we would die if we ate from the tree.

Snake: And you believe Him? He's just trying to keep you down. This tree's fruit will make you the same as He is... wouldn't you like that?

Eve: Sure, I would, but I'm afraid to die. He told Adam that if we ate from the tree, we would die!

Snake: God's not going to know. He's not even around... come on, have a taste, they're really good. You'll see that nothing is going to happen. I'll protect you.

Eve: But I really shouldn't... good, you say?

Snake: They're delicious, try them. I told you I would protect you. God has no power over me. I ate from the tree, and nothing happened to me... and yeah, they're really delicious.

Eve: Are you sure?

Snake: Of course, I'm sure. God's going to tell you anything to keep you from eating from the fruit of that beautiful tree. Come on, look at it, how can the fruit from that tree hurt you? And besides, He's not around.

Eve: I better not.

Snake: I'll tell you what, I'll make certain that this guy God doesn't bother you and Adam will be really happy with you when he sees that you have the knowledge and power as that God guy that's bulling him around.

Eve: You mean we'll be able to get him out of the grip of God?

Snake: Yeah! Now you got it! Don't you want your man to be proud of you?

Eve: Well, sure, I live for my man.

Snake: Well, if you do this, Adam will be so proud of you... and don't forget, I'll protect you from God.

Eve: Are you sure that Adam won't get mad at me?

Snake: No... He'll be proud, and he'll finally be rid of that God guy who doesn't let him know all the secrets of the universe, but you got to get him to eat from the tree too. Come on, try it. You'll see just what I'm talking about.

Eve: Yeah, and how is it that you can talk, anyway?

Snake: I ate from the tree, and now I'm invincible. I can do anything I want and that God guy can't do anything about it. Come on, little girl, take a couple of those beautiful apples and go tell Adam the deal.

Eve: Okay... if you're sure that he'll be all right with it.

Snake: He'll be just fine, and this fruit, the best-tasting fruit in the garden... just tell him that you want him to be like God, and this apple is the ticket. Tell him that you're looking out for him, and that if he loves you, he'll do this for you. He loves you, doesn't he? Make him prove it! Now, take some of the fruit and tell Adam what you want him to do for you... here he comes.

Satan got his way, convincing Eve to disobey the first and only rule that God had put in place for this human couple. He used the same deceptive technique then as he does today. He appeals to our weakness and convinces us that it's going to be better to disobey the Word of God; he'll be there to protect us from God.

Now I'm pretty sure if this wasn't the conversation between Eve and that talking snake and I did have some fun writing it, but I'm absolutely positive that the gist of the conversation was similar to the banter above; besides it could have been exactly like this. Who really knows the truth, only God, Eve, and that cunning creature, the snake... that's who.

"The woman saw that the tree was good for food pleasing to the eye, and desirable for gaining wisdom. So, she took some of its fruit and ate it; and she also gave some to her husband, who was with her, and he ate it. Then the eyes of both of them were opened, and they realized that they were naked; so, they sewed fig leaves together and make loincloths for themselves." (Genesis 3:6, 7)

As you can plainly see, Eve got Adam to eat the apple. She did what the demon asked her to do... convince Adam to share the delicious treat with her. Then the eyes of both of them were opened, and they realized that they were naked. These were the first sins, lust and jealousy. They didn't have these feeling about their sexuality nor were they jealous of God's authority until they disobeyed God and followed the advice of Satan.

Original sin was the disobedience to God; however, the result was the discovery of the most offensive and displeasing action that we as human being can display. The human body, well, most of them with the exception of mine, is a beautiful creation. The greatest artist of the universe designed it and designed it with specific purposes in mind.

God designed the body to function as a temple of the soul. He designed it for the continuation of the species by the mating process. God designed the body as a thing of beauty; however, mankind from that point and on has uncovered and revealed the bad side of the scenario. Mankind now saw the lust in the act of sex and the jealousy for equality opened the door, and they realized that they were naked, so they sewed fig leaves together and make loincloths for themselves.

Sex shared between two people in love for the procreation of children was the pure design of the specie's sexuality, and it was and is a good thing... all agree, even God. But now that man has learned the secrets of good and evil, he gained the knowledge of the impure nature of the act, the lust and desire for the animal act of sex. This was and still is the core result of the thing we all call original sin, our animal sexual instinct.

We're going to get to a point in this book where we see that there was a woman born in this world without original sin and conceived a child without the "knowledge" of man. This is highly significant and truly important for us to understand why this had to be so, and it leads right back to this first act of disobedience, the original sin of Adam and Eve.

If an apple was such a bad thing, why can we eat them now without consequence? But it wasn't the fruit; it was the act of disobedience, the insubordinate choice of mankind to listen to the "snake" and not the Master. Man, chose to obtain the knowledge of good and evil and then learned the sinful nature within himself.

Eve at this point was "tricked" into the act, but she had been given the opportunity to merely ignore the cunning snake and just listen to the Master. If she had done this, we would not be in the situation that we're in right now.

"When they heard the sound of the Lord God moving about in the garden at the breezy time of day, the man and his wife hid themselves from the Lord God among the trees of the garden. The Lord God called to the man and asked him, "Where are you?" He answered, "I heard you in the garden; but I was afraid, because I was naked, so I hid myself," Then He asked, "Who told you that you were naked? You have eaten from the tree which I had forbidden you to eat!" The man replied, "The woman who you put here with me, she gave me the fruit from the tree, and so I ate it." The Lord God asked the woman, "Why did you do such a thing?" The woman answered, "The serpent tricked me into it, so I ate it." Then the Lord God said to the serpent: "Because you have done this, you shall be banned from all the animals and from all the wild creatures; On your belly shall you crawl, and dirt shall you eat all the days of your life. I will put enmity between you and the woman. And between your offspring and hers; He will strike at your head, while you strike at his heel." To the woman He said: "I will intensify the pangs of your childbearing; in pain you shall bring forth children. Yet your urge shall be for your husband, and he shall be your master." To the man He said: "Because you listened to your wife and ate from the tree of which I had forbidden you to eat, "Cursed be the ground because of you! In toil shall you eat its yield all the days of your life. Thorns and thistles shall bring forth to you, as you eat the plants of the field. By the sweat of your face shall you get bread to eat, until you return to the ground, from which you were taken; for you are dirt, and to dirt you shall return."

"The man called his wife Eve, because she became the mother of all the living. For the man and his wife, the Lord God made leather garments, which clothed them. Then the Lord God said: "See! The man has become like one of us, knowing what is good and what is bad! Therefore, he must not be allowed to put forth out his hand to take fruit from the tree of life also, and thus eat from it and live forever." The Lord God therefore banished him from the Garden of Eden, to till the ground from which he had been taken. When He expelled the man, He settled him east of the Garden of Eden; and he stationed the cherubim and the fiery revolving sword, to guard the way to the tree of life." (Genesis 3:8–24)

I'm not sure how much of this really needs an explanation, but I want to explain a few of the lines we just read. The first line is: "The Lord God called to the man and asked him, 'Where are you?'" The Lord God knew exactly where Adam was, He knew exactly what the two of them had done. He didn't need Adam to answer Him and let Him know his location, but this was simply the first judgment of mankind.

God wanted Adam to account for his actions. He was asking for acknowledgment of the act. And so, the answer, "I heard you in the garden; but I was afraid, because I was naked, so I hid myself."

So, Adam admitted that he did eat from the tree, but he blamed it on Eve... another common sin of today, rationalization for an act you are responsible for committing and placing blame somewhere else or in this case on someone else.

Next, "because I was naked, so I hid myself." Adam couldn't have known that he was naked unless he gained the knowledge of good and evil.

That's the point when the first judgment of man took place. God simply asked Adam to take responsibility for the action, but Adam blamed his wife Eve: "The woman who you put here with me, she gave me the fruit from the tree, and so I ate it." I think that our God, merciful as He is, would have forgiven this man if he had taken responsibility for his action, just as God will do today if only, we admit it was our will that made the choice.

God made them one body, one soul, a married couple. They were one in the same as far as God's is concerned. Then God gave Eve the same chance to fess up. But she didn't and took the easy road again… "The serpent tricked me into it, so I ate it." This is so commonplace in our society; we allow ourselves to succumb to the lies and misdirection of… well, all who tell us something that makes us do what we want to do anyway, and if it's wrong, we simply pass the buck.

And passing the buck really seems to annoy the "Big Guy," so naturally, he got a little upset. And now the "Chief" now had to flex his muscles and put the guidelines on the "test."

I'm really having a weird thought about this Satan/snake thing right now, so I'm going to stop and pray and talk to God before I go on… I'll resume once He tells me know who is putting these thoughts in my mind.

New day…

Here's the trouble with listening to voices in your mind; sometimes the thoughts are from the evil one; you must proceed with caution and pray for the guidance before carrying out any of these thoughts or actions.

I'm positive now that the last things I was hearing yesterday were not from the "Chief," but from the snake himself. So, I stopped before I wrote them down. The stronger you get in the Grace of the Lord, the more the evil one hates the thought of not having control of your mind, heart and soul, but today my mind, heart, and soul are with God.

Now because the Lord was a little annoyed with the situation,

He had to react and react correctly, and He did by making the following first judgment. "Because you have done this, you shall be banned from all the animals and from all the wild creatures; on your belly shall you crawl and dirt you shall eat all the days of your life. I will put enmity between you and the woman, and between your offspring and hers; He will strike at your head, while you strike at his heel."

Now some may interpret this verse to say that non-humans have souls and now the Lord just banned Satan from having power over them. This is not true; animals do not have souls.

What this does say, however, is that the Lord took away all control that Satan had or wanted to have over the beasts of the world. He placed the authority directly back into the hands of man and Himself. Satan would not be able to influence the evolution of these creatures. He would not be able to upset God's order, by which God had given dominion over these creatures to the man on the sixth day. Satan lost any and all control of those breasts from that day forth. In fact, "on your belly you shall crawl" is the amount of control that Satan has over these creatures... none. He is the lowest in this chain whenever he takes the form of the snake, and as far as God is concerned, "dirt you shall eat all the days of your life."

"Dirt you shall eat all the days of your life" is also symbolic of another order set by this decree... last line of the passage: "Until you return to the ground, from which you were taken; for you are dirt, and to dirt you shall return."

Satan is trying his best to influence man, and he is trying his best to capture as many of the souls that were ultimately meant to be God's. However, Satan's existence has a limit; it will be over when the final judgment takes place, but what about the eternity of hell, you ask? Imagine knowing that you will die, and there is nothing after death. That's the true existence of hell. Sure, there is a place now with the fire, brimstone, and pains of separation, and it is hell. It's one of the three universes... or, more understandable in human terms, "dimensions" of this universe that we inhabit and it is most assuredly real. But it is a temporal plane of exist-

59

ence, a "rest stop" so to speak for the souls who do not pass this test. We'll get into that subject later in this book, and I'll show you to the place where it specifically says this in the Bible, for the skeptics.

God couldn't just punish the snake for this act of treason. There had to be consequences for the humans with souls. Eden was the place where God placed these first two humans. He offered them an existence free from worry, work, the troubles of life, and offered them the easiest test of all, one rule. But man, couldn't then and can't now, seem to listen to God's authority. We all have a choice to follow our "heart" because of free will and so we all risk the loss of "Shangri-La."

I'll tell you this and it is coming straight from the Master... He wants us to pass the test. He wants us to live forever in happiness with Him in His Kingdom of Heaven. He doesn't want to lose even one of the souls; they're all a part of Him. His plan provides us the opportunity to gain eternal life; it's just as simple as understanding that He is part of every human being we come in contact with.

It's just as simple as looking at the image and likeness of God in every human that we encounter. That's the reason "rules" were established. I'm getting to them, but you must understand that these rules were formulated for this specific reason and the reason is to look at God as the master and to look at every other human as another "living god," so to speak. It's very simple; look at this human life as if you were looking through the eyes of a child. Look at this test with a pure heart, with an innocent heart, and then and only then will you pass this test.

Now then, what say we give these two kids a chance to be alone and have some kids, so they can fill this place to the east of Eden with our ancestors... well, some of our ancestors. Someone reading this is just about to ask themselves how that happened, Adam and Eve had two sons, Cain and Abel. How did all of us stem from that family? Did they have daughters?

Okay, guess we'll answer that question and see how that happened.

This world at that point in time had many humans inhabiting it, but the two that were put back into the mix, Adam and Eve, were the only ones who had souls. They bore two children initially according to the records, Cain and Abel… male children. Cain was the first, and Abel was the second son born to this couple. Abel grew up to be a shepherd, and Cain became a farmer. These two sons had the gift of the soul, and well, so would all the children that Cain would father, because Cain killed Abel over a little misunderstanding that was a result of an offering made to God. God punished Cain for this killing and sent him to the land of Nod, which was further east of Eden. There Cain took a wife, one of the humans inhabiting this region. What happened next?

Cain and his bride had a child, and they named him Enoch. Cain also became the founder of a city that he named after this child… Enoch. Pretty lonely city if it was just the three of them, don't you think? But there were plenty of non-soul humans around; in fact, at this point in time, five generations later, according to scripture, man had developed refined skills. The people of this era could play musical instruments and forge bronze and iron. That's pretty amazing for five generations, about 150 years, don't you agree?

But the gene pool that came from Cain was not going to be the genetic line that God would choose to found the first tribes of Israel. This task would fall squarely on the shoulders of Adam and Eve's third son, Seth. However, Adam's first son Cain did do his part in the repopulation of this earth by fathering a child, who fathered children, and so on, and they all had a precious soul.

"At that time men began to invoke the Lord by name." (Genesis 4:26)

So now we're going to move on to the flood. Some say true, some say folklore, I say, let's see for ourselves. But keep in mind, this book of the Bible was written by Moses. Moses was one of the few men that lived here on earth that actually saw God face to face. He got the story firsthand from the "Boss." But as things typically go, the story does change as it is told.

What Moses was simply trying to convey in the Book of Genesis was the fact that God and only God is responsible for the creation of everything. Moses was trying his best to get the story right, but other human helped write and pass down these stories until they finally were put in their final form.

What the historians tell us about the formation of the Bible is that Moses lived around 1400 BCE and probably wrote the first five books. But they're not 100 percent sure of the fact that this first book of the Bible was the first document pertaining to God's creation story.

However, truth is this: God gave Moses the information because too many records were destroyed, and the truth related to creation needed to be recorded.

Truth is that the book of Job is the first documentation that this generation of man had been able to recover from the long-lost past. Truth is that Moses did get the rest of the information from God directly, but he had the information from the book of Job to work with and other information passed down by prior generations. How could there have been a Hebrew nation that could believe in this God of theirs... well, ours... without some prior information? How could there have been so many other civilizations on this earth if the earth was only two thousand years in the making based on their assumed time lines.

These civilizations in those times had gods, they were up to speed in the arts, wine making, metal forming, and the only thing that we don't know is if they had some technologies that were similar to the technologies of today. Who built the pyramids? Think about that! It wasn't aliens... guarantied.

Think about this also, for just a minute, this Adam and Eve event happened in 13,671 BCE, but there were other humans "unlike" us inhabiting this earth then, weren't they still humans who could use reason? They were intelligent. Isn't it possible that God's plan was to refine this creature until He felt that the "time" was right to place the soul? Couldn't there have been other civilizations that had developed into civilizations similar to the civilizations of today before Adam and Eve and were lost? As we move on, think about those possibilities.

Chapter 6
That's a Lot of Water

Humans want answers, answers that compute; this does not compute, Will Robinson! This was dialogue between a young boy and a robot from a TV series in the late 1960s. This TV series was a precursor for the new technology humans we were about to be introduced to in the late twentieth century.

We were not prepared to fully understand what changes were about to happen to the civilized world. We were going to be gradually eased into the acceptance of the possibilities that there could be other life forms living in this vast universe, new technologies, and certain beliefs that we as humans had of the "facts," which would possibility have not made any sense to us; they didn't compute.

The flood does not compute to most of the present-day scientists. Most are in disagreement that conclusive evidence of this global catastrophe is sufficient. The claim is that no one, including this family and ark filled with the animals, could have survived if this did in fact happen the way that it's described in the Bible. The argument is that the amount of water from this flood would have drastically changed the atmosphere so that the air would not be suitable to support life; the atmosphere would be too thick.

Many scientists say that they would have all literally drowned in the thickness of the oxygen because the moisture would have filled their lungs and collapsed them, if in fact there was enough water to cover the entire planet.

Another argument is that there is not any evidence of the earth landmasses being submerged in water for that length of time. It would have left sediment at a uniform level, which would have been easily seen with some minor excavation.

Of course, the assumption is that the time line was four thousand years ago, so all the research has been conducted on that inaccurate time line assumption. For thousands and thousands of years, humans have been here on this earth, but only in the most resent 15,700 years or so have these beings been separated from the category of animals. With God's Day in the garden, and the institution of the "breath of life" in the human, the earth was about to change. But it didn't get to the point in history that we have all assumed to be this 2000 or so BCE time line in a mere 1656 years as some believe.

There were 7,625 years between the Adam and Eve incident and this Noah's Ark event and yet another 4,600 plus years before Moses arrived on the scene. If researchers would look past the accepted interpretation of the Bible and other texts, they might just be able to attain that much-needed information and evidence that all have been looking for... the evidence that does compute.

Please understand that the Bible has only just been written in the "grand scheme" of things. It is a collection of the known history and events of our passed times. It is what we have salvaged from the past after the elimination of the "animal" man because of this "flood" event. It is very accurate and absolutely true, but it's often not interpreted correctly.

Now also, we must all accept the fact that this work of literary brilliance was originally written to support the faith of the Jewish people, the once one true people of our God. Later events and a change in the religious basis caused the "purification" until we had the current version of the Bible of today, which is the basis of the Christian religion.

Unfortunate as it may seem, some of the time lines do not correspond to such an event, and we have no scientific data to support many of the time lines. Furthermore, there is no supporting evidence apparent to the scientific community to prove that this event actually took place other than the four chapters in the Bible, which, incidentally, they do not accept.

Genesis 6 through 9 inclusive... this does not compute... so says that community.

So, let's proceed, but we'll proceed cautiously, and we will take a look at the verses in these four biblical chapters and bring them into perspective; you then can evaluate the words and decide for yourself if they do compute. Not everyone will agree, and in fact, most might disagree, but I didn't write the text; I'm just going to tell you what I believe it means.

"When men began to multiply on the earth and daughters were born to them, the sons of heaven saw how beautiful the daughters of man were, and so they took for their wives as many of them as they chose. Then the Lord said: "My spirit shall not remain in man forever, since he is but flesh. His days shall comprise one hundred and twenty years." At that time the Nephilium appeared on earth (as well as later), after the sons of heaven had intercourse with the daughters of man, who bore them sons. They were the heroes of old, the men of renown." (Genesis 6:1–4)

In verse 4, you will find the word *Nephilium*. Let me define the word; this word means "giant" and can also be interpreted as a large version of man. This man surfaced in the evolutionary chain around 30,000 BCE. They coexisted with the current primitive man for quite some time until the present-day man was the remaining result. However, no one is completely sure the exact time line of the total disappearance of that primate.

Some theologians have also made claim that the Nephilium were angels who were free to roam the earth and act as humans. This is also incorrect; angels are totally spiritual beings. They do not want or are even capable of physical relationships nor do they have to be subjected to this "test." It is true; however, that there are angels among us then and even now but they are here for one specific purpose.

"What's the purpose?"

Thanks for asking. I'll be happy to tell you.

There are two different types of angels, the good angels and the bad angels. The good angels were created before the disturbance occurred and are the true faithful spiritual beings of the Lord God Almighty. They are the beings that did not compromise their faith during the battle of good and evil that caused this entire situation in the first place during the battle that took place in the first universe.

The bad angels were also created before the disturbance and are the faithful followers of Satan. They are tried and true to his beliefs that they should not have to worship another celestial being, especially one who claims to be their God. All these bad angels believe that they are the true masters of these universes. But their leader Satan, the one who started this whole mess, is the boldest of the bunch and has the most power of any of these angelic beings.

But contrary to popular beliefs, these beings, all angels, cannot cross into the physicality of this dimension or universe without God's permission. They are limited to the spiritual interaction between their spirit and our soul or as I like to call it, our living spirit. They're purpose and only purpose is to assist our living spirit in making the choice of which direction to follow, the path of good, the good angels, or the path of evil, the bad angels.

We're all familiar with the two angels sitting on our shoulder, one cute little one with a halo and one dressed in a devil's costume complete with the pitchfork, right? That is basically true and factual. There is at all times of our life here on earth at least two "angels" assigned to each and every one of us... yes, all of us, even the two without sin, one good, one bad. They are in direct contact with our living spirit and are trying their very best to lead us to their side.

That's were our free will comes into play. We get to choose if we are going to do what is right and just in the eyes of the Lord or what is offensive to Him and pleases the demon and that's what free will is, the ability to choose between good and evil and "own" that choice; free will is totally owning our choices...

I know that this last paragraph is a little out of place, but the urge to write this was very strong and I really had to write it, so I did, so…

From the time of Adam and Eve until the tribes of Noah, Shem, Ham, and Japheth were an incredibly long time in our perception of time… 7,625 years. Mankind had every opportunity in that time to prove to God that he was a worthy creature and was capable of performing his mission here on earth, the mission of passing the test. God gave mankind ample time to make his intension known, would he choose good, or would he choose evil. But mankind in general was still an animal because of the "giants" who still roamed the earth… Neanderthal man, this new man's ancestors.

Let's assume these as accurate dates of these events, Adam and Eve, 13671 BCE; Noah and the boys, 6046 BCE. And let's also assume that in 7,625 years of "being fruitful and multiplying," the earth's population was somewhat similar to today's population. Additionally, let's assume that the morals of then were similar to today's morals. Let's really go out on the limb and assume that those people had a somewhat similar lifestyle; many of the creature comforts that we enjoy today. Let's say that there were many nations inhabiting this planet, and the social standards of those people were also similar to today's social standards, can you see it?

No wonder God had to get rid of them; I wouldn't be surprised if He's considering something similar for today's society. This is a morally corrupted society that embraces the power of lust, greed, envy, and "bad will" toward their fellow man, and a very similar type of end for this society is coming, but not water… something far worse.

That society then was just as guilty of the moral corruption as this society. Some theologians claim that the passage, "My spirit shall not remain in man forever, since he is but flesh. His days shall comprise one hundred and twenty years" was in fact a warning to those people. A time limit to get their acts together so to speak. God was putting down the law; you guys have 120 years to straighten this mess out, or I'm going to be forced to do something about it. That's the reason it ended up in the current location of the text and is at Genesis 6:3. But it doesn't belong there; it belongs in the fifth chapter, it should be verse 33, in my humble opinion, because God was issuing a warning; I'll explain.

First and foremost, it would have taken much more than 1,656 years, the assumed time from Adam to Noah, to eliminate this planet of all the "man creatures" that did not possess a soul. Fact is, there are still some primitive cultures among us today. That 120 number is and always has been the maximum lifespan of a human being. It is not factual that any human has every lived to be over that age; well maybe, check the world record book… none since we've been keeping score.

But in 7,625 years, the repopulation process eliminated a very large percentage of humans without souls. True that some of the old "man creatures" were still around, but it was a very small percentage… just like the primitive cultures today.

And in the 7,625 years, man had an opportunity to become the "gods" that we think we are… just like today's societies and people. There was ample time for the development of societies, cultures, trade between nations, tools… all limited to that man's intellectual capability. Don't discount that intellectual capability either; it was similar to ours. The "man creature" has been here for many millenniums and has the highest intellectual faculties of all the creatures that populate this earth. He was also the chosen of God to carry the soul in his physical being. There was ample time for man to lose himself inside himself and find that separation from God that is so evident in that society who was about to be destroyed by God.

The whole meaning around the story of the flood is that man was about to be eliminated from this earth… all the corruption, all the sinful ways, all the "man creatures" left on this earth, eliminating those with and without a soul, with the exception of the four "chosen" tribes, and yes, I said tribes: Noah, Shem, Ham, and Japheth, and the select animals.

Genesis 6:5, 13: this section is entitled "Warning of the Flood."

"When the Lord saw how great was man's wickedness on earth, and how no desire that his heart conceived was ever anything but evil, He regretted that He had made man on the earth, and His heart was grieved. So, the Lord said: "I will wipe out from the earth the men whom I have created, and not only the men, but also the beasts and the creeping things and the birds of the air, for I am sorry that I made them." But Noah found favor with the Lord. These are the **descendants** of Noah, a good man and blameless in that age, for he walked with God, **begot three sons**: Shem, Ham and Japheth. In the eyes of God, the earth was corrupt and full of lawlessness. When God saw how corrupt the earth had become. Since all **mortals** led depraved lives on earth, He said to Noah: "I have decided to put an end to all the **mortals** on the earth: the earth is full of lawlessness because of them. So, I will destroy them and all life on earth."

If you noticed, there are five words in bold in the passage above. Two of these are key in understanding that there were three other "tribes" that stemmed from the "tribe" of Noah. The most important word is *descendants*. Followed by the words *begot three sons*; these words appeared in the St. James Version as, *generations* of Noah and His generations walked with God. These *generations* were Shem, Ham, and Japheth, so the only true interpretation for this is that there were three other tribes that came from the Noah tribe. However, purifying sometimes has an opposite effect, and in this case, it did. I truly believe that the interpreters got a little overzealous in their translation of this verse. I grew up reading the St. James Version and now read both the text, including the New American version, daily in fact, so I am familiar with both texts.

The other two words highlighted are the same word, *mortals*. In the previous text, this word was flesh. All flesh was to be eliminated from the earth. God was mad, He was mad at man, so mad that He was about to destroy all flesh, all living creatures including the Neanderthal man—*mortals... no souls...* they had to go!

Funny thing about words; they have multiple definitions. Let's take the word *flesh* for instance. My seven-language dictionary, three volumes, has thirteen definitions listed for *flesh*. I also looked up the word *mortal*, and it has eleven definitions. I'm not going to list them all; I only want to make this one point: words are interpretable.

This original text was written in the Hebrew language. I don't know how many of you have ever seen the Hebrew language written, but when you have a chance, take a look at how it is written. It's a very fascinating language; it only has several "letters," but their arrangement defines the word. The translators of this text really had to work diligently to come up with an accurate English translation for us to read.

They did their best and the religious authorities, including the most important of the all, the Son of God, approve it. He approved the text because in basis, these are the chain of events that happened in the formation of this world. These are how the people of those times were created and were evolved, and what ultimately led to their destruction. However, Jesus also was known to apply the use of parables to explain the truth of the events, so why should we, knowing all that we claim to know, expect anything different from Dear Old Dad? That apple didn't fall far from the tree... did He, Dad?

But anyway, let's get to it. It's raining this morning and has been raining all night. There is a large pool of water collecting in my rain gutters that I have to clear, so we need to address this flood now so I can get to that problem.

The flood story in the Bible has never been accurately confirmed scientifically. In fact, the newest explanation of the theory is that the flood in the Bible is actually based on the Babylonian text entitled *The Epic of Galgamesh*. It is theorized that this flood occurred about a thousand years prior to the Noah flood event.

Both have similar points in common. However, the epic account is said to have happened locally and did not cause a catastrophic flood on all the landmasses on the entire earth. I actually watched a documentary on the Discovery Channel some time ago on this newest attempt to discredit the Noah story.

However, what has been scientifically confirmed is that around 6200 BCE, a "minor ice age" occurred, and it took about six hundred years before things were back to "normal." Gees, bees, Louise, isn't that a coincidence? They've uncovered scientific evidence that shows that this region... the Middle East, because that's where the entire text of this book originated, specifically the Black Sea, was the region where this significant change occurred.

Two senior Columbia University scientists said in essence, that because of this ice age, ten cubic miles of water flowed through the region each day; that's about two hundred times the amount of water that flows over Niagara Falls each day. They say that this was the case for about ten months... three hundred days.

Now an "ice age" is caused by the drastic reduction of the air temperature of the earth, specifically the northern or southern poles of the planet. The glacial caps are expanded to cover landmasses that are normally not covered by ice. When the temperature rises again, the thaw occurs, and so that melted ice has got to go somewhere. In this case, it flooded the region where it all started, the area of the development of these people of God.

All right, right here it is in the nutshell, here's the deal; I'm going to go over this fact by fact...

First, we'll start with the words used; in fact, all words used then and now do have more than one meaning... fact! Each individual can interpret the way a word is used differently... fact! Any and all written word when translated into another language will typically lose its effect during the translation process... fact!

Secondly, man was and is a corrupt being, both these new and improved men and the old men of that period on this earth... fact! Man, was separated from a true union with God Almighty; man, was influenced more by the "snake" and followed in the snake's ways... fact! God Almighty was provoked to the point of action... fact! All "flesh" was not destroyed from the face of the earth, with the exception of the chosen... fact!

Third and most importantly, all the "flesh" on the entire planet was not eliminated; this was not a global catastrophe... fact! Scientists cannot find evidence of this global catastrophe because it does not happen... fact! God was dealing with this group of people who He Himself gave this gift of life and was setting the stage for yet another phase of the refinement of this man... fact! God was about to cleanse this planet from the corruption that this man had partaken in when he chose the ways of the "snake"... fact! The difference between man and animal is that men are conscious of the eventuality of their death and animals are not... fact! Man, has been trying to explain away this existence of God in one way or another from the beginning of that initial separation in the Garden but only when blame is needed man will acknowledge God and then will blame Him for our failures... fact! That culture in that era had to be punished by God... fact!

God saved four communities or "tribes" of people, not the eight individuals we always have been led to believe... truth!

Let's read this, shall we?

"Make yourself an ark of gopher wood, put various compart-ments in it, and cover it inside and outside with pitch. This is how you shall build it; the length of the ark shall be three hundred cubits, its width fifty cubits, and its height thirty cubits. Make an opening for daylight in the ark, and finish the ark a cubit above it. Put an entrance in the side of the ark, which you shall make with bottom, second and third decks I, on my part, am about to bring the flood waters on the earth, to destroy everywhere all creatures in which there is the **breath of life**; everything on earth shall perish. But with you I will establish my covenant; you and your sons, your wife and your sons' wives, shall go into the ark. Of all other living creatures, you shall bring two into the ark, one male and one female, that you may keep them alive with you. Of all kinds of birds, of all kinds of beasts, and of all kinds of creeping things, two shall come into the ark with you, to stay alive. Moreover, you are to provide yourself with all the food that is to be eaten, and store it away, that it may serve as provisions for you and them." This Noah did;

he carried out all the commands that God gave him." (Genesis 6:14, 22)

Let's talk about this first line: "Make yourself an ark of gopher wood, put various compartments in it, and cover it inside and outside with pitch. The Hebrew word used for ark in this sentence is *teivah*; it could mean *ark*, or it could mean *word*. The original Hebrew word used was *go'fer*, which has no meaning and has never been accurately translated. It has been changed to *gopher* through time. This word *gopher* is used, but cypress is the wood common to the region and also is the material of choice for the construction of vessels. However, this simple little word *go'fer* indicates this construction may not have been a vessel at all.

The word *ark* also has several meanings, as does the word *word*. Perhaps God was simply establishing a covenant with Noah and his people: "But with you I will establish my covenant."

Perhaps this ark was actually an *arca*, which was the origin of this Hebrew word *teivah*. The word *arca* means to hold off or defend. It also means chest, coffer, covered basket, another closed receptacle, or a hutch.

I don't know; maybe this civilization was much more advanced than we give them credit for, and perhaps they're technologies were more advanced than we know. Perhaps these people were in the same standings then with God as the people of today seem to be... because I assure you, God is certainly angry with today's society.

I'm going out on a limb here... build a hutch, as a gopher would could conceivably be the translation today; we have such retreats borrowed into the ground. Today's safety retreats have been built in the event of a global catastrophe and are a safe haven for the leaders of our planet.

There are a great number of these hutches... dugouts through-out this planet and were built primarily as a precaution in the event of global war. Perhaps we can't find this elusive ark because it was not a vessel at all, perhaps it was a hutch... dug out from the side of the earth.

Are you beginning to wonder if the Bible is indeed accurate? I assure you that it is! But please understand, this ancient text had to make some kind of sense to these people and of course there was the Epic of Gilgamesh that was not only a verbal story that was being passed down, but it was on tablets for them to read.

And please understand that we are not as advanced a creature that we assume to be. Just because we have electronic technology and have mastered manufacturing of many products that we take for granted on a daily basis, this does not necessarily mean that our cultures are the most advanced creature in our history of this planet.

If we are so advanced, we would truly understand the needs and wants of our fellow human beings. We would see the soul inside every living being and treat them as if we were addressing God himself. That, my friend, is the ultimate goal in the civilization of this species.

"This is how you shall build it; the length of the ark shall be three hundred cubits, its width fifty cubits, and its height thirty cubits. Make an opening for daylight in the ark, and finish the ark a cubit above it. Put an entrance in the side of the ark, which you shall make with bottom, second and third decks I, on my part, am about to bring the flood (waters) on the earth, to destroy everywhere all creatures in which there is the breath of life; everything on earth shall perish."

I thought you could see this again with a different perspective. It says that this "ark" has different levels; it's pretty big, too, about the length of the block that my home is on, twice as wide as the street in front of my house and about twice the height of my home. It was huge, and it was supposedly made from gopher wood. We can't manufacture a seaworthy vessel today with those dimensions and with the "wood" materials available today. Many of our supper tankers made of steel use to transport oil aren't even that big... the *Titanic* wasn't that big!

Let's say that Noah and the boys were really four different groups of people. They were all descendants of the original clan of Noah. Let me give you an example of what I mean. The United States of America was formed as a branch of Great Britain... true? We, the Americans, were originally the "generations" or "sons" of England, a term that would fit in any conversation to be had or any written document that we would read... true? If there were a global event that could threaten the existence of mankind these two nations would join forces and together would try to preserve the species. And of course, other God-fearing nations would be invited to join this cause as well... how many takers?

Here's how I interpret this text; there was about to be a flood, caused by the melting of the frozen northern ice caps. These three other nations that originated from Noah were "just" in the sight of God and were going to join the crusade.

Let's look to where it says this in these three chapters.

First place... Genesis 7:6: "Noah was six hundred years old when the flood waters came upon the earth."

Okay, if the verse in Genesis that refers to the age that a man shall live is indeed accurate and men lived a maximum lifespan of 120 years, then Noah couldn't have been six hundred years old. And if the tribe of Noah or Noah himself was born in of about the year 6,046 BCE, isn't it feasible that if "Noah" was six hundred years old when the floodwaters came that the year 5,446 BCE fits the theory of the two Georgetown University professors' time line? They said this minor ice age had its thaw around 5600 BCE, but it could have been as late as 5400 BCE.

"In the six hundredth year of Noah's life, in the second month, on the seventeenth day of the month; it was on that day that All the fountains of the great abyss burst forth, and the floodgates of the sky were opened." (Genesis 7:11)

Pretty specific on the day, don't you think? Look, this Bible is infallible on doctrine and belief. It is also totally accurate on the rules governing our behavior and conduct required to get past this testing period. However, and I can't stress this enough, it is a well-written literary piece of work. It also is written in the "parable" format because we need to interpret for ourselves the true meaning of each of our own existences. The answers to every question are contained in this work of art given to us by God Almighty.

I'm sure that the "February 17" day as we date today has some meaningful reason for being in this verse, but I really don't think that I care to ask God to answer that question. I'm pretty sure it's only placed in the verse because the writers or tellers of this story were indeed looking to get the readers' and listeners' attention; they were being dramatic, or perhaps it's deeper, but it's not important.

What is important is the use of the word *abyss* again. According to Old Testament translators, this word can be interpreted as oceans surrounding the earth. And then the floodgates of the sky were opened... so before it started to "rain" the great abyss burst... hum. Let's look at this passage really quick too: Psalm 104:5, 9.

"You fixed the earth on its foundation, never to be moved. The ocean covered it like a garment; above the mountains stood the waters. At your roar they took flight; at the sound of your thunder, they fled. They rushed up the mountains, down the valleys to places you had fixed for them. You set a limit they cannot pass; never again will they cover the earth."

This passage is entitled "Praise to the Creator." This passage is speaking directly of this event. It confirms that this flood was indeed a result of this "ice age" thaw. The oceans covered the earth like a garment, so much so that they covered the mountains. That's what happens when the polar caps are frozen and the caps are extended; the water needed is water absorbed from the oceans, from the lakes, from the rivers, but primarily from the oceans. It stretches across landmasses and covers them completely with ice so that no land is seen… like a garment covers us… well, not like some of the garments of today, some you indeed couldn't consider coverings; might as well be naked. We'll get to that later…

Then God's command… the roar… they took flight and rushed through the areas chosen by God. This was the flood that caused the catastrophic elimination of the flesh of this earth. And God set a limit to where this water would go, and in fact, this water did not cover the entire planet, just this specified area that God was "cleansing." And it won't happen again… not by God's hand, but by ours… did you ever hear of global warming?

And really, let's not forget the opening line: "You fixed the earth on its foundation, never to be moved." God was fixing the problem; man was the reason for the foundation of this physical earth. And this man is never to be moved from this earth.

Now what does that mean? Today, we advanced humans are actively exploring space. We are in search of other planets that could sustain our live forms. We want to colonize Mars for fear that our natural resources will soon run out. We are afraid that there is no repairing the damage we've done to this planet by stripping it of what we feel are the necessities of life.

Do you think it was the same then? Ever hear of the myth of the lost city of Atlantis? I'm not going to write about it; there are plenty of materials on the subject, but I do want to show you one more place in the Bible before we get back to the "flood" chapters in the text. I'm only going to site two verses from this chapter and finish with this section because I really, really, really want to get to the meat of this mission… the "rules."

"The Lord came down to see the city and tower that the men had built. Then the Lord said: "If now, while they are one people, all speaking the same language, they have started to do this, nothing will later stop them from doing whatever they presume to do." (Genesis 11:5 and 6)

Please think about that! Back to the flood...

"Those that entered were male and female, and of all species they came, as God had commanded Noah. Then the Lord shut him in." (Genesis 7:16)

"I wonder why God had to shut Noah in; couldn't he close the door? Do you think that the "ark" was maybe, just maybe, a secure dugout or underground shelter... can't be. In verse 17, it states, "As the waters increased, they lifted the ark, so that it rose above the earth." Again, *ark* from the Hebrew word *teivah* is also interpreted as word. So, what this really could mean is as the flood continued, the word of God Almighty rose above the earth and His decree was to be carried out."

"The Lord wiped out every living thing on earth; man, and cattle, the creeping things and the birds of the air; all were wiped out from the earth. Only Noah and those with him in the ark were left." (Genesis 7:23)

I can't help thinking that God is indeed a fat Italian guy, smoking a big cigar every time I read this verse. I then am, certainly; made to his image and likeness... little of my humor. God wiped them out! I can see it now; he put a "hit," a "contract," out on the "mutts."

You know, God's really okay with humor; it's part of life. Just because we have to take this test doesn't mean we shouldn't have some laughs on the way. Lot of beautiful things here, and laughter's one.

This was the decree of God. He commanded the "eradication" of all those living creatures in which there is the *breath of life*, but it doesn't say the entire earth, just those on the earth with the breath of life. It was localized to certain areas that God needed to cleanse.

"Gradually the waters receded from the earth. At the end of one hundred and fifty days, the waters had so diminished that, in the seventh month, on the seventeenth day of the month, the ark came to rest on the mountains of Ararat. The waters continued to diminish until the tenth month, and on the first day of the tenth month the tops of the mountains appeared." (Genesis 8:3, 5)

Now there was localized flooding as well as flooding in other regions of the earth. However, this story of Noah is specifically about this particular region of the earth. This story is a combination of Noah's adventure and the epic found in the ancient Babylonian tablets. The reason for this text is to try to explain that God was so angry at the way that man had developed that He had no other choice then to get rid of the bad "seed."

When this was revealed to the author of these writings Moses, you must understand the situation that Moses was in at the time. He had just led his people out of Egypt, and they wanted some answers. They wanted to know about the past and how their future was going to shape up. About four thousand years had gone by since this event, and the only writing that existed to assist Moses with this difficult situation was the Babylonian text. So, it was an easy and plausible transition to the Noah story. But please don't misunderstand what I'm saying; this catastrophe did in fact occur.

God did cause a great flood to eliminate the evil from this earth. The four groups of people and the animals were preserved, but how could Moses tell them that they, the chosen people of mankind, were in most ways less superior in technologies and social standings than the people of those times. Plus, God knowing that man would return to these ways allowed Moses to use the basis of this story as the explanation to an unconceivable event.

This is evident in these passages we just read. This one for example makes the case for the thaw; 227 days… seventh month, seventeenth day, the ark came to rest on the mountains of Ararat.

The real significance of the "location" is not for us to be searching for a ship on the mountain, but to identify the region. Perhaps we should be looking for some large hidden cavern in the region.

The significance of the time is to support the scientific evidence we would eventually find. It goes on to say 301 days—tenth month, first day. This is the evidence presented by the scientists from Georgetown University… it took about three hundred days.

And if you're still not convinced, Genesis 8:13:

"In the six hundred and first year of Noah's life, on the first day of the month, the water began to dry up on the earth. Noah then removed the covering of the ark and saw that the surface of the ground was drying up."

So, a year went by from the point that these people supposedly boarded this ship, but why, oh why, did Noah have to *remove the covering* from the *ark*? So, he uncovered the ark and saw the earth was drying up; strange, isn't it?

The very purpose of the Bible is to instruct us. To lead us to the end with a passing grade. But we must do this on our own. The text is a study guide so to speak. If God were to reveal everything that brought us to this point in time, this test would be totally meaningless. If we knew factually and without any "gray areas" what our past were, fear would keep us on track, not love for God.

Fear of us losing this chance to exist forever. But that's not what God wants.

God wants us to make the choice and He wants us to pass the test, but we must use the "free will" option that He gave us to take this test; remember, free will… it's the choice between good and evil that we alone make and own the choice.

Is this starting to compute?

Want a fix on the time line? Read Genesis 11–17 from the New American Version and chapters 10 through 17 in the King James Version of the Bible. Add the applicable numbers in the chapters and verses until you get to Abraham himself and then do the math. I suggested something similar to this back in chapter 4; did any of you do it? If you did you need to go a little further and look closely at both of these texts. If you got it right, you should be placed perfectly at the time line that we know factually that Abraham lived. This is my little test for you. I know that it works out. I did it; you try it.

Chapter 7

Oy, vey... here's a rule – more accurately, a covenant.

And it is a doozy; ya think God could have skipped this one? The year is 2,453 BCE. Check the math then check the records available.

"When Abram was ninety-nine years old, the Lord appeared to him and said: "I am God the Almighty. Walk in my presence and be blameless. Between you and me I will establish my covenant, and I will multiply you exceedingly." When Abram prostrated himself, God continued to speak to him, "My covenant with you is this: you are to become the father of a host of nations. No longer shall you be called Abram; your name shall be Abraham, for I am making you the father of a host of nations. I will render you exceedingly fertile; I will make nations of you; kings shall stem from you. I will maintain my covenant with you and your descendants after you throughout the ages as an everlasting pact, to be your God and the God of your descendants after you." (Genesis 17:1, 7)

Always keep in mind when reading the Bible that it is the absolute and literal truth, but sometimes it can surely be assumed that it may be different than it first appears.

You're going to need to think about that for a while; you know what? That will be answer number 2 at the end of the book.

I'm sure that we discussed the fact that Abram was not in fact "Abraham," in an earlier chapter and contained within this passage is the confirmation of that fact. Likewise, I'm sure that many may not agree with that statement. And that's okay. Everyone has an opinion, and you are entitled to think what you will. However, my opinion is that Abraham was the entire tribe that stemmed from this man Abram...

Anyway, every human doesn't have what's necessary to comply with this required procedure that this chapter is focused on. It's limited to the male population... go figure. But this is the way it was back then, and of course, the basis of this covenant had to be established with who those cultures believed to be the dominant sex. All males of the time were the masters of their household, and that is a fact. No Hebrew woman of the time was considered equal to a man no matter what the case, and that, sorry to say, is also a fact.

Now we're going to see a shift in direction. Instead of four tribes as we saw in the previous chapter, we're going to see that the twelve tribes of Israel were descendants of this tribe of Abraham. God didn't save the original twelve tribes that were established from the time of Adam through Noah and the boys; they weren't the chosen ones.

Did you know numbers in the Bible have a great deal of religious significance? For example, the number 4 refers to the four directions in this instance—north, south, east and west, and if you haven't figured it out yet, Noah and the boys... the four directions; I guess I should have told you that in the last chapter, just a little oversight. Twelve is another significant number; I'll tell you why later.

When Abram was ninety-nine years old, the Lord appeared to him and said, "I am God the Almighty. Walk in my presence and be blameless. Between you and me I will establish my covenant, and I will multiply you exceedingly."

So, at the ripe old age of ninety-nine, Abram got his face-to-face with the boss Himself, God Almighty. The more likely case is that this "person" Abram was the individual that God did speak with but this was a direction that the tribe of "Abraham" was to follow.

They were a group of righteous men who were about to make a covenant with the Lord God Almighty. This was going to be a very serious covenant, which involved a painful ritual... one that would separate the men from the boys, so to speak.

The next line is "This covenant was going to be established and this people would multiply exceedingly... " and they did and still do. This covenant took the Hebrews from just a people to the basis of the Jewish religion, which was the foundation of the yet to come Christian religion. Basically, this opening statement says that God was choosing the Hebrews to become His followers, His people. He would now call them His own.

"My covenant with you is this: you are to become the father of a host of nations. No longer shall you be called Abram; your name shall be Abraham, for I am making you the father of a host of nations. I will render you exceedingly fertile; I will make nations of you; kings shall stem from you. I will maintain my covenant with you and your descendants after you throughout the ages as an everlasting pact, to be your God and the God of your descendants after you."

All right, here's the guy we're looking for: Abram. So, during this face-to-face with this group, God chose one individual and made a decree that this man would be the man that He would establish His covenant with and this man Abram would be the father of an entirely new religious community, the confirmation that the tribe of Abraham was from this man Abram, the establishment of the people known as the Hebrews.

The number 99, Abram's age, is also a significant number and in fact verifies that one individual was getting the go-ahead to be the head of this tribe. The number 9 has several meanings when used. It can mean consolidation, it can mean conservation, it can mean humanness, and most importantly, it can mean to serve as a minister of God. That's the true reason that Abram was ninety-nine years of age. The first 9 in this number refers to the consolidation of the tribe of Abraham. The second 9 refers to the person Abram as the minister to God. Abram was now being named as the leader of a new group of people that would change the history of mankind.

"I will give you and your descendants after you the land in which you are now staying, the whole land of Canaan, as a permanent possession; and I will be their God." God also said to Abraham: "On your part, you and your descendants after you must keep my covenant throughout the ages. This is my covenant with you and your descendants after you that you must keep: every male among you shall be circumcised. Circumcise the flesh of your foreskin, and that shall be the mark of the covenant between you and me. Throughout the ages, ever male among you, when he is eight days old, shall be circumcised, including the house born slaves and those acquired with money from any foreigner who is not of your blood. Yes, both the house born slaves and those acquired with money must be circumcised. Thus, my covenant shall be in your flesh as an everlasting pact. If a male is uncircumcised, that is, if the flesh of his foreskin has not been cut away, such a one shall be cut off from his people; he has broken my covenant." (Genesis 17:8, 14)

"I will give you and your descendants after you the land in which you are now staying, the whole land of Canaan, as a permanent possession; and I will be their God" … oh, how true this is… for thousands of years these people have inhabited this area. I don't see them leaving anytime in the near future either. The territories of Canaan were first limited to the Mediterranean coastal region of Lebanon; that's where this covenant was established. Then these people migrated and expanded the territory to Gaza in the south.

By the time that Moses showed up on the scene, about a thousand years later, these people with the help of Moses were about to occupy all of the land west of the Jordan River and the Dead Sea including Jerusalem. This area and regions are currently the hub of the Jewish religion. God, our God, their God, my God, your God, has been with us each and every single day since this covenant was established.

God also said to Abraham, "On your part, you and your descendants after you must keep my covenant throughout the ages. This is my covenant with you and your descendants after you that you must keep: every male among you shall be circumcised. Circumcise the flesh of your foreskin, and that shall be the mark of the covenant between you and me. Throughout the ages, ever male among you, when he is eight days old, shall be circumcised, including the house born slaves and those acquired with money from any foreigner who is not of your blood."

I wonder how many people today would be willing to undergo this painful rite and ritual that the males of this tribe had to undergo. I mean, God just told them that this circumcision was required, but he wasn't talking about eight-day-old children. He was talking about grown men. They had to comply with this covenant and undergo this procedure without the clinical conditions that exist today.

I can only imagine how much that hurt. I remember when my circumcision was done. I was only a day old, and boy, it hurt so much, I couldn't walk for a year. I'm laughing out loud right now; that's too funny.

And why was circumcision necessary anyway? Couldn't God come up with something else to seal this covenant, something that didn't require the drastic and extremely painful removal of a man's foreskin? Well, let's talk about this procedure and what the benefits actually are to having this done.

In these times of this covenant, many cultures performed this ritual because they were convinced that it did in fact improve hygienic conditions and prevented infectious diseases.

The Egyptians, for example, had performed this ritual as well. It is actually depicted in the carvings and paintings on the walls of many of the structures still around today. Many of these Egyptian structures date back thousands of years before this covenant took effect. Some scientific evidence suggests that this ritual may have been performed for as long as ten thousand years, but they're certain of the date or the culture responsible for the first circumcisions.

Remember that these cultures were guilty of the same lustful desires as we are today and they were subject to the same risk of diseases as this society of today. God had already wiped out the world once before because the people had become so sexually deviant and totally engrossed in the pleasures of the flesh. This new religion now had the opportunity to seal this covenant with God by cutting off the "root" of the evil, by barbarically removing the foreskin. This covenant now acknowledged that the conduct of sexual deviance by His people was unacceptable to the Lord God Almighty.

But it was a double-edged sword. Yes, the commitment to God was an important part of the thinking, but the flip side of the sword was their concern about the diseases that they knew were related to the foreskin retention and the improved hygienic conditions that this procedure would supposedly provide.

"Circumcise the flesh of your foreskin, and that shall be the mark of the covenant between you and me. Throughout the ages, every male among you, when he is eight days old, shall be circumcised, including the house born slaves and those acquired with money from any foreigner who is not of your blood."

The mark that is a result of this procedure is so highly significant along with the eighth-day requirement. This tribe was the first to actually acknowledge the fact that they, along with all humanity, were a sinful species.

They conceded to God Almighty that the sin of the flesh was one of the reasons that mankind was separated from God and were at that point willing to make this pact and bear the sign. This was pleasing to God because finally man had seen the light and was willing to acknowledge this sin.

The eighth day is also very significant because of its symbolism. This culture and race still perform this rite on the male child on the eighth day, if they are in fact strict in the practice of their religion. The symbolism is evident in the number itself. The number 8 has these three symbolic meanings when used in the Bible. First, it means a new birth; second, it means new creation; and third, it means new beginnings. In this covenant, all three meanings are applicable and sealed this bond with God Almighty.

Of course, all households of those times were totally united. The oldest male was the master of his family. I guess *master* might be too harsh of a word for some, especially in these days, where hopefully, there is equality among men and women, but in those days, it wasn't the case. The oldest male truly reigned as the "master" of his household. So, if this covenant was put in place, all male members of any of these households were subject to this mark of the covenant by decree of its master, the eldest male.

"Yes, both the house born slaves and those acquired with money must be circumcised. Thus, my covenant shall be in your flesh as an everlasting pact. If a male is uncircumcised, that is, if the flesh of his foreskin has not been cut away, such a one shall be cut off from his people; he has broken my covenant."

And so, it was: the very first requirement and new rule since Adam was established by God. The first covenant was between this "chosen" people and God Himself.

We're not going to spend too much more time on this subject. If some of you would like to research this more, you can. If you choose continue reading Genesis, you will find the two sons of Abram. Ishmael was the son who was already born to Abram and his Egyptian concubine Hagar. Sarai, who would be renamed Sarah, would bear Abram a son within the next year: Isaac.

Isaac is the son who is the important figure in the Bible. His descendants are the ones who we will be following for the rest of this manuscript. Ishmael was also an important figure but would go his own way and establish another religious group—Ishmaelite, or as they're known today, the Muslims. There are many similarities between these two religions; however, if you have chosen that path and decided to follow the Muslim beliefs, then you will have chosen incorrectly—and that's a fact Jack, another truth.

For right now, let's summarize this rule... covenant... and move ahead to the important rules.

This requirement, the circumcision rule, was and still is a basic rule within the Jewish religion. It is the requirement and rule that shows that man is admittedly a sinner. His first sin is the lustful desires of the flesh. That is really the significance of this requirement. All men of the religion were admitting that the source of the most basic of sin was man's animal insistence to follow their desire for sexual pleasure.

Now don't take this the wrong way, sex is okay... but the problem is the sexual activity that we humans engage in, more often than not, is not holy nor pleasing to God because lust is the motivator.

We couldn't continue the species without sex, no human life would survive. However, and I think you know what I mean, man's desire is obsessive; we're going to see that very soon.

Oh, one last thing; look at this...

"Thus, saith the Lord God: No stranger, uncircumcised in the **heart**, nor uncircumcised in the flesh, shall enter into my sanctuary, of any stranger that is among the children of Israel." (Ezekiel 44:9)

See it?

God is telling us we must also acknowledge the sinful nature within our heart, our lustful ways, if we do not, we cannot enter into His sanctuary. This is the essence of this covenant; now on to the rules.

Chapter 8

The Rules… It's about Time!

There are a number of Jewish traditions, rules, and customs that are currently in effect most of which I suppose serve some purpose, but quite frankly, simply are not that important in passing the test of life. They mainly pertain to do with preparation of meals, rites, rituals, and penalties for noncompliance with the observance of the practices and performances of these rites and rituals.

If you questioned what I just wrote, then perhaps someone should remind me later to go to Matthew 22. I will try to remember, but I would appreciate if someone would shout it out… thanks.

I would also suggest that you read the rest of the book of Genesis or you might not understand how the Hebrew people who were just promised the land of Canaan as their home in fact got into Egypt. Long story short, Isaac had two sons, twins, in fact; Esau and Jacob were their names. Jacob was a son who when grown, traveled, migrated, and his son Joseph's descendants ended up in Egypt.

I mentioned somewhere in this book that many wonder if slaves or aliens from outer space in fact built the pyramids. I assure you that aliens had nothing to do with the construction. Men and muscle built these structures. Need to see it for yourself, then sit back and relax…

Exodus 1:8, 14… entitled "The Oppression."

"Then a new king, who knew nothing of Joseph, came to power in Egypt. He said to his subjects, "Look how numerous and powerful the Israelite people are growing, more so than we ourselves! Come, let us deal shrewdly with them to stop their increase; otherwise, in time of war they too may join our enemies to fight against us, and so leave our country." Accordingly, taskmasters were set over the Israelites to oppress them with forced labor. Thus, they had to build for Pharaoh the supply cities of Pithom and Raamses. Yet the more they were oppressed, the more they multiplied and spread. The Egyptians, then, dreaded the Israelites and reduced them to cruel slavery, making life bitter for them with hard work in mortar and brick and all kinds of field work; the whole cruel fate of slaves."

The Ten Commandments is an epic film, but it is historically inaccurate. The Egyptians themselves built the pyramids with the assistance of this slave labor that did all the related work. The slaves made the bricks and did all the trivial labor related to the construction of the structures. I couldn't imagine that this proud people, the Egyptians, would allow this group of slaves to have any meaningful part in the building of the tombs of their living gods, when the Hebrews did not believe that these kings were in fact gods. The loyal and dedicated Egyptians are responsible for the construction of the pyramids.

Not to bash this movie, I watch it every time it's on, around Easter... well, Passover... but the fact is that the movie was a Hollywood production designed to make money. The depiction of the Hebrew slaves is only half accurate in the sense that they were directly involved in the setting of the stones and the final carving and shaping of the structure; that task was done by the Egyptians alone... and that is the truth.

But it does give us a somewhat accurate picture of the magnitude of the flight of the enslaved Hebrew people. It depicts the escape back to the land of Canaan, which was the Promised Land via the covenant between God and Abraham about a thousand or so years prior.

However, the parts about the two brothers fighting for favor in the eyes of the Pharaoh, the struggle for the love of the princess, the enslavement of Moses, the walk through the desert, and please, "so let it be written, so let it be done," all Hollywood. But it is a great film. Unfortunately, too many people have based their actual beliefs on those events shown in this moving picture.

Moses was not a man who was educated and treated as an heir to the throne of Egypt. In fact, I know someone will get offended by this statement, but please forgive me in advance, I got to use it; Moses was treated just like a "red headed stepchild." This information is located here... look and see.

"Pharaoh's daughter came down to the river to bathe, while her maids walked along the riverbank. Noticing the basket among the reeds, she sent her handmaid to fetch it. On opening it, she looked, and lo, there was a baby boy, crying! She was moved with pity for him and said, "It is one of the Hebrew children." Then his sister asked Pharaoh's daughter, "Shall I go and call one of the Hebrew women to nurse the child for you?" "Yes, do so," she answered. So, the maiden went and called the child's own mother." (Exodus 2:5, 8)

His sister, Moses's sister, was one of the maids, a slave girl of the household asked Pharaoh's daughter, "Hey, should I get somebody to nurse the kid or what?"

"Yes, do so," she answered. So, Moses's sister went home to get Mom to suckle this kid. Mom and his sister set it up so Moses would have a chance to be free from slavery. They played Pharaoh's daughter like a fiddle and capitalized on the vulnerability of her desire to have a child.

They were hoping that Moses would have an opportunity to gain freedom from slavery, but he blew this opportunity.

It wasn't a secret to anyone in that household that Moses was a Hebrew, not as depicted in the movie. When he grew into a man, he killed an Egyptian for striking one of his kinsmen. When Pharaoh heard about the murder, he got a little perturbed. He wanted to put Moses to death, but Moses fled the scene of the crime and fled into the desert, ultimately finding the land of Midian, where he met up with Reuel's clan.

Moses identifies himself as an Egyptian to gain favor and marries one of Reuel's daughters Zipporah. Reuel was also known as Jethro. Moses had a couple of kids with Zipporah; the eldest went by the name of Gershom and a later son named Eliezer. Everything was good for the couple until one day when Moses was leading the flocks of his father-in-law Jethro across the plains and came to Horeb… the mountain of God. This mountain is also known by most people as Mt. Sinai, which is located in the mountain system of Jebel Musa.

This is where it all starts to really happen for this man of history. Up to this point, he's just an average Joe, living in the desert, hiding out from the law… the Egyptians, trying to get on with his life… living within the house of Jethro, his father-in-law, who was the priest of Midian.

What better instrument could God have picked, a man who wasn't convinced either way of the reality of either religion, wanted for a murder by the Pharaoh, a man who was familiar with the customs and religious beliefs of both peoples, a man who spoke the languages of both. He was the perfect man for the job; well, almost, he still lacked the communication skills necessary for the task.

I'll show you that soon, but first, the burning bush. This bush wasn't far off as depicted in the film; remember, Moses peering off to the mountain, then climbing up the side of the mountain, crossing the flat vista and finally coming upon the bush.

No, no… Moses was herding the flock and saw the bush; it was pretty close to him. Then an "Angel of the Lord" appeared to him in fire flaming out of the bush. He looked at the bush and was surprised that it wasn't consumed. So, he decided to go closer and see what this was all about… naturally, wouldn't you?

The Angel of the Lord called out to Moses, "Hey, dude, what's happening?"

Moses: "Wa's up, my brother from another mother?"

The Angel: "Dude, what did you step in? Take those nasty shoes off, man, I don't want any of that sheep crap on His floor! Hold on a minute... I'll get Him..."

Okay... not true... but I'm laughing... and so the initial meeting of the two via the Angel.

God then introduced Himself, as I Am Who Am, and then told Moses what the people were to call him I AM for short. God then explained that He knew of the trouble in Egypt and that Moses was going to go there and lead His people back to the land of their heritage.

Moses wasn't happy about this situation, but God Almighty assured Moses that everything would be cool. He showed him a sign to prove to Moses that He was on the up and up... the little thing with Moses's hand... but Moses still wasn't convinced he could pull it off... look here.

"Again, the Lord said to him, "Put your hand in your bosom." He put his hand on his bosom and when he withdrew it, to his surprise; his hand was leprous, like snow. The Lord then said, "Now, put your hand back in your bosom." Moses put his hand back in his bosom, and when he withdrew it, to his surprise it was again like the rest of his body. "If they will not believe you, nor heed the message of the first sign, they should believe the message of the second. And if they will not believe even in those two signs, nor heed your plea, take some water from the river and pour it on dry land. The water you take from the river will become blood on dry land." Moses, however, said to the Lord, "If you please, Lord, I have never been eloquent, neither in the past, nor recently, nor now that you have spoken to your servant; but I am slow of speech and tongue." The Lord said to him, "Who gives one man speech and makes another deaf and dumb? Or who gives sight to one and makes another blind? Is it not I the Lord? Go, then! It is I who will assist you in speaking and teach you what to say." Yet he insisted, "If you please, Lord, send someone else!" then the Lord became angry with Moses and said, "Have you not your brother, Aaron the Levite? I know that he is an eloquent speaker. Besides, he is now on his way to meet you. When he sees you, his heart will be glad? You are to speak with him, then, and put the words in his mouth. I will assist both of you and him in speaking and will teach the two of you what you are to do. He shall speak to the people for you; he shall be your spokesman, and you shall be as God to him. Take this staff in your hand; with it you will perform the signs." (Exodus 4:6, 17)

So now Moses is on a "Mission from God." He's been given his marching orders and is off to see the Pharaoh. He is appointed as spokesman, with the assistance of his brother Aaron to set the people free from slavery and bondage. Great... he still doesn't have a clue. But being the good soldier that he was, he did as instructed. Big and bold as a man could get, he confronted Pharaoh and said the immortal line: "Let my people go!"

And so, the staff into a snake, the plagues, with the frogs, the gnats, the flies, the pestilence, the boils, the hail, the locusts, the darkness, and the one that broke Pharaoh's back: the death of the firstborn. Free at last, free at last, oh, thank God, we're free at last!

This last plague, the death of the firstborn sons, is the inspiration of the ritual of Passover... for all you out there who don't know, it goes something like this: The family should procure a lamb; if the family is too small, they should share one with their neighbors. The lamb should be a one-year-old male, free from blemish. Now, you should keep the lamb and care for it for two weeks (fourteen days) before you slaughter it in the twilight hours. Roasted — not raw or boiled — whole, with its head and shanks and inner organs. Then eaten with unleavened bread and bitter herbs. You must eat it all or burn the remains the new morning as a sacrifice to God. You must be dressed as if you were ready to flee and the blood of the beast should be put on the door lintel as a marker so the "Angels of Death" will know that your house is protected. Also, for seven days afterward, you must eat unleavened bread, nor can the house have leavened bread in it or you have not completed the ritual correctly and are banished from the group.

This rite is actually supposed to be practiced in this fashion by this religious community as a memorial of the freeing of the people. However, I can honestly say that I have never been part of this ritual performed in my lifetime. Anyway, this is the ritual of Passover for all of you out there who observe the holiday. The exact rite is specified in Exodus at chapter 12:1–20.

So, yet another inaccuracy in the film: these people, the Hebrew slaves, observed this rite before departing. They didn't leave Egypt like "thieves in the night." They took their time, gathered their possessions, and in fact, got articles of clothing, gold, and silver from the Egyptians. They even had time to exhume the remains of Joseph so that they could take his "bones" out of the land of his captivity... by his request. The film shows that the very night that this firstborn death occurred was indeed the night that these people "blew out" of town... not true.

The chase by Pharaoh is also inaccurate; yes, he did get mad and pursued them, but it wasn't after he held his son in his arms, cursed Moses, and pitched that fit as it was so dramatically depicted in the film. The chase occurred, in fact, when the Hebrew people were stalled in the desert and Pharaoh had the chance to think about the lost slaves and benefits of the "free labor." That's when he went after them to recapture this people. God wanted this to happen so that He could show this Egyptian people that He and only He was God. Take a look...

"Then the Lord said to Moses, "Tell the Israelites to turn about and camp before Pi-hahiroth, between Migdol and the sea. You shall camp in front of Baalzephon, just opposite, by the sea. Pharaoh will then say 'The Israelites are wondering about aimlessly in the land. The desert has closed in on them.' Thus, I will make Pharaoh so obstinate that he will pursue them. Then I will receive glory through Pharaoh and all his army, and the Egyptians will know that I am Lord." This the Israelites did. When it was reported to the king of Egypt that the people had fled, Pharaoh and his servants changed their minds about them. "What have we done!" they exclaimed. "Why have we released the Israelites from our service!" So, Pharaoh made his chariots ready and mustered his soldiers... six hundred first-class chariots, and all the other chariots of Egypt, with warriors on them all." (Exodus 14:1, 7)

Our knowledge and experience in life is always influenced by what we are subject to and what we have seen, felt, or heard. Most have seen this epic film, and if you ask any person who has how the Hebrew slaves left Egypt, many will give you the version that they have seen in the movie... but it didn't happen that way. It happened just like you just read. I don't know about you, but I really don't care to see the Egyptians drowned so we're going to skip that part and move directly to the where these people, the Israelites get to Sinai, because that's what this is all about.

Ah! There it is, the Mountain of God, Mt. Sinai. It took the Hebrews three months from the time they left Egypt to make the journey to the desert surrounding this mountain. They are pitching camp and getting ready to meet the one and only God of their fathers. What... what's this?

"They can't come up here with you, Moses." What a bummer.

God instructed Moses to gather the people around the base of the mountain but not to let them come close enough to even touch the base of the mountain. In three days, after they clean themselves up, God was going to descend upon the mountain and lay down the law.

So, in three days... count: 1, 2, 3... the cloud is descending upon the mountain — that's God.

Moses is climbing the mountain and the people are standing around in wonder. Thunder and lightning are beginning, but the people aren't fazed by this; what's a little rain... it's a welcome event in the desert anyway.

They're starting to get a little antsy, and they're moving closer and closer to the mountain... well, when is something going to happen? Closer and closer they get. Meanwhile...

"Then the Lord told Moses, "Go down and warn the people not to break through towards the Lord in order to see Him; otherwise, many of them will be struck down. The priest, too, who approach the Lord must sanctify themselves; else he will vent his anger upon them." Moses said to the Lord, "The people cannot go up to Mount Sinai, for you yourself warned us to set limits around the mountain to make it sacred." The Lord repeated, "Go down now! Then come up again with Aaron. But the priests and the people must not break through to come up to the Lord; else he will vent his anger upon them." (Exodus 20:21, 25)

And so... Moses climbs down the mountain; *not* with the two tablets in his arms, hair *not* as white as snow, approaching the people shouting to them to... move back!

And now the moment we've been waiting for... "His Rules." The people are still full of doubt, expressing the lack of faith that all men are guilty of, questioning the instrument of the Lord, Moses, and this is when, with the greatest voice ever heard by man, came thundering out of the mountain:

"Then God delivered all these commandments:

"I, the Lord, am your God, who brought you out of the land of Egypt, that place of slavery. You shall not have other gods besides me. You shall not carve idols for yourselves in the shape of anything in the sky above of on the earth below or in the waters beneath the earth; you shall not bow down before them or worship them. For I, the Lord, your God, am a jealous God, inflicting punishment for their father's wickedness on the children of those who hate me, down to the third and fourth generations; but bestowing mercy down to the thousandth generation, on the children of those who love me and keep my commandments.

You shall not take the name of the Lord, your God, in vain. For the Lord will not leave unpunished him who takes his name in vain.

Remember to keep holy the Sabbath day. Six days you may labor and do all your work, but the seventh day is the Sabbath of the Lord your God. No work may be done then either by you, or your son or daughter, or your male or female slave, or your beast, or by the alien who lives with you. In six days, the Lord made the heavens and the earth, the sea and all that is in them; but on the seventh day he rested. That is why the Lord has blessed the Sabbath day and made it holy.

Honor your father and your mother, that you may have a long life in the land which the Lord, your God, is giving you.

You shall not kill.

You shall not commit adultery.

You shall not steal.

You shall not bear false witness against your neighbor.

You shall not covet your neighbor's house.

You shall not covet your neighbor's wife, nor his male or female slaves, nor his ox or ass, nor anything else that belongs to him." (Exodus 20:1, 17)

The Ten Commandments were actually delivered to the people directly by God Almighty. There wasn't the drama as we saw in the film; well, actually, this effect would have been much more dramatic, but how would Moses get the tablets carved by the "finger of God" to present to the people if not for the movie's creative department. The tablets came after the second trip.

This event scared the bejesus out of the people, and so they're moving back from the mountain, panicking and screaming, "Help me... help me... we don't want to die... oh, Moses, help!" One would think that the Hebrew people should have expected this after all the thunder, lightning, trumpet blasting, smoking mountain, and this thunderous voice... since God just delivered them from the Egyptians. Maybe these people were all bosses; you know, what have you done for me lately, forgetting everything in the past...

What did they expect? A wimpy little voice, saying, "Okay now, I just rescued you nice people from those nasty Egyptian captors; this is what I'd love you to do for me since I just got you out of a terrible jam...

Come on, this is God the Almighty, the Master of all creation, the Author of all life. The time was right for God to lay down the law to his chosen people and expect them to comply with the rules, and He wanted to let them hear the rules firsthand.

With fear in their hearts, they asked Moses to help them... and here's what he said:

"Moses answered the people, "Do not be afraid, for God has come to you only to test you and put His fear upon you, lest you should sin." (Exodus 20:20)

Matthew 22... you said to remind you!

Thanks, but not yet.

Chapter 9
Rules 1–3

I chose the title for this book for one simple reason and it's this: You know when you go into a bar and there's a pool table there, and you get in line to play a relaxing game of eight ball, you may discover the rules for the table may vary from place to place. Well, that's how I feel about the Ten Commandments. Depending whose table you're playing on, that determines what the rules are concerning the winner of the game. In essence, the result is to get all your balls in before attempting to sink the eight ball, sink the eight ball, and you win; however, the rules concerning the way you play are not the same in every case. They refer to these as the "House Rules."

So is it when we interpret the Ten Commandments. It depends on your religious denomination and that is the final determination on the way any religion adheres to these rules. These variations are very similar to the game of pool. The owner or manager of the bar made the game's variations in all cases so that the game would best fit the skill level of that person… the owner or manager, just like any variation of any of the religions available for us to practice today.

But there is an actual set of rules on how to play the game, and they are the real rules of the game… just like the Ten Commandments are the actual rules governing the way we play this game of life.

So, if we learn to play the game—either game—incorrectly, we may never learn to play either game as intended, and when we come upon an opponent who knows the actual rules and plays by those rules, we feel that they are cheating us.

So now that y'all... sorry I had to do it, Carole... you all know the why I chose this title, let's get to it.

First rule:

"I, the Lord, am your God, who brought you out of the land of Egypt, that place of slavery. You shall not have other gods besides me. You shall not carve idols for yourselves in the shape of anything in the sky above or the earth below or in the waters beneath the earth; you shall not bow down before them or worship them. For I, the Lord, your God, am a jealous God, inflicting punishment for their father's wickedness on the children of those who hate me, down to the third and fourth generations; but bestowing mercy down to the thousandth generation, on the children of those who love me and keep my commandments."

Over the years, man has shortened the first and most important of the commandments, to this version: "I am the Lord thy God, thou shall have no other gods before me."

Now I ask you, how did we ever get this one-sentence rule from the paragraph delivered from the mount in the presence of the chosen people? It must be one of those house rules. But this isn't the rule... I am the Lord thy God; thou shall have no other gods before me. It's only part of the rule; it's a variation of the rule so that it fits the skill level of the players now playing on that table. We have omitted the true essence of this first and most important rule, and that, I suppose, is okay if you truly understand the meaning behind the entirety of this most important rule.

We're going to take it line by line and see what this means and why even one word of this rule should have never been omitted, because God didn't give us the "short" version of the rule.

"I, the Lord, am your God, who brought you out of the land of Egypt, that place of slavery."

"I, the Lord... " God has just identified Himself; He would appreciate if we would call Him Lord. God has many names in this the twenty-first century. He is called by so many, that it is almost impossible for anyone to name them all. If you recall on Mt. Sinai, when Moses was first introduced to God, God told Moses to have the Hebrew people call Him, I am, and so the next words, "am your God... I AM."

And what does the word Lord mean? Again, like every other word, we have come up with throughout our history, has many meanings. But in this instance, the word Lord absolutely and positively carries one meaning... Master of the House.

He is the only God, the God who brought you out of the land of Egypt. God is now telling them with authority that He's the one who was responsible for bringing "you" out of the land of Egypt, not one of the gods of Pharaoh and not one of the gods of any other religion. Incidentally, "you" refers to all of us that believe in our one true God, the Lord, then and even now in the twenty-first century.

The nation of Egypt had many gods, and they were believers in what we now call the pagan religion. And of course, we know that the kings themselves believed that they were living gods, so our God wanted them to know that He and He alone was the God who freed them from the bonds of their slavery, and that place of bondage.

You shall not have other gods besides me, and oh, how many gods we have. We are constantly adoring, loving, and worshiping everything and anyone that gives us pleasure. We fail to realize that God is the Supreme Being responsible for all that we have in our lives. We give credit to ourselves for our accomplishments and possessions when in fact; we couldn't even take the next breath if God had not permitted us to do so. We couldn't take the next step unless God were there to hold us up. The Lord grants by His mercy and His love, all the pleasures we have in life.

Sure, we can be proud—but not boastfully proud—of the life we've made for our families and ourselves, but give credit where credit is due: to God Almighty. We should have pride in our love of God and pride that He is the source of all that we are because He is the one and only God… not to be confused with the cars, properties, money and "bling" that all strive to adore.

"It is easier for a camel to pass through the eye of a needle than for one that is rich to enter the kingdom of God." (Mark 10:25)

This is exactly what Jesus was talking about when He made this statement. He wasn't saying that we should be poor. He was saying that men love possessions and makes them their gods. The worship of those gods will doom our live and keep us from passing this test of life. And if you are truly not sure, that this is what God is saying, He makes it crystal clear in the next line by defining for everyone that He knows just what a man is capable of loving and worshiping in His place.

"You shall not carve idols for yourselves in the shape of anything in the sky above or the earth below or in the waters beneath the earth; you shall not bow down before them or worship them."

"Seeing is believing" is a common cliché, which dates back thousands of years. In fact, Missouri is one of the states in this country, which is nicknamed the "Show Me state." Man has always had the need for a visual aid, and so he produces objects to satisfy that part of him that is in need of the visual effect. Consequently, he will often allow his imagination to get the best of him because of his separation from God and it's only because man creates too many idols that he will often substitute to replicate the true image of God.

We're a faithless species, lacking trust and belief in our God. We lack genuine love for God, and we create a substitute in our hearts, minds, and souls for the God who we don't yet know. We fashion images that we can see, substituting them for what we cannot… we then love and worship those images as if they were

God. Could you imagine that our Lord, who created us in His image and likeness, wouldn't know what the people then and now were and are capable of doing? He knew from the beginning of time, for He is time, what this creature of flesh, blood, and bone would conspire in his mind, and bring into his reality, but it's not God's reality...

He gave us all our emotions, all our intellect, all our physical abilities to do with what we please; and He did that for a reason.

He planned this so that only the persons with true faith and love for Him would survive the test of our physical life throughout time as time has been set for this testing.

Our Lord and God will not find mercy for the faithless; He will punish those who take no heed in his words, for just like the creature He made in His image and likeness, us, God is jealous of anyone or anything that doesn't gets the respect due to Him and Him alone. Read the final sentence of rule one and you shall see what God is saying in this, the first rule: "For I, the Lord, your God, am a jealous God, inflicting punishment for their father's wickedness on the children of those who hate me, down to the third and fourth generations; but bestowing mercy down to the thousandth generation, on the children of those who love me and keep my commandments."

And certainly, it is important to mention the society of... well, then and now and how people have come to worship everything other than God. The moon, the stars, good old "Mother Nature," the gods and goddesses that some people believe that they are due to this "new age" belief and the sorriest of them all, the "snake." My God, look around at today's newest generation, the new-age bands, the blatant disregard and the disrespect of God and you'll know just what God was referring to; He knew what His humans were going to do. They were going to break this rule and this rule is placed as number one because it is the most important of them all. Without God, we are nothing; we are truly dust and to dust we will return.

Second rule: "You shall not take the name of the Lord, your God, in vain. For the Lord will not leave unpunished him who

106

takes His name in vain."

All right, simple rule, don't you think? It should be that simple that we could obey this one, but we can't.

This rule is all about the use of the Lord's name without love and honor for Him. Some don't even know what to call God, but we sure can come up with some tremendously creative variations. I often wonder if Jesus had a middle name, and if his middle name started with the letter H… I know that some use it as if it were.

Some say that I have a vulgar mouth and can't believe that I am as religious as I actually think. Well, hypocrite and sinner that I am, I rarely, if ever, use language that breaks this rule. If I do, it's under extreme circumstances. Immediately upon the use of inappropriate use of His name, I immediately pray for forgiveness. I truly am sorry for the slip of the tongue on the rare occasion when this may occur and beg the Almighty for his pardon.

So, let's talk about the hypocrites and sinners that we are; people that condemn the language that I or anyone else might admittedly frequently use. It makes me laugh actually. These people get on their righteously high horse and criticize what you or I might say and then, show no moral fiber whatsoever. They have little regard for anything but themselves and are putting on a "show" for those around to illustrate their assumed morality. Shame on them, and actually shame on me, for no one should ever say anything or judge another person's words, thoughts, or deeds. I apologize to anyone who might take offense, but this is really the way it is with the human race.

Vulgarity, on the other hand, is offensive to God, but it is not a violation of this rule. It is offensive in the fact that God gave us all the intelligence to communicate without the use of those vulgar terms. In fact, when we use those terms, the meanings of those words are often interpreted as an improper sexually related act. Caution to those of you who overuse these words, they are only to be used to vent anger and not to be used as a part of your everyday communication; however, some use them as if they were a comma, as is the case when I choose to use this type of language.

However, I limit the use of this type of language to certain situations... I'm in the construction field... got it?

Oh, and let's not forget swearing to God... For the Lord will not leave unpunished him who takes His name in vain. Not only does God not want to use his name in vain as we do when we curse, but woe to the man the vows or makes an oath by the name of God...

Matthew 5:33–35... no, this isn't the Matthew I asked you to remind about...

"Again, you have heard that it was said to your ancestors, 'Do not take a false oath, but make good to the Lord all that you vow,' but I say to you, do not swear at all, not by heaven, for it is God's throne; nor by the earth, for it is His footstool; nor by Jerusalem, for it is the city of the great King."

To wrap up this rule, number 2, let me just say that the only time you should take the name of the Lord God Almighty is when we are praying to Him. It should always be used in the deepest reverence and honor, for He is the Master. Those little *gosh darns* that we use are nothing more than a shorter version of the actual slander and should be avoided, unless you chose to break this rule.

Number 3:

"Remember to keep holy the Sabbath day. Six days you may labor and do all your work, but the seventh day is the Sabbath of the Lord, your God. No work may be done then either by you, or your son or daughter, or your male or female slave, or your beast, or by the alien who lives with you. In six days, the Lord made the heavens and the earth, the sea and all that is in them; but on the seventh day He rested. That is why the Lord has blessed the Sabbath day and made it holy."

Got to love how people go out of their way to break this rule. The national average for the United States of America is about 20 percent participation at Sunday service.

And, boy, oh boy, can people come up with all kinds of excuses for non-attendance and non-participation.

Oh, I know: "Sunday is the only day I get off," "I'd like to sleep in, get up around ten and then read the Sunday paper and have my coffee," or another of my favorites, "My house is my church... I worship God in my house so that I don't have to be around those people who just go because the want to look good." The most extreme, on the day of rest: playing golf, going to the park, going for a ride, going out with the family to breakfast... they're going anywhere but to a church to honor the Lord. What a beautiful thing, the literal translation that we humans have come up with in the interpretation of this third and very important rule.

And yes, I can read and I am fully aware that it doesn't say that you must go to Sunday services. It says, "Remember to keep holy the Sabbath day. Six days you may labor and do all your work, but the seventh day is the Sabbath of the Lord, your God."

Let us look at the word *Sabbath* and find its meaning. The Sabbath is defined as a day of rest. However, it is also a day set aside for devotion and prayer and a day for the dedication to religious practices. Additionally, among Christians, the day gradually became the day commemorating the resurrection of Jesus, hence the "Lord's Day."

On this day, we are required by all religions to attend service. Great... required. Hence, most defiantly decide not to participate, but I assure you that attendance to a service alone isn't enough to become close to the Lord; you must participate.

Let me tell you how to interpret this rule. God wants us to pace ourselves. If we work all the time, we will not only lose track of the reason that we were placed here, but the traps and snares of this world will overtake us. We will not have a focused outlook on the test. We will become enthralled in the physicality of this plane. We all need to stop and smell the roses, so to speak, and while we smell them, we need thank the Almighty for putting them here for us to enjoy.

I start every day and finish in prayer… every day. I try to focus on the Lord throughout the day; I try to look for God in everything and every person I run into. And when the day is over, my last thought is not of the daily rigors, but it is of the appreciation that God has allowed me one more day to try to gain a "passing grade."

Here's what God wants:

He wants us to publicly show our respect for Him.

He wants us to mirror His actions.

He wants us to acknowledge that we are made in His image and likeness.

He wants us to be in paradise when this life is over.

He wants us to enjoy this and the next life.

He wants us to love Him.

And now, thank you for reminding me.

Matthew 22:37, 40: This is Jesus. The question was, which is the greatest commandment…

He said to him, "You shall love the Lord, your God, with all your heart, with all your soul, and with all your mind. This is the greatest commandment. The second is like it; you shall love your neighbor as yourself. The whole law and the prophets depend on these two commandments."

We could stop right here, and if everyone could understand this, there would be no need to go any further. But unfortunately, because man does not have a close relationship with God and has free will, he chooses not to live to the essence of this statement.

Man makes excuses for his actions, and he is a defiant creature. There are some circumstances when he cannot attend service to acknowledge his Lord. If the reason is valid, God will understand. But we find validity for non-attendance in the lamest ways. "I was out last night and I'm tired… oh, poor little me." Or "I work on the weekends, and I can't get to church on Sundays... God will forgive me." Yea, He will if you make an effort to visit Him on another day and observe the Sabbath during the week. All men, women, and children want to go to heaven... well, most of them, not all... and to get there, you must obey the rules. There are ten, but if you take a close look at what Jesus said to the Pharisees just a few seconds ago, the first three are rules are based on the love of God and the next seven are rules on how to love your fellow human being. By loving your fellow human, you are loving God, His image and likeness.

To love God with your whole heart, soul, and mind is the essence of these first three rules. I don't know how anyone could say that they love God without at the very least going to service once a week.

Why would anyone want to spend eternity with God if they can't spend one hour a week with Him? Yet most people are convinced that they are in God's Grace and don't see the harm in missing Sunday Service on the "Sabbath."

My advice to you is this: Instead of trying to "find" God, find yourselves. God is not lost, we are lost; we're in a dimension separate from God. Ask God to find you; He knows where you are so it wouldn't be very difficult for Him to locate you... not at all.

Then, ask Him to be your friend, a true friend; God wants nothing more from you and me than to be our friends. That's the reason He gave us this gift of life and offered us the opportunity to take this test. We can only pass this test with His support. He is the teacher, He is the master, and He is the Lord.

Sunday Mass: I'm Catholic, so we call the service — celebration — Mass; well, some call it church but the church is the building and not the service. It gives us the weekly lessons that we all need to stay in the friendship of God. We can't know him unless we spend some time with Him. Once you start to do this, it will be very difficult for you to stop. You may even learn to pray to God daily... prayer is nothing more than a conversation with God. And once you develop a firm relationship with your "new friend," you will have the world at your fingertips. You will be able to seek and find, you will knock and the door will open, for everything is possible once you are a friend of God.

Chapter 10

Who's Your Buddy? Rules 4–10

The next seven deal with us and our relationships with the other human beings that we come in contact with on a regular basis. They are also the rules that most of us ignore on a regular basis. We do this because we believe *we* are the most important living creature on this earth. We can't help this fact because throughout our lives, we are constantly concerned with our physical survival and well-being. It's rare without some special occasion that most would go out of their way for someone that was not very close to them, related to them by blood, or for another purpose.

This is human nature at its worst, not to be confused with its best. If we could just love our "neighbors" as we love ourselves, we would really have no concerns and God would provide. But who is our neighbor, you ask? Is he the guy or gal next door, or is he or she the person who lives halfway around this planet?

This is as clear as I can state this; everyone you will ever meet is your neighbor. They are just as important as you are. Fame, power, or wealth have no bearing on one's importance, for in the eyes of the Lord, we're all the same.

Yet in human eyes, these are the gauges that we, as humans, use as the litmus test. People judge others by their success in this physical plane and often try to mirror and imitate their actions. That's okay, I suppose, if your goal is success in this life and have no concern with the eternity set before you. I am going to do my best, with the grace of God, to cover all of the variables of these next seven rules.

But before I start, I want to explain one thing, if you please. "Love one another as you love yourself… "

113

We are an extremely judgmental race of beings. Some say that they love someone, but if that someone offends them, they often hold a grudge because they have judged them to have done something that is unforgivable in their eyes. This is because they fail to see their own shortcomings in this life. They could have done what this person may have done somewhere along the course of their lives, but they casually forget that offense to that other person. We as a people fail in most cases to look within our own being to see the sinful mature of ourselves and hold those persons accountable for an act that we ourselves may have done or something equally as wrong in the sight of God. There are two passages in the Holy Bible that clarifies this. One in Luke and one in Matthew. This one is from Luke 6:41–42; I don't think I've used Luke yet.

"Why do you look at the speck that is in your brother's eye, but do not notice the log that is in your own eye?" Or how can you say to your brother, 'Brother, let me take out the speck that is in your eye,' when you yourself do not see the log that is in your own eye? You hypocrite, first take the log out of your own eye, and then you will see clearly to take out the speck that is in your brother's eye."

You see, we judge others and seem to forget we are the same as the other person and in many cases worse when it boils down to our sinful nature. That's what keeps us from finding the true love for our neighbors. But if you can remember those offensive things that you have done, it may become easier for you to find the love for you neighbor.

Rule 4:

"Honor your father and your mother, that you may have a long life in the land of the Lord, your God, is giving you."

I just had a thought: In today's society, we have come up with a term to describe a good percentage of the families — dysfunctional. *Dysfunctional* means one that fails to serve a useful purpose in society. What a negative term, don't you think, but acceptable in describing how we perceive some family units. Overused if you ask me, and almost always misunderstood.

The term originated recently in this society. This society is trying to understand how families are changing. They're changing because the divorce rate is escalating to an all-time high and the children are confused. There're not sure who to be loyal to in the splitting couple: mom or dad. Of course, mom wants the kids and so does dad, a good percentage of the time. So, mom and dad will often "poison" the minds of the kids to try to win them over to their side and gain their love and loyalty.

We, as a society, have become so engrossed in this subject that we actually have shows on television daily with experts in the fields related to the particular dysfunction. Not only are we doing our society an injustice, but more so, we're adding fuel to this fire... a fire that we may not be able to extinguish.

It all starts with noncompliance to this rule. This rule doesn't just say that we are to honor our parents; it's much deeper. Very deep in fact and we're going to spend some time here. We want to start out with the basics: who you would you consider to be your father and mother.

Father: male.

Mother: female.

One of the biggest topics in the news in recent years in the United States of America is the acceptance of same-sex marriages. Some states have put a ban on this union, and some states have allowed and actually legalized the unions to take place. Some people who are not from these states where this union is legal have defied the state law and have been joined in the state of matrimony, and in fact, the television media has covered this spectacle and tried their best to sell it to the public as an acceptable union. Just recently, a former president openly congratulated and praised a professional athlete for announcing he was gay.

What a shame! Shame on you, Mr. President, and shame on the media for their support of this lifestyle. The media presents something almost daily related to the gay lifestyle. I assure you that God is not happy with this development and this lifestyle. He didn't create Adam and Adam in His image and likeness, nor did He create Eve and Eve. But I'll tell you who is responsible for this twisted chain: none other than the "Prince of Darkness," Satan himself.

Let's look at this passage.

"If a man lies with a male as with a woman, both of them shall be put to death for their abominable deed; they have forfeited their lives." (Leviticus 20:13)

This passage goes both ways... ha, that's funny... sorry, God, but you let me write it. This passage also refers to women as well. God sees the acts of homosexuality — as well as lesbianism — as an abominable deed. The death that this is referring to is the loss of our soul to the fires of hell. We should already know that death is the end of our physical life, and when the initial judgment of our soul happens immediately after this death, some souls will be sent to hell. However, at the final judgment, hell will no longer exist; hence, death is the punishment for this deed.

And this "lifestyle" is becoming more and more acceptable; live and let live is how most handle the presence of this abomination. It has become such an issue that the Vatican is now considering conversation regarding this epidemic, which has now become so popular only because of the pressures by the people who live in this lifestyle. And the Vatican is right to a point related to the rule of loving your neighbor to consider conversation strictly related to acceptance of the person related to the pastoral care and spiritual assistance for their souls.

But this lifestyle is only the beginning of the reasons for the high divorce rates and dysfunctionality of the family unit. Just a small percentage of the unions between men and women dissolve because of newfound lifestyles.

Lust is a large contributing factor in the escalating divorce rate. Lack of commitment between the two is the other major factor in the dilemma. Lust is something we're going to cover in another one of these rules, so let's focus on the lack of commitment for a moment.

There is a genuine issue with the lack of commitment with people today and, actually, for all times past. Because of our inability to see God in every human being, we are incapable of true love for our neighbor. That neighbor is, in fact, going to be the one that you choose to be your spouse, if you choose marriage. Sure, you love them, I guess, but if you truly loved them, could you be without them ever? And if you were separated from them, your thoughts would be of them, if you truly were in love... true?

I read a little of an article on the Internet one morning while I was checking my e-mail. It was some new information regarding affairs in the workplace. This article basically stated that 20 percent of the women today, in the workplace, are involved in an affair. That's one in five... pretty scary. It went on to say that their reasons were typically the lack of physical romance and/or a non-affectionate husband.

I also seem to recall that the figure for male affairs in the workplace was much higher, from a different article I saw a few months before this particular article. Now, what that must mean is that the women are having affairs with more than one man in the work environment for this to be true. If my memory serves me, the figure was 35 percent. That article went on to say that the male population in general—workplace and beyond—had an overwhelming affair rate of 50 percent, if my memory serves me correctly. That's one out of two... shocking!

By now, you must be wondering what this has to do with this rule. Doesn't this have to do with rule number 6? Well, yes, it does; however, this is an important factor in the base of this rule.

How could any child honor their father and mother if they present no honor in the family unit?

Honor is defined as the respect due to another person. If that other person, a parent, dishonors the family as a whole by not totally committing to the family, then this honor cannot and will not occur.

I am a product of one of these dysfunctional families. My parents divorced in 1973, and I struggled with this rule for many years afterward. This is one of the sins that I had an extreme amount of difficulty trying to get under control. Human as I am, I had to work diligently to fully forgive both of them for the acts that brought this situation to the reality and the finality of their union.

I struggled with this constantly and their attempts to "win" me over to their side. And I know, hypocrite that I am, that it was wrong for me not to totally forgive them. Try as I might, I couldn't seem to convince them that I didn't want to be subjected to the situation. Because of their influences, I held in my soul this sin for years. I am not a sinless man, and truly that is the key to finding the way to holiness: the admission of sin and guilt.

"Honor your father and your mother, that you may have a long life in the land of the Lord, your God, is giving you."

I prayed daily so I could accept the fact that I had this monster within me, the judgmental beast that can't seem to find love and honor in the essence of this rule. I prayed constantly to God for His forgiveness and prayed I would find peace in the fact that I was not at fault. I ask God to forgive them for the sins of their lives that have caused this sin to occur in my life. I felt responsible for being judgmental and hoped and prayed that this pass... and it has.

Now, in our family, both our sons know the meaning of this rule. I love my wife in the deepest way and that love fills our home. Yes, I am a strict parent because I want nothing but the best for my two sons, and they know that I sometimes I am an ignorant dummy, but they also know my motives. One of those motives is that my boys never break this rule and fall into the same "sin" that their father had to struggle with daily. Because of my penance for my ongoing sin, my wife and I have created the correct environment and model home for our children.

It really is the parents' responsibility to assure that the children never cross the line on this rule. The parent shouldn't expect respect unless they command respect. If there is love in the home and proper guidance of the children onto the righteous path, this rule should never be broken.

To summarize this rule, if the parents show the correct honor and respect within the home, they will in turn get the honor and respect that they deserve from their children. This is the true essence of this rule, and it starts with the ones closest to you, your spouse, and your children; that's why this one was first of the seven... 'nuff said.

Rule 5: "You shall not kill."

Killing someone is a very serious violation in the test of life. When you kill someone, you take away their chance to complete the test on their own terms. Every person has the right to attempt to succeed in this test and make their way Home... heaven... without someone else having the responsibility of "buying" their ticket.

Now don't give me that nonsense about predetermination of each person's life. God does know when and where our life will end. He is the Lord, the all-knowing Lord, but He doesn't set the stage, so to speak, nor does He script our lives. We are typically in control of our physical death in many cases, and we alone, are responsible for how we affect our neighbor's lives if we decide to break this rule and steal someone chance to have control of their death.

When we take another's life, we have committed the most serious violation imaginable. If we even consider killing, we still, in the real sense of this law, did the crime. Now, not... I'm gonna kill him! That's just anger. It's wrong, but it doesn't break the rule

119

unless you truly would like the other person dead and want to kill them.

And what about the sanctioned killings of abortion, war and capital punishment? Let me pray on this before I write any more. I have an opinion, but that's not important. I want this to be uninfluenced by my personal thoughts on the matter.

I write in the morning just after I pray, which is after I get up around 3:30 AM. Tomorrow is Sunday, and Sunday is the Sabbath... the Lord's Day. Tomorrow morning, hopefully, I will be able to continue on this subject, the fifth rule, but I fear that I am going to get this wrong if I continue today. See, I am absolutely opposed to killing of people of any kind, and I need God to tell me if there are any circumstances in which someone can justly take from another His precious gift of life.

So, you see my dilemma. God almighty, make clear the path that we will take.

I will continue to pray until tomorrow...

Good morning, it's Sunday, and my mind is clear!

I got to tell you: God is awesome. He took me to a party last night where the host of the party was a hunter... no, not just a hunter, but he had a 1,500-square-foot room filled with trophies of game that he killed. Now I know that this is not the subject at hand, but it is soon going to be covered in this rule. But while I was there, all kinds of revelations were coming to me. I didn't sleep, well, about four hours, because I needed to get up and ask God to direct me to the issue at hand, and He did. I've been up for about two hours and have a lot to share on this topic.

First, abortion. This is murder plain and simple. The child that the parents and God created is a living being from the moment of conception. Yet because society has deemed the fetus as "not a person" we have wholeheartedly embraced this act of murder simply because it's legal. They say it's a woman's right because it's her body but, I gotta tell you, they're wrong. The Catholic as well as many Christian faiths do have exceptions related to abortion due to rape and/or if the woman's life is at risk but, based on this rule, this would be the only time killing this innocent life would even be considered acceptable.

I can tell you with certainty that God will hold those accountable for this act of destruction of His creation of life. He granted the two parents the privilege of assisting in this creation, yet more times than not, when this occurs, it's an act of selfishness on the parents' part to ignore this blessing from our God.

But, in today's society, sexual relationships outside of marriage are the norm and are usually the reason for these "unwanted pregnancies." So, in our infinite wisdom as a society, we have established "choice" to justify the result of this sinful practice... the part of today's society that agrees with this type of murder is so wrong!

Second, war is waged because of many reasons. Typically, the leaders of a people convince them that it is in their best interest to go to war and usually they use God as the inspiration for the act of war. "God is behind our efforts" is most often their claim. The most recent war that comes to mind is the war on terror. On 9/11/01, we were attacked in our own "yard," and our reaction—slow as it was—was justified by our leaders as retaliation to this particular attack. However, when this happened, a good thing happened: We openly prayed to God, as a nation.

The motivation of men to go to war is too often influenced by other objectives, disguised and given a new façade: the façade of righteousness. I'm trying right now to be totally objective and keep my opinions out of this, so I look to God again to direct me back to the subject at hand: war.

"They will expel you from the synagogues; in fact, the hour is coming when everyone who kills you will think he is offering worship to God." (John 16:2)

Those were the words of Jesus Christ. He was talking to His twelve chosen about His upcoming death. He was trying to shed light on why men kill.

121

The act of war in all cases is not the choice of the soldier. The soldier is convinced that it is his duty to protect his country, follow orders, kill the enemy, and ultimately make the conditions we live in safer from our aggressors. The decision however, is often sold to us as an act of freedom and protection with God at the side of the country who claims that war is inevitable to secure it people from harm's way.

When men go to war, they are put into a situation beyond their control. They have one choice: kill, or be killed.

In this circumstance, self-preservation is the driving factor. As unrighteous as it is for a man to be put in this situation, those men put in this situation are totally absolved from this sin of killing. More often than not, these wars, in fact, are unavoidable because Satan has been carefully choosing the souls of the men that are responsible for inspiring these retaliatory responses by other governments and leaders of people.

In the cases where these retaliations are merited, wars are indeed righteous. We are bound by our love for others to defend others from the men inspired by Satan. Throughout the ages, men have indeed raged war for land, power, wealth, control, and so on. These men I assure will bear the total responsibility in the face of God for the deaths of the innocent men, women, and children who lost their lives due to the decisions made to follow the evil one's influence.

So, in the eyes of God, the men and women who are involved in the war effort and are merely "following orders" are not guilty of the crime of killing, if their intension isn't just for the sake of killing another human being. However, if any man or woman in this situation needlessly and wantonly takes another's life without just cause, they have committed the crime and have broken this rule.

Now, capital punishment is as old as society. Men invented capital punishment, not God; and, for that reason, I purposely avoided going any further through the Exodus book back in the previous chapters.

We sometimes put our own little twist on the words of God when we read the book of Exodus. Man had to have some control on the society, and again, wanting to be godlike, man decided to put rules into place that gave him the power to judge and to end another's physical life. In essence the death that is often referred to in the Bible as punishment for any crime, is the sole decision of God and that death is limited to our soul, not our physical life.

Man started to be judge and jury in a civil fashion to show that he was not going to put up with the disobedience of the God or man's laws. So, society back in those days, the days of Exodus, stoned a person to death if they broke a rule that they decided was a serious offense to God or man. A barbaric and cruel way to end someone's life and through the ages... we have become more civil in the ways that we approach taking of human life in the capital punishment theater. Nowadays we use a more civilized and humane procedure to accomplish this feat, the lethal injection, administered so that the person who is about to die feels little to no discomfort. How humane we have become!

"Let the one among you who is without sin be the first to throw the stone at her." (John 8:7)

Jesus made this statement to the faithful followers of the Law of Moses, Abraham, and the other prophets. They were about to kill a woman for being caught in the act of adultery.

At that time, according to their law, this act was punishable by death and apparently, it wasn't the Sabbath because they couldn't kill on the Sabbath day, either, go figure. I guess that killing someone wasn't considered rest.

This culture was under the reign of the Roman Empire who had also devised an extremely barbaric type of capital execution known as crucifixion. Citizens who were found guilty of breaking certain laws, according to their legal system, were subject to this horrific and brutal death; and at least one time, to my knowledge, someone who was innocent of any crime was also subject to this brutal execution.

Mankind must have felt that the murder of the "guilty" should be done in a more civil fashion. I'm not going to go through all the changes in the process of capital punishment but man has found that the disposal of life should be done in a more humane way so as not to offend the public. Of course, their concern is for their image among men, and they appear not to be not too concerned what God or His Son thinks about this subject.

"Let the one among you who is without sin be the first to throw the stone at her."

We, the normal human, are not without sin, not one of us. This capital punishment issue is the focus right now, and according to the Son of God, Jesus, it ain't right. This decision on the person's death for disobedience to the "law" is reserved for someone who is without sin, and we ain't him or her.

Yes, I know, someone killed your loved one, and you want the "eye for an eye." You want revenge! But revenge is also sinful, and I suggest, hard as it may be, to leave this judgment to God because God will affect the ultimate penalty to this person. If you remain righteous in the eyes of the Lord, you will see the wrath of the Almighty at His judgment, and your soul will be comforted.

However, society thinks it needs to be in control of evil people and thinks they need to deal with their evil deeds. We need to protect society and expel these people from society is typically the general consensus regarding this issue.

So, we as a society, have agreed that the death of these people in this public display of authority is justifiable. However, it seems as if we aren't really sure if we should proceed with these executions and allow the convicted amble time to appeal the verdict. It is not like in times of past where the execution occurred immediately after the verdict because we have become more civil and refined.

For the most part, we as a society view these people as mentally unstable and most often that will be their legal defense. This, in itself, is also an injustice to the society, but I won't expand too much on that subject... maybe a sentence or three. Yes, there are people with mental deviances and our consideration is merited; however, in many cases, it is only a mask, a cover-up for the evil inside these people. But because we are creature that make excuses for our lack of righteousness, faith, and genuine love for God, this does not give us the right to take the life of the convicted in this public display that we have masked an act of justice. That is reserved for one authority beyond the human level: God.

There are alternative solutions to capital punishment. We are a narrow-minded creature, with little insight to the truth; and that, in itself, prevents us from finding the alternative solution.

Self-gratification is the driving force behind this punishment and man has "grown" in his view of this sinful display. But I assure you, he has not grown enough because revenge and the control issue of one man's authority over another man's destiny are still the real culprits behind this punishment.

Now, the killing of animals in the sports of hunting is another subject that we must cover in this commandment. God gave us animals as a food source. Hunting them and killing them for this purpose is fine, I myself am a hunter and enjoy harvesting a mature buck if given the opportunity. Also, as far as the food source itself, we have become so civilized that we in fact have made a business of the supply of meat for food and have domesticated many animals for this exact purpose.

Animals do not have souls. I know that some of you think that cute little cat or dog you own is just like a part of your family and is a creature with a soul. Well, we own a dog and a cat; however, they are merely life forms that God has put here for us to enjoy and nothing more. And it's really difficult not to love them... but they have no soul.

I going to keep this brief: Killing any animal without a reason is wrong. It is a sin to waste our resources, but it is not an offense to this rule.

Sport killing was developed because we no longer have to hunt and kill our food. The food industry makes it simple for us to have most any animal on the dinner table that we could desire. Sport killing is also necessary to control the population of the animal kingdom so that there is a balance on this earth. If left without control the animal population would soon be overwhelming and become a nuisance. They would destroy crops, property, and cause too much trouble for society as a whole. Man has actually done a good job with this control in recent years. He realized that he was needlessly killing many species of some of these creatures and has gained some control of their preservation. Yet we have a long way to go in the "balancing" of these remaining endangered species.

But man, he is a funny creature, and he likes to kill. But if he has the need to satisfy that desire, he does have other options. For example, many target shot, which seems to satisfy some of this animal instinct.

However, any killing of an animal must be for the purpose of food or to control the species. Man cannot kill just for the sake of killing. We cannot destroy any life that God has put here, just to destroy a life.

We must also stop killing these creatures for his profit. Whales for example have been and are killed for the oil that is a product of their blubber. We have no need to do this in the twenty-first century; we have the technology to reproduce this oil by other means.

Elephants are another creature that man needlessly kills for profit. The ivory that the tusks produce is a very valuable commodity, but then the animal is left to rot in the sun… what a waste of life. Get the picture?

There are only two reasons to ever kill any living being, human or animal and they are these: self protection and self preservation.

Rule 6: "You shall not commit adultery."

Let's start out with Fact 1, and it is that mankind is truly an animal, an animal that has too many desires. Mankind is never satisfied with anything; it's never good enough. There is always something better in his or her mind, than what they already have.

Fact 2:

Mankind is guided by two spirits: your guardian angel, the good, and the demon placed beside you by Satan, the bad. The good spirit is doing their best to keep you on the path of righteousness, and naturally, the demon is trying to have you damned.

The good spirit is guiding you toward the path, which is of the spiritual plane. The demon is guiding to the plane of the total physical pleasures within this dimension and is doing his best to convince you that this life is the only life you and I should focus on.

Now that we are again aware of these facts, we can proceed in finding the reasons that humans love to break this particular rule. I seem to recall a saying about this... it goes something like this: A woman needs a reason to make love, but a man only needs a place. However, according to current statistics, this saying looks to no longer be valid because men and women are now participating in these adulterous relationships with an equal amount of enthusiasm.

There are so many things running through my mind right now; I not sure where to start. I guess I should start with the "bonding" of the man and woman.

Okay, a man and woman get married. They take a sacred vow to love, honor, cherish, in sickness and in health, until death... unless they decide they want a "mulligan." That's a term used in golf for a do-over. Marriage in itself has fallen apart. In today's society, it is commonplace for the two — most times, man and woman — to try it out before committing to the union. They want to be certain that it will work. The "it" is usually related to the sexually performance between the two. This part of the union and the relationship is the tell-all to some of these couples. Sure, they want to know if there are compatible in their personalities as well, but

127

most often, the primary reason for two people to live together is based on the "it": the sexual relationship.

And of course, sex between men and women starts at a very early age. Sex is now for "sport." And yes, hundreds of years ago, men and women had sexual relationships at an early age as well, but they were married at an earlier age. Man's typical lifespan was much different then; they didn't live to be in their eighties and nineties. This was not the norm; the norm was sixties and seventies only, because we didn't have the advances in prescription drugs as we do today. Those people had a much different view on the sanctity of the union; it was 'til death do us part a greater percentage of the time.

However, today it's "'til I find someone who will sexually satisfy my animal needs better than you to the nth degree." Adultery has been around since the beginning of mankind. God destroyed Sodom and Gomorrah because in this place, the biggest sin was the sin of sex between men and women, between men and men, and between women and women... and so on. Sex in itself is not sinful; God's first order to man was to be fruitful and multiply, but he also put guidelines on the mate that man was to multiply with...

However, Sodom and Gomorrah were a "monastery" compared to the standards of today. Today we are bombarded by these sinful influences in every direction that we look... on the newsstands, in the media, in the workplace, in our neighborhoods, in our own families, and just about anyplace else that you can think of, and of course, we as a whole, don't put up a decent battle to fight off the urges of falling into this trap of sin.

Everybody wants to be a part of this age-old sinful practice. We express our own desires to participate in this activity in a countless number of ways... in the way we dress, in the way we walk, in the way we talk, in the way we think. We think that there is no harm in this; it's perfectly acceptable in the standards that we have set as a society.

"Everyone's doing it, so why can't I?" is the justification that comes out of our minds. Yet some still "resist" the temptations of this soul-destroying act, but some are still guilty in their minds and hearts of this offense.

"But I say to you, everyone who looks at a woman with lust has already committed adultery with her in his heart." (Matthew 5:28)

That's right, even if you think of the act, you have committed the sin in the eyes of God. Even if you think of part of the act; you've done the deed. Even just a little contact that is inappropriate and done to satisfy your lustful desire is an infraction of the rule.

I'm thinking of a past president right now. He denied ever having sexual relationships "with that woman" until the evidence of the dress... oops, I guess that's considered a sexual relationship too! And to think, half of the American people couldn't find this to be all that wrong. They were willing to overlook this as a small slip-up, and not because they found mercy in their hearts, but because they truly didn't consider this as an adulterous deed. Imagine that!

God created man and woman and, in His creation, as in all His creations, there is beauty. There truly is no harm, no foul, if you are merely looking at the beauty of His creation. However, when the lust overtakes your heart and mind and you react to the physical aspect, then you have committed adultery.

All humans, including myself, commit this sin, no matter who you are; you are not immune from falling into this trap. It's part of the deal, "the test," and this issue is spreading to both sexes. Typically, in years past, most men were viewed as "pigs," but nowadays, it is no longer just the men who have been branded with this title.

Women have joined the crusade and are seemingly pleased to be part of the group, the "Ms Piggies." Well, what can you do? It's that equality thing, I guess.

I don't want to beat a dead horse, so let's say this and move on. You can't control some of the thoughts in your mind when it comes to this subject. However, you can ask God to grant you the graces necessary to get you through the temptations of the mind. However, you must practice this virtue, pray and practice, then pray and practice... 'til you get it right; you may never get this right but you must try, try, and try again.

And you can resist the act of adultery. You can take a proactive position in this epidemic simply by saying no... difficult as that might be for some. But some will never be able to "just say no" because they have no real relationship with God. They are the disciples of the demon.

God doesn't want to lose even one soul to the Satan, and mankind does have the choice in this matter. Man makes the final decision on this rule, and if he can't overcome this physical temptation, he will not pass the test.

Genesis 3:11... let go back to this for a second.

"Who told you that you were naked?"

It all started in the garden when the first rule was broken. It was part of the rule, don't you see? When Adam and Eve's eyes were opened to good and evil, they then discovered the sins in the flesh. When you commit adultery, you not only break rule number 6, but you undo the completeness of the union between man and woman. You have not only failed your spouse; you have failed yourself because you are one body, one spirit, and one soul and this sinful practice of adultery is the basis of evil, part of the first original sin.

Rule 7: "You should not steal."

I wish this was as simple as this: If it's not yours, don't take it. But it's not.

All right, let's try that again: If it's not yours, don't take it. Still didn't work, did it?

I told you earlier that I was a Catholic — Catholic school education and everything. When I went to school, my teachers were mostly nuns and priests. This religious order constantly influenced my education. I learned all of the rules at a very young age; in fact, we had a religion class every day of my academic life while attending grammar and high school. Even though I still am guilty of making fun of the system, I would never trade my education, even if I could. The sisters and priests not only taught me the rules, but also the potential consequences and penalties of breaking these Ten Commandments.

I was recently shocked to learn that some of the penalties had in fact been lessened since my youth. There have been several changes in the doctrine of the Catholic Church since I completed my fundamental education in 1974. One such change is related to this particular commandment. When I went to school, I was taught that if you broke this rule, you committed a mortal sin. But now the sin is prorated so to speak; there are two degrees of severity for this sin: mortal and venial. Imagine my surprise when I learned this... well, it was about thirty-five years after I completed high school.

I learned that because we humans steal on a regular basis; the degree of the theft determines the degree of the sin. Incidentally, there have been other changes due to our society's tolerance of the infractions of these commandments. Ain't it a shame!

We as a society have become extremely greedy. We look at others with more envy than any other time in the history of the world. We all believe that it is unfair that one individual could have so much while others have nothing. We decided that this is wrong, and we now take the possessions of others without fear of consequence.

We take these items big and small; feel no guilt or shame and never consider this to be wrong. For the most part, we as a society share this position. For example, when you go to work and you need a pencil or two for the home, don't you just take them home? Are you doing work at home or are the pencils for the kids? Not one of us considers this as stealing, right? We took them because it was easier for us to do that then go to the store and buy some pencils, or we saw no harm in taking them because the company has lots of pencils, right? Generally, people do this on a regular basis, and yes, even I have been guilty of this sin.

Companies have actually made provisions in their operational budgets to offset this "accepted" practice. So not only has the Catholic Church changed its policies on this matter, corporate America has also become lenient to the point of acceptance.

But the pencils are only one example of how we have become thieves and like it. We take paper, envelopes (these two items are incidentally the top two items of theft from companies), staplers, paper clips, pens run a close second, and whatever we want — and it's okay.

How I learned that this was no longer a serious sin was when I confessed my theft in the sacrament of confession. Yes, I took some office supplies, and before I did, I asked my supervisor who gave me permission. I felt guilt for doing this knowing that these items really didn't belong to the supervisor but belonged to the company, and confessed this sin.

I told my priest that I had permission to take but still felt that I had sinned. He then explained that the rule changed and assured me that it was no longer considered a "serious" sin when taking these types of items.

That in itself has prevented me from any further infraction of this rule. I was literally shocked into reality. We have become so tolerant of theft that its now considered an "excuse me" offense with a minor penalty attached to the infraction... what a shame!

And this is just the tip of the iceberg. Because of our acceptance of these newfound freedoms to break this rule, our theft level has escalated almost beyond control. I find myself putting valuables in our safe when we have company over. I do this because once we had a ring stolen from the house by a visitor who was part of a group of people invited to our home for a party. Now, we don't have definitive proof that it was any one particular person, but the ring was on the bar and when the party was over, it was gone. Actually, now that I think about it, this happened on two different occasions. The second was when my son invited some friends over after school one day. We were not home from work yet, and one of my wife's rings was taken off her dresser. We suspected one of the children but, again, we had no proof. This ring was very special to her: It was the only thing she got from her father who died many years before from colon cancer, a non-replaceable item.

I'm laughing right now. I'm thinking about the time two of my friends and I were playing cards and we all commented that "we should get new friends"; we were talking about these incidents. They themselves have experienced the same problem in their homes, and all I can say is, "What a shame!"

There are different degrees of theft, agreed; but here's the deal, if it ain't yours, don't take it. Whether it be a pencil or the Hope Diamond and you gain possession of the item (s) without the true and rightful ownership; it is stealing and stealing is wrong!

I can assure you of one thing, come Judgment Day, you and me will answer to the Lord. He is not going to be as tolerant as society has been when He is judging each of us. He will consider each and every infraction of His law. And there will be no infraction missed, big or small.

Then God will do the condemnation on mankind, so don't be confused, I am not condemning mankind for his misdeeds, I am part of the crowd. I myself am guilty of these same sins and these infractions of the law of God, and I will be in the line of judgment right alongside of you. However, I am conscience of the humanity within and I am always striving to take control of my sinful ways, which we were both born with, and which we need to overcome.

Rule 8: "You shall not bear false witness against your neighbor."

I was once told that lying was an occupational hazard. At the time, my profession was in sales. Can you imagine anyone could make such a comment? But they did, and it made me very angry because the stereotypical image of a salesperson is that they are liars.

Salespeople will tell you anything that you want to hear to secure the sale. They can't be trusted; in fact, they are considered the least likely person to be truthful: those used-car salesman! Fortunately, I was in another industry and was not subject to too much of this stereotyping; however, I did get my fair share of those negative feeling from people at the initial contact.

When the customer got to know me a little better, they then saw that I was trying my best to be an honest and truthful man. This gave me great success in the profession of sales. Quite often, my peers and supervisors would ask me what the "secret" is to my success in the field of sales. I would chuckle and tell them, "The truth will set you free. Nothing more, nothing less." But they don't get it; they just can understand that this could be the "secret" to my success, and for the best of me, I can't myself understand how people could not see this to be true. People want honesty in their day-to-day contact, even though they themselves may not always be as truthful as their expectation of others.

Lying or bearing false witness for the most part could be merely an extension of the truth. It may be the truth as some individuals perceive it in their own mind. It is how they want it to be, but not how it really is factually. Pride is the chief motivator in most of these "extensions" of the truth, and pride is also one of the seven deadly sins. We'll talk about those seven deadly sins later, I assure you; but for now, our focus is on this commandment.

This commandment is a funny little commandment, a Catch-22, so to speak. Funny in the respect that everyone, except for those two who lived or will ever live, breaks this rule. No avoiding it, no way around it. The other nine of these rules… well, at least there is a fighting chance that we could avoid breaking at least one of them, but this one, no one has a chance to never, ever break this rule, and that is absolute truth: Everyone lies!

If pride doesn't get us to break this rule, then fear will be the motivator. Fear that some harm will come to us if we tell the truth; we want to protect ourselves from an outcome of our actions. If it's not fear, then jealousy could be a contributing factor, and so on. So, you see, this is a tough rule — no, an impossible rule to never break.

Hence, the venial and mortal sins were introduced by the authorities of the churches so long ago. Unfortunately, God doesn't see much of a difference in the two types of sin. God is hurt when we sin, no matter the degree. Be it serious or be it minor, sin is sin. So, we do have a reference point in the Bible to go to and see for ourselves when this introduction of mortal and venial sin was made. It was then refined and defined by the Catholics and still in place in our religion.

It's at 1 John 5:16-17.

"If you see any brother or sister commit a sin that does not lead to death, you should pray and God will give them life. I refer to those whose sin does not lead to death. There is a sin that leads to death. I am not saying that you should pray about that. All wrong-doing is sin, and there is sin that does not lead to death."

Let's look at the two types of untruths and see which one is which. Which one is an "oops," and which one is a biggie?

I have a headache and don't feel like going to the mall shopping today. This is a good example of a common lie told by most husbands. It's usually told between September and January at or around noon on Sundays. The headache finally eases up at around 7:30 PM. Fortunately, an afternoon on the couch watching football, drinking beer, and eating snack foods is the most recommended prescription for this annoying affliction. Most wives see right through this mistruth and are somewhat tolerant of the telling of this universal and accepted untruth.

My wife, on the other hand, will watch the game with me on game day and has actually learned enough that she does in fact — I think, unless she's lying — enjoys the game. That's really unfair to her; I'm sure that if she didn't want to watch the game, she wouldn't. I know that she does because she will put the game on in the kitchen so that if she has to leave the living room for that pesky task of preparing the dinner, she can follow the game without interruption. I'm 100 percent sure that she does like to watch football… I think.

Or "I'm going over to my buddy's house to help him on a project he's working on around his house, and he can't do it without my help," when, in fact, you had something else in mind is another fairly common mistruth. Now if your plan is to go to the jewelry store and buy your "girl" a nice present for that special occasion, well, that's actually just an oops. But if your intension is to go to the local pub and you and your buddy have another agenda on your minds… oh boy, that's a biggie!

The biggie is the lie that hurts another individual in any way. Your neighbor is everyone, so it makes no difference if you know that person that you are telling this type of lie about or not. Any and all meaningless mistruth that is told to keep someone "uninformed" so that you can do something nice for him or her without him or her finding out is the type of lie that we can tell without any serious consequences… the *oops*. However, if the lie affects your neighbor's happiness in any way, real or perceived, you have broken this rule and told the biggie lie.

Let's go to this. for some guidance and see if this, "the oops," is covered…

"Nothing that enters one from outside can defile that person; but the things that come from within are what defile." (Mark 7:15)

If you look ahead a few verses, the explanation:

"He said to them, "Are even you likewise without understanding? Do you not realize that everything that goes into a person from outside cannot defile, since it enters not the heart but the stomach and passes out into the latrine?" "But what comes out of a person, which is what defiles. From within people, from their hearts, come evil thoughts, lack of chastity, theft, murder, adultery, greed, malice, deceit, licentiousness, envy, blasphemy, arrogance, folly. All these evils come from within and they defile." (Mark 7:18, 23)

This place is a good place. We're going to spend some time here later, but for right now...

It all starts with what comes out of our mouths. Sometimes we can't control the feelings within our hearts, and from those feelings, the words spew from our mouths. Most often, if these words are not truthful, they will lead to the more serious infractions of the rest of the rules.

I just happened to take a break for a minute and asked my wife if the weatherman had given the forecast for today yet. It's raining right now, and my grass needs to be mowed. The forecast is for clearing this afternoon, but it might be too wet to mow. I said to my wife, "If I don't mow the grass soon, you won't be able to see the small tree anymore." We planted a small red maple; it's about a foot tall. She said, "Really, is it that high?"

I responded, "No, I'm lying."

Telling a lie for the entertainment value or to make a situation funny isn't a lie at all, provided the person or persons do, in fact, understand that it is for amusement only. For example, fictional writing and/or movies that we know are based on an untruth. If it is obviously an untruth and is presented in such a way that we all understand it to be a lie, it isn't a lie at all. However, it should be made crystal clear that the information is fictional and has no basis in truth and this should be done in a definitive manner.

Unfortunately, much of the entertainment of today doesn't differentiate between the truth and fiction. The general public is confused on the reality of reality. We have accepted for so long the fact that untruth is an acceptable practice, and now some can't tell the difference between fact and fiction. It all stems from the infraction of this rule, a simple little rule, but the beginning of the end of our awareness of our reality.

My advice to you: Tell the truth. If you speak an untruth, confess to it then or when the time is right. If you're surprising someone, they'll know anyway when they get the gift; if not, tell them. You will start to look at life in a different way when you become honest with yourself and with others around you... important: with yourself first. Don't live in a fantasyland. Honesty starts with you; know who you are and be proud of who you are because of your honesty.

Think of it like this: You're a child of God. God is truth. Being one of His children, it's in your "genes" to be like unto your "daddy." Talk to your Father; He will be more than happy to help you and guide you to be like Him. He will never turn His back if you simply ask, and if you ask for righteousness and honesty in your life, this does please our Dear Old Dad and you will receive the grace to become honest.

I know that this was one of the struggles I had in my early years of life until I finally asked God to give me the grace necessary to maintain an honest and truthful presence on this earth. I still, every now and then, tell a little "white" lie, but it's always followed by the confession, "no, I'm lying." And I only do this in situations where I am basically putting a little levity into a situation, easing the tension, protecting someone, or making light of the topic at hand.

This test we are taking is about you, it's about me, and it's about us. We can't pass the test if we cheat on the test. God is the proctor and monitor of this test. He sees everything, and try as you might, you can't avoid being caught cheating. Honesty starts with you, and honesty is the key to the passing grade. Imagine how wonderful this world would be if everyone told the truth. If you could depend in everything someone told you all the time.

Try this today. Speak to others with this in mind; I'm not going to say anything that will be untrue, and I'm not going to hurt them with my words in any way. It's really not that difficult to do if you do unto others, as you want them to do unto you. You've heard that before, and you're going to hear it again soon.

One other tip on how to succeed...

We all come into this world the same way, and we are all going to leave it the same way. That makes us all equal. Pride is the main motivator when we break any rule.

The Lord is not impressed by what you think you are and what you think you have, because you only have it because He allows you to have it.

However, God is impressed by what you want to be and is extremely impressed if what you want to be is proud to be His child.

Your brothers and sisters, His other children, are extremely important to Him as well. When you speak about them in an untruthful way, you are, in essence, speaking about Him; and, by hurting them, you are hurting Him.

If you hurt God, you are following the ways of Satan. And if you decide to continue to follow the ways of Satan, God will allow you to do so. That choice is yours and yours alone. But if you need His help overcoming Satan and the forces that take you down this path, He will be there for you.

We're going to look at the next two rules and talk about them together. They belonged together in the beginning and should never have been separated. I can see it now... Cecil B. DeMille presents *The Nine Commandments*. Well, they were separated long before the movie, but I got a little chuckle out of the line.

Rules 9 and 10: "You shall not covet your neighbor's house. You shall not covet your neighbor's wife, nor his male or female slave, nor his ox or ass, nor anything that belongs to him."

This commandment is simply an extension of a prior rule. However, it is so important that it had to be said again. The rule, number 7, "You shall not steal"; these rules—9 and 10—are the reinforcement of this particular rule.

Let's just start with the word *covet*, shall we? What does this word mean? Well, it means to wish earnestly or to desire something or someone. This is the first definition in the dictionary and, for all intents and purposes, this is the definition that applies to this rule.

Envy is one of the forces that drives us toward breaking this commandment. Greed is also a contributing factor, and let's not forget jealousy; all three are applicable.

There's no denying it, to even try to convince anyone, even you, that you have never broken this one, is a bald-faced lie. I myself felt a great deal of envy for someone else's possessions. I was guilty of coveting my neighbor's goods. A couple of rules ago, I told you I was at someone's house for a party. I told you that he had a game room filled with hunting trophies. I didn't tell you about the rest of the six-thousand-square-foot house filled with—well, everything: art, expensive furnishings, marble floors, four full baths, a Lamborghini in the garage, and so much more.

When we left, I told my wife that I had felt this envy and that I was ashamed of myself for having these covetous and envious feelings. I know better; I know that having all those earthly possessions don't make a bit of difference in the salvation of my soul. But I couldn't help having those feelings because of the abundance of one person's possessions and then to wonder why they could have so much more than us... totally overwhelming. I'm over it now, thank God, but I felt the envy for a couple of days.

I suppose I needed to experience that because it has shed some insight on the subject at hand. God does work in mysterious ways, no denying that.

So, what else can we as human beings covet? According to these two rules, we aren't supposed to covet someone's house, their wife, their slaves, their beasts of burden, or anything else that they might possibly own, correct? Correctamundo!

But slavery has been abolished since this commandment was given back in the day, right? Wrong, some cultures still enjoy this practice of ownership. I don't want to get too deeply involved in the subject, but I will tell you how the slave trade started so that you can understand a little better why that was included in this commandment.

Slavery began some ten thousand years ago or so. The premise behind the practice was to use captured soldiers from wars to perform hard labor. A slave was a prisoner and was forced by their captors to work under their control until death. The captor would provide food, shelter, and clothing for the slave in return for the services rendered; however, the captor had total control over that individual's life in almost all respects.

Well, this practice evolved into a trade of "flesh" so to speak, and by the time that many ancient cultures such as the Greeks, the Romans, the Athenians, and the Egyptians, among others, had become world powers, slavery was an industry. It was common practice and accepted by all — with the exception of the slaves.

Now, of course, man in his quest to become a god twisted this practice into what we can remember in our recent history as a despicable and unacceptable control of another's life. What I'm talking about is how mankind lost the respect of the sanctity of another person's freedom. Think about it: when this started, it was very similar to the way we as a society deal with criminals. You can find this practice just about anywhere in any civilization today. Our criminals are locked up to protect us from any further offenses, yet we put then to work on road crews and basically force them to perform tasks to defray the cost of their imprisonment. Or we use them in the manufacturing of many common items; the most recognized was the license plate for your car. This was the concept behind slavery, yet mankind, in his infinite wisdom, twisted it into this shameful practice as history unfolded.

The society that this rule was first given to had certain guidelines on slavery, and they, once being slaves themselves, understood the root concept behind this practice. When the slave had served his or her time to the "master," they were set free. These people were the "cutting edge" in those times and were striving to be righteous in the eyes of the Lord. However, they still practiced this control of another's life and debt to another person was the chief reason for this practice to continue in that era.

And truth be known, we still practice this act of slavery. Don't some people have servants, maids, butlers, pool boys, gardeners, or the more sophisticated class, the nanny? Don't some people bring others into this country illegally to work for basically food,

141

shelter, and clothing? You know what I'm talking about, right? Anyway, I didn't really want to get that deep into this subject, so I'll stop this thought and get back to the subject at hand: rules 9 and 10.

Here's what they say: Don't be greedy, don't show envy for another's goods, and don't be jealous of something or someone that another possesses. It is very difficult to obey this rule because of one important factor: human nature. Human nature is a nature of want and desire. It is a nature of self-gratification, a nature of self-indulgence, and a nature of want and desire for every earthly possession imaginable... greed, envy, and jealousy!

Before we go anywhere else, I think that we should look at those nasty, seven deadly sins. If we have an understanding of the sins, then we might stand a chance of becoming a better and more tolerant individual in regard to our humanity.

Because, my friends, that's really all there is: nothing more, no other reason for us to live this physical life. This, in itself, should help you understand why these last two rules are highly important.

The bottom line is this: We can't worry about what someone else has because it's not important at all. Our possessions in this life have no bearing whatsoever on the final outcome of any of our lives here on earth, so please be thankful for what you have because God provides what we need but doesn't always provide what we want.

Chapter 11
Seven Comes in Eleven: How About That!

There was a movie out—I can't remember how long ago, and I guess it really isn't important enough to look up when it made the box office for the first time—but it was called *Seven*. It was a movie about a serial killer who chose his victims based on their worst traits and characteristics. Each time the killer murdered a victim, he left evidence that he was the same killer and established a pattern of his victim's selection, which was based on the seven deadly sins. The movie runs on cable every now and again, and if you like murder mysteries, this is a decent flick, but...

The worst thing about this movie is that these types of murders do indeed happen. It's unfortunate for the most part that some may imitate what they see in the movies. Many people don't realize that these productions are in fact for our entertainment and should be viewed as fictional, but are they really fictional in some minds?

Again, the media and greed for the almighty buck is the culprit, which movie will gross the highest opening dollar figure. That's always a good indicator of the movie's total initial run revenue.

Media capitalizes on human weaknesses. They need us to be interested in what they are offering; if not, it's a flop. When they offer a subject in which the main character displays one of these seven sins, it is generally a box-office hit. I often wonder why we, as humans, want these seven destructive characteristics ever present as an influence in our lives. Flaunted constantly and daily, anywhere we look in the media today... but it sells!

The more violent the act, the bigger the response by the media group presenting the "facts." Is our concern the sorrow for the tragedy, or is it our curiosity that drives us to either watch or read the presentation on the matter? If you can honestly answer that question, then you will know how you're doing in the test so far, but honestly, I mean, deep down in your heart, no one else has to know... just you and God.

Pause and pray... ask God to show you the way to your heart. Please take a moment for your own sake.

I found it funny this morning when I went on the Internet to get the correct order of the seven and the correct words used in the list itself. Funny because on the first site I visited... well, the only site I visited... there was an offer to purchase a T-shirt that had the seven deadly sins displayed. See what I mean? Commercialism is everywhere, the search and desire to capture the almighty dollar, and the constant preying on our weaknesses. My weakness, in this case, was the accurate list of words. You see, the Internet is nothing more than an extension of the information media around us. I frown and feel sad that I have to be exposed constantly by these intrusions in my life, but I cope, I accept, and I pray for strength.

Okay, let me list them and then we'll go over them each of them, one at a time:

> Pride
>
> Envy
>
> Gluttony
>
> Lust
>
> Anger
>
> Greed
>
> Sloth

Incidentally, *sloth* is a word I couldn't remember, and it was the reason I had to look the list up this morning. Not that it matters, but I just thought I share. I couldn't remember this word because I am normally not guilty of this particular sin. Might as well start with this one; it doesn't really matter if we don't take them in the order just listed.

Sloth is the avoidance of physical or spiritual work. Lazy... that's what I was thinking and couldn't remember the word *sloth*... but it's very early in the morning and I haven't an ample amount of caffeine yet.

That's probably why I'm not lazy. I drink too much of this drug in too many forms. It's one of my vices in life, but it's certainly not one of my worst.

Now that I'm thinking about it, I am guilty of this sin...

I've had two major back surgeries in my life, and I do avoid many of the everyday physical tasks to prevent higher levels of pain and further injury to the affected area of my lower back. But I still do everything that I am physically capable of and quite often do too much, which aggravates my existing and never-ending condition.

I have substituted many of these physical tasks with spiritual tasks to help me from committing this sin. Example: this right here.

An idle mind and idle hands are the devil's workshop... or something like that. That's sin in the sin of sloth. When we have nothing to occupy us, we open the door to the demon. We allow him to enter our hearts through our minds. Work requires concentration and attention to the project. When we are idle, we are open and vulnerable to the direct influence of this demon. Our mind wanders, and unless you are impervious, you will lose.

Sloth not only can cause problems with our spiritual well-being, but it can also cause problems with our physical wellness.

Laziness — sloth — causes death, both physical and spiritual. We know why sloth may cause death of your physical life, but the physical life isn't as important to us in an equal degree, as the spiritual life is. Let's take going to Sunday services for an example, shall we?

145

Most people who miss Sunday services miss the service because they are lazy. They've worked so hard all week long that they deserve the time in the "rack" on Sunday morning. They deserve to get ten to twelve hours of rest because they've earned it! Trouble is, they don't give credit where credit is due. God allowed them to make it until Saturday night, and they should be anxious to thank Him on Sunday morning for the gifts He has given them during the week, but they're not! True that! I learned this term from a younger employee that I work with; it means that the statement is correct and 100 percent accurate... I like it.

But men give too much credit to themselves for their own simple accomplishments: their simple accomplishments of completing the day-to-day endeavors. Because of our slothful ways, we avoid the basic yet required activities to maintain the state of grace to prevent the death of our soul. Men seem to avoid the spiritual tasks with so much more conviction, almost like they are purposely and consciously attempting to do so. But why?

Pride, also known as vanity. Vanity is absolutely the sin that all other sins arise from and should have been first, but because I couldn't remember the word *sloth*, I chose to go with that one first instead.

Pride is excessive belief of one's own abilities, which interferes with any individual's recognition of the grace of God Almighty. Vanity, another word for *pride*, is the demon's favorite sin. He encourages us constantly to embrace this feeling of power, to flaunt and/or strut our "stuff."

Now don't get this wrong, pride to a degree is acceptable. Pride in your accomplishments after hard work on any task is a good feeling, but realize that God gave you those abilities and the graces to succeed in those and all endeavors. Without His guiding hand, your simple accomplishments could never occur... true that!

But we take pride to an extreme level, and we're boastful to the max. We encourage the sin of envy in others. We want them to want what we have, and we like the feeling that we get from this;

it's a rush for most people who display this characteristic. You know these people, they're the people who you are jealous of and want what they have. They're easy to identify; they are the ones who got it all. You think they do?

No, my friends, they have nothing but the sin of pride, vanity buried deep inside their hearts, mind, and soul. All their wealth, all those possessions, all the gold do not buy the eternal life of the soul. It does not buy one more second of life here in this physical plane, which is so important to these folks.

This sin of pride is covered over and over again in the Bible. The main thrust is in the Book of Proverbs or sometimes referred to as the Book of Wisdom, a truly accurate name for the information contained in this work. In fact, Jesus Christ and His apostles often expressly quoted the Proverbs.

If there are no objections, let's research The Book of Proverbs and have a look around, shall we?

Proverbs... circa 850 BCE.

Hey, here's a good one right here.

"The fear of the Lord is to hate evil; Pride, arrogance, the evil way, and the perverse mouth I hate." (Proverbs 8:13)

This chapter is entitled "The Discourse of Wisdom." It basically says just about what I said so far. It speaks of truth, honesty, how to deal with material wealth, and speaks of this pride issue. But if you look forward in the chapter, it is actually speaking of Jesus Christ as the savior and how from the beginning of time itself, He was part of the plan. This is a very good read; read it when you have a moment.

Here's another, Proverbs 16:18: "Pride goes before disaster, and a haughty spirit before a fall."

And another, Proverbs 29:23: "Man's pride causes his humiliation, but he who is humble of spirit obtains honor."

If you take anything away from this experience, this "book," please take this little tidbit of understanding. The Book of Proverbs has got just about everything you'll ever need to survive this test. There is a lot of information, all true, within the entire book of the Bible.

But this section is the "goods." When you finish this book, you should make it a practice to read this section entitled Proverbs. Then read it over and over again so that it becomes part of your life. If you do this, I will have succeeded in my task and will have given you the opportunity and information needed to pass this test!

I've struggled with vanity, pride, arrogance, and those boastful ways for most of my life. But what gets me by is the effort I put forth in my attempt to gain control of this nasty sin, this sin that causes me to sin every other sin. We all are sinners; it is part of our being. I've come to realize that in my life, and I have accepted that as a fact. Most of my sins come to fruition because my pride has been hurt; just like everyone else, I'm no different. And so, I turn to this verse, which we all just saw moments ago, for the strength I need to control the beast within me.

"Man's pride causes his humiliation, but he who is humble of spirit obtains honor."

And then there's envy, which is a direct result of one's pride being injured. Envy is the desire for another's traits, status, abilities, or situation. We all experience envy sometime in our life, some more often than others, some constantly, and some occasionally, but no one is immune to this deadly sin...

Fortunately, it is rare for me to experience this sin... well, at that party, but not since. I am happy with who I am and what I have; I know that I have plenty of material wealth. I'm not filthy rich, but we have more than enough to eat, to drink, to pay the bills, to support charities, to help the needy; and I thank God that I have all these basic necessities of this physical life covered, so I am rich.

I thank God daily for all the wonderful gifts He has allowed me to obtain in my life. I thank God for what He has not allowed me to gain as well. Each righteous person is given what he or she will need to survive and pass this test.

Be assured that we don't have to get everything we want, but some can't make the distinction between the two; their wants become their needs. They want what others have and that is envy. They want those things so badly that the desire becomes an obsession and that obsession turns into the force that causes their sinfulness.

There is no justifiable feeling of envy. It is negative and has no merit or saving graces. We'll talk about the saving graces as soon as we get through these deadly sins, but this little four-letter word, *envy*, is in my opinion, the worst four-letter word of them all... way worse than the "f" bomb, for sure...

There is a section on the Bible that addresses our envy and desire for material wealth... well, more than one... but one in particular that I'm thinking of. It is contained in the Gospel of Luke. It is entitled the Parable of the Rich Man. I'll just highlight some of the content of the section, but feel free at any time to read this section in the Bible on your own. It's located in Luke 12:16–21, and while you're at it, read the next section entitled "Dependence" on God (Luke 12:22–34). This really says it all when it comes to the issue of material wealth.

The section on the rich fool basically says that it doesn't matter how much you attain in this life, how rich you are or how rich you will become, those riches don't matter to God. He provided you the ability to get them, but they are not of any importance to Him in the least. The next section speaks of how God will provide you with all the things in life. In fact, there are several lines that say, if you are a righteous person, God will grant you more than you need and all that you want. Read it for yourself: Luke 12:29–31.

So, there is absolutely no reason for anyone to ever feel this emotion of envy if they are righteous in the sight of the Lord. Righteous in knowing that He will provide to you and me all the things we need to survive, but what about the poor? The people who are unfortunate and have little material wealth, what about them?

I'll tell you what about them, one of your missions as well as my mission, is to help these people; help these people with commitment, showing the true love for your neighbor. We all can see what's going on around us; millions upon millions of our neighbors don't even have enough to eat, forgetting the fact that they could ever afford all those golden bulbuls and bling we're so proud to show off. Then we have the audacity to say, "Oh, what a shame," as we jump into our SUVs, which we are currently making that outrageous monthly payment on, and head to the mall to shop for things that we really don't need; we simply just want those things, blinded to the cause of charity, charity toward our fellow man, only because envy has turned into greed. Pity the fool.

I heard you...

The answer is yes and no. Yes, if you want to be a saint, truly a saint in your heart, with no other objective in mind other than to go straight into heaven when you complete this physical life. Yes, then give it all away, freely and passionately. The Lord will provide for your earthly existence more so than you could ever imagine. No, charity begins at home. If you have dependents that are in need of your material support, you can't abandon them for your own sake. You can still become a saint without giving everything away, but after you have provided for the family, then extend yourself to your neighbors. God will never be outdone when it comes to charity; the more you give others, the more God will give you, caution needed.

Do not give with the expectation of receiving something back for your generosity. Give it freely, no strings attached, no expectations other than you'll be helping someone in need of your charity.

There are plenty of millionaires in heaven. My closest angel just corrected me and said that they all live like millionaires, every one of the Saints in Heaven, because if you pass the test and make it into heaven, you will never experience another want or desire for the rest of eternity. All those who make it into heaven are, in fact, saints, just thought I'd throw that in here; maybe you did, maybe you didn't know that fact.

But greed keeps us from earning our "wings," because greed is envy to the most extreme degree. I can assure you this, and I'm not hearing any correction, there are no greedy people in heaven; they're all in hell. Their never-ending desire for the possessions and wealth of this physical plane has earned them the pains of everlasting torment and want.

Their never-ending desire to retain everything for themselves, never sharing with their fellow man, is a direct and inexcusable sin against God and His children here on earth. But man, is a fool; he has no faith, he has no trust, and he lacks true love for his fellow human being. Love is sharing, love is caring, and true love is freedom for our souls.

Everyone feels the power of greed sometime in his or her life. Yes, I said that everyone feels the power sometime in their life, but only a select few embrace the power. The wise person will defeat this ugly beast, while the fool will embrace this beast. There is a difference between the two; if you love Satan, you love greed.

I told you earlier that I was not a filthy rich man, but I am comfortable. I once quit a job where I earned a six-figure salary year after year. I took a job at half the pay. I did this because life has more to offer than a paycheck. I've positioned our family well, and we are very happy regardless of the money. The new position offered me some freedoms and extra time to do the important things in life, which I never had the time for before this change.

My friends said I was crazy, but I don't care what they think. If greed had been my motivator, I would have never discovered the pleasure in the quality of life that I am now experiencing. I still make plenty of money to support my dependences and to give to the charities of my choice, not wanting any more than I already have, because I have more than enough.

I have overcome greed; I have eliminated this emotion from my life. What a feeling not to be controlled by this beast, and what freedom I feel in my soul. I thank God for where He has brought me in this physical life, and if He decides to take it all away, I still know that I will be free from that evil, dirty, and ugly sin of greed.

I've come to realize that it's so not important to have material wealth; it doesn't buy you the happiness that love for your fellow human and charity toward the needy can buy. All money buys are things; I never saw an armored car following a Hearse in a funeral procession carrying their money to the grave either. Have you?

But I suppose the true fool might have done this, and I wasn't around to see it.

Take a little advice from me; the guy whose friends thought he had it all and threw it away for a better life; money is a necessity in this world, but it isn't, nor should it be your motivator. However, it can be the driving force for most that can't control this beast and often results in the ignoring of the health of their spiritual being.

Moving right along, let's look at the deadly sin of *gluttony*.

Gluttony is a good choice for the next one, since it goes hand in hand with the sin of greed.

Of course, you're now wondering why and how the two could go hand in hand. Well think about it for a second; gluttony is an inordinate desire to consume more than which one requires, by definition.

It's not limited to the consumption of food, as most could assume. It's the unusual and burning desire to take in an excessive amount of anything, whether it be food, clothes, and money; the list could go on and on and on.

True that people who are extremely overweight are more than likely gluttons, possibly overeating every meal to a point where they think their stomach is about to burst and continuing this practice day after day. But also, true that we can be gluttons for material wealth. Just a few paragraphs back, I told you about the change in jobs I had. I also told you I wasn't rich, merely comfortable, but I didn't tell you this...

When my wife and I got married, we didn't even have the proverbial pot. We actually opened the cards from the wedding to go on a three-day honeymoon by car to Vermont. Upon our return to Pennsylvania, we had a balance of $300 with an accumulated debt between us of about $3,000. We were deep in the hole, but it didn't matter, because we were in love... we're still in love today... a little more, I'd say, if that's even possible. But it's not because of the material wealth we've gained through the years; it's because when we took those vows in 1976, we meant them.

We've experienced some hard times, as have every other married couple; there's nothing special about that, but what is special is that we have never tried to put money in the front position in our lives. Nor have we ever been gluttons when it came to any of these necessary material goods to keep us alive and healthy.

We know when we've had enough—except when she makes that one dish with the chicken, broccoli, and sharp cheese; we are admittedly gluttons. We make fun of it, because we will definitely overeat that meal because it's gooooood!

But you need to set limits on what you eat. You shall not kill is one of His Rules, yes? You shall not kill yourself by becoming so overweight that you put yourself in danger of any of the physical troubles associated with being overweight—heart attack, stroke, heart disease, and so on.

And you should also know the risks of possessing too much material wealth as well. Having too much affords you the opportunity to... have too much. Money can buy a lot of things, good and bad. The unfortunate part is that when you are too rich, others who are envious of gaining your wealth, will do or offer anything to you to capture "their share" of your stuff... money, gold, property, and so on. Sometimes, their offer is hard to resist and that little demon on our shoulder convinces us to accept the offer, and boy oh boy, we sure can do the wrong things then.

I read in the newspaper the other day that a man who pleaded guilty to a crime made that exact claim. The press quoted it: "The devil made me do it." I know the man. He is what most would consider rich; he's got plenty of money. He allegedly sexually molested a teenage girl and offered her money to "keep it quiet." But the girl didn't... good for her. Is he a dirty old man, or does he have too much wealth? Only God knows for sure.

The result was that this man was given probation because of a few acceptable reasons according to the court's opinion. I know the judge, as well; and I was very surprised with his verdict. He should have known that gluttony, not the devil, made him do it; gluttony for the sins of the flesh... lust.

Lust... where should we start with this one? Anywhere, I suppose, because lust is everywhere. Everywhere you turn, everywhere you look, and everywhere you go.

Lust is the exaggerated and inordinate craving for the pleasures of the body. It's everywhere!

You can't turn on the television, open the newspaper, go to the grocery store, look on the Internet, go to work, go to a show, go out to dinner, go to the mall, go to buy a soda pop at the local convenience store... well, you get the picture. Everywhere you go, it is there, and you can't seem to avoid staring at its ugly face.

Here's a little story: Several years ago, well, about ten now, one of the people I work with, a man forty years old at the time and had been married for almost eleven years was getting the "itch." Because I was older than he and have fought this battle, I decided to help him through his trying time. Now, I don't know if he's ever scratched this itch prior to this event, nor do I really care to know, it's none of my business. But what I do know is that his lust deal is for real.

I've worked with this man for a long time, I've known him since he was a small child and I don't mean working with him at a job, I mean working with him on the salvation of his soul. I think by that time he realized that fact. But anyway, every time I saw that gleam in his eyes when a pretty girl walked by, all I would say is six and he knew what I mean, referring to rule number 6, the adultery rule.

God made every person beautiful in so many ways, some more physically attractive then others, but all so beautiful. God does this for a reason, He's never told me why; maybe I'll ask Him someday, maybe I won't. I don't really need to know.

When I see a pretty girl, an entirely different thought comes to mind: God was paying attention to His work that day. But this guy's thoughts were lust for the flesh.

But believe this; I am not immune to those thoughts. I fight the fight even today. I don't live in a bubble, nor am I going to say that this sin doesn't have a hold on every living being on this planet, including me, because it does. This guy wasn't any different than any other person walking the planet, and neither am I!

The biggest difference between this guy and me is that I feared that he might scratch the itch, and I know that I won't. But—and I think that we covered this when we were talking about number 6—if you even think about lustful desires, you have, in fact, committed the sin. So, I am not completely guilt free or without sin in this matter, because on some rare occasions, those thoughts come into my mind, too. Do you feel better now?

Long story short with this guy and that girl: He did scratch that itch. Both ultimately left their spouses for this relationship. When I asked them if this was actually happening, prior to their new and unholy relationship announcement, they both adamantly denied this to me several times, in fact. They both lied to me. I was truly upset when this happened and have since dissolved our friendships.

Had they both told me the truth when I asked them, perhaps I could have counseled the both of them and saved them from violating their marriage vows. We speak now and again, but we are no longer friends in the same sense are we were prior to this situation. I have forgiven the both of them in my heart and soul, even though neither ever admitted lying to me nor asked for forgiveness for this hurtful act of trust betrayal. I pray for them and hope that God will forgive them of this adulterous union, "forgive us our trespasses as we forgive those who trespass against us."

Lust is strictly physical and is the demon's completion of the sin of pride. Think about that, and then you'll have the strength to fight the fight because the demon is all about the physical relationship to this physical life.

And the demon doesn't make it easy for anyone to not be affected by this sin of lust. He puts it in our face day after day, because lust is an express ticket straight to hell.

This test we are all taking is the test of this physical plane. Lust is totally physical, and there is no spiritual influence whatsoever. It's the present-day apple in our Garden of Eden here on earth.

So many people will be lost to the fires of hell and ultimately experience the loss of their spiritual life because of this completion of pride, which is lust.

Heaven is not about the physical; it's about the spiritual, the completion of love, which is the opposite of lust.

Hell, on the other hand, is all about the physical; it's all about how you and I deal with the challenges we face daily here in this physical world. Do we lust after the pleasures of the flesh, or do we respond to the physical in a spiritual manner? That's the greatest judgmental factor.

The express ticket to hell is issued by the ticket window attendant Satan in response to our lust for the flesh… guaranteed.

In the beginning, God created man and woman. He created them to be fertile and multiply. He created them to be one with one another, not to be one with everyone that they craved. The human's lustful heart drives them to sexual acts with so many variations; it's almost sickening. Yet we encourage these activities because of our rights to be free. We accept this unholy practice and embrace it as if it were natural…

I ask myself, *Oh God, what are we doing?*

I'm just sitting here praying right now, praying for the next line to come into my hands. As you can plainly see, my personal feelings have taken over, and I fear that I'm getting too emotional, and this is not about my emotions, it's about the truth. Please give me a moment.

Thank you, Lord!

"Do not love the world or the things of the world. If anyone loves the world, the love of the Father is not in him. For all that is in the world, sensual lust, enticement for the eyes, and a pretentious life, is not from the Father but is from the world. Yet the world and its enticements are passing away. But whoever does the will of God remains forever." (1 John 2:15–17)

The emotion that was taking over was anger, anger with mankind and his obsession with lust. One morning when I was on the third or fourth writing of this book… I can't remember which, regardless; there was mass media coverage of a New Jersey governor who resigned because he had a gay love affair. Of course, the public's reaction to this "news" is appalling.

About half of the people seem to think that this is his own business and it's okay; he shouldn't have to express any remorse for his actions. What a sorry state we live in when we think that this type of sexual behavior is perfectly acceptable and we even encourage this type of lifestyle, lust.

Lust… what else can I say?

It's a struggle that we all must deal with, every one of us. If anyone thinks that he or she is immune to this sin, they are wrong.

Get a little angry about it, pray for help. I know I do, and you should, too; pray for strength to keep out of this sin's path.

Anger is also a deadly sin if not used correctly. Mild anger is a healthy emotion especially if you use it to correct a personal flaw. I'm remembering a scene from a movie I once saw; I don't remember the name of the movie or the characters or the type of movie, but I do remember the main character leaning out of a window in a city high-rise, screaming, "I'm mad as hell, and I'm not going to take it anymore!" He was a newscaster.

That's what I'm talking about: getting angry at the ways of this world. Getting angry to a point that you just don't want to have any more negative influences in your life. Getting angry and doing something positive to correct your life and the lives of those around you.

But anger can go too far; it can be the most destructive force in your universe and in your life if not correctly used and controlled.

Anger is always manifested in the individual who ignores love and embraces fury instead, overcome by the feeling of wrath and rage. That's when anger is taken to the next level, that's when it is categorized as a "deadly sin."

Example:

Someone insults you and your immediate and natural emotion is anger. So, what's your reaction? Do you fire back with an equally insulting response or do you just "grin" and bear it? But you're still very angry and vow in your heart to get them back. Or do you use the anger correctly and "hear" what they said, using the anger to positively correct that flaw, which could actually exist within yourself. Something inspired them to make this insulting comment and this something was directly related to you!

Unless of course they are just a nasty and ruthless person... oh no, they don't exist... well, yeah, they do, the demon's children. But you don't know for sure if they are his kids and you won't know that until judgment day. In fact, you're not even the judge, so don't presume to judge these people yourself.

I've been an angry man most of my life. I still am an angry man, but now I channel that anger into positivity. When something angers me, I search my heart and soul to find out why. I no longer turn that emotion into wrath and rage or any other destructive force; I merely use the good within the emotion. Fortunately, I've never killed another human during this developmental transformation, but I've physically hurt quite a few. For that I am sorry. But once I learned that this emotion is more destructive than anything else, it was fairly easy to learn to control this emotion.

That's the difference between this being an emotion and being a deadly sin: the ability to control this force, embracing its positive power and using it for good, not evil. If you use this emotion to hurt another person, it hurts you far more than any thought, word, or action they may have done to you; that is evil.

Get mad, get over it, move on with your life, and avoid the evil in this emotion!

We're going to go to something a little more positive next. Boy, oh boy, I'm glad that's over!

If you feel like I have been scolding you, I am sorry, and for that I apologize, but good can come from bad. One of the keys to life is knowing who and what you are... really are! No one can correct a flaw unless they first admit that a flaw exists within them. Hopefully, this somewhat-negative chapter has hit home for some and a new way of thinking will begin in your mind, your heart, your soul. That's my hope, that's my prayer. My hopes and prayers are continually focused on the changes in your life, as well as mine.

Next chapter, the seven graces.

Chapter 12
The Good Things in Life

Ice cream is good, stepping up to the plate and hitting a home run is good, sharing a private moment with your spouse is good, believing that there is honor amongst all of mankind is good, working on a project that you believe in is good, because everything within this physical universe that God created is good if you want it to be good.

We make things bad because we have not used the tools available to us to keep all these things good.

I said that I was going to keep this chapter positive, so I will.

The good things in life are all around us; we merely have to reach out and grab the "brass ring." Life is a gift, a gift to enjoy, a gift to find pleasure in, and a gift to use to its fullest.

Someone said to me some time ago that they really like me because I was the first truly honest person that they had ever met. That was a good thing in life for me especially since I only knew that person for a short while. I was extremely humbled to hear such a flattering comment.

Now I don't believe for a moment that I am the most honest person in this world. I know plenty of people who I consider to be much more honest than myself. I thanked that person and told her that he should meet some of my friends; those friends are truly honest people.

I then told her that I have to work hard on being an honest person because it doesn't come naturally to me or any other person who practices this trait. I told her what she was really noticing was my love for life, not physical life, but my spiritual life. She was young, about thirty-five, and I'm sure she didn't fully understand my statements. So, I explained a little further because I could see the puzzled look on her face.

Incidentally, I am not ashamed in the least to talk to anyone about my religious beliefs. So, the conversation shifted to what we are now going to talk about now: graces. The conversation was fairly brief because it was near time for us to leave for the day, but it was a good conversation nonetheless. I liked this kid… she was a good kid and took her under my wing; I felt compelled to help her.

As I feel compelled to help you… because you're good kids too!

Prayer is a wonderful thing, and I'm sure I've told you already that I pray most of the time. Even when I'm not praying, I'm trying to pray. Prayer is any thought, word, or action, which is pleasing to God. My focus is on the good of this world so that I can pass the test and enjoy forever the goodness in my eternal existence. That's who wins this game, that's who passes the test, not the guy with the most "toys." You need to pass the test too so we can meet.

And so, I pray to God to grant me the graces to keep me strong and on the path back to Him. This God, our God, is such a good God! He never lets me down; sure, I have crosses to bear, plenty of them… Oh the crosses, but none as heavy as the one He asked His Son to carry for us.

He grants me the graces, and He'll grant you the graces if you only ask Him for them; our Father will not say no to graces ever!

But don't confuse monetary gain with graces. Don't pray for the winning lottery ticket to end up in your hand… well, if you feel like it, and if you please, pray that it ends up in my hand… sorry, I couldn't help that… I'm just kidding, I don't need it because that's all that God will grant, our needs.

Prayer opens the floodgates to all graces. They will pour out upon you like the waters of Niagara Falls; you will be drowned in their power. Once you feel these overwhelming forces in your life,

161

you will crave them like an addiction to a drug. And this addiction is an addiction you will never want to beat.

Most people don't know how to pray; they have little or no clue. There are many prayers that we can learn, I know many, and I say many, but the best ones are the one that are conversational and unrehearsed. God knows even before we ask, He wants to give us anything and He will. Trust me on this one, will you? He has given me, a miserable sinner, so, so much. I really can't thank Him enough for all that He's done. Ask for nothing, and He will give you everything. Show Him how much you love Him, and He will show you His love in more ways than you can fathom.

This work is a prayer, a plea to Almighty God for Him to grant all those who might read this, the graces to change their lives for the betterment of humanity. The more we help each other grab that brass ring and embrace the desire for life eternal, the more graces to do the right things in this life will be showered down upon us.

If you learn anything at all from this, learn this one thing, sharing your love for life and the desire to continue your life, even after the physical death, will get you the passing grade on the test, and the keyword is sharing. Don't be that bully who takes his ball and goes home because he's mad that he couldn't play. Let the other use the ball and play; watch and learn, practice and develop your skills, and you will eventually get in the game.

So here are the graces that are needed to combat the seven "deadly sins."

Faith: belief, trust, fidelity, loyalty and conviction.

Hope: desire, reliance and expectation.

Charity: generosity, benevolence, helpfulness and mercy.

Fortitude: strength, courage, endurance and resoluteness.

Justice: impartiality, fairness, equity, righteousness and dispassion.

Temperance: moderation, restraint, self-mastery, frugality and sobriety.

Prudence: discretion, thoughtfulness, carefulness, wisdom and vigilance.

These seven graces are the strongest forces in this physical universe. With these seven graces stored in your "utility belts," you can be the superhero who will defeat this archenemy that wants nothing more than your soul. This archenemy wins some of the battles, but you my friend can be the one who wins the war against this evil nemesis, and he is evil, no other evil is an evil more dangerous and cunning than this enemy Satan.

You might think that some individuals are the enemy, but they're not. They are your brothers and sisters and are in need of your help. Be the superhero, embrace the force... no, not that force, Luke Skywalker... great series of movies if you like science fiction... a little bit of a stretch... maybe—but the force I'm referring to is the force of these graces.

Because with these graces, all is possible, every trouble will be resolved, and you will be protected from the worries of this earth.

But wait, there's more. There is a prayer that opens a door and gives you access to yet another seven additional graces for you to store in that "utility belt."

God has given us the opportunity to ask for "favors" from many sources. God alone is not the only source of grace; God shares. He has shared His powers with all those who have made it back to His heavenly home. He has given one woman the crown and has made Her the queen of this universe, the purest of the pure, one of the two that ever existed on this earth free from sin. I know I just spilled the beans, but I'm sure you probably looked on the last page already anyway. We'll, at least most of you have if you already didn't know the answer to the question I asked in the beginning of this book. Well, I'll have to say it now, I opened the door, it's the Blessed Mother and the prayer is the rosary.

Perhaps some of you don't know this way to pray. It's kind of easy actually; I say the rosary every day of the week. Some days twice. Now you can say the rosary anytime or anywhere, but I prefer to say it on my front porch in the morning. Sometimes if I'm in the car for the required time, I might also say the rosary.

If you're not familiar with the rosary, there are many prayer books that describe the prayers used and the sequences in which they are said; I'd advise you to get one of these books. They're small and easy to carry.

If you say the rosary with regularity and consistency, these are the graces that Our Lady of the Rosary, another name for the Blessed Mother, will grant to you without hesitation and without any bias of any kind, guaranteed. I know because I receive 1 through 5 and I'm sure 6 & 7 will happen at the time of my death.

These are the promises that the Blessed Mother made to all of us and the graces she will give us if we simply say this prayer:

"I will grant peace to their families."

"They will be enlightened about the Divine Mysteries."

"I will console them in their pains, and I will accompany them in their work."

"I will give them as much as they ask for as long as it does not oppose the will of my Divine Son or the sanctification of their souls."

"I will defend them in their spiritual battles with the infernal enemy, and I will protect them at every instant of their lives."

"I will visibly help them at the moment of their death, and they will see the face of their mother."

"I have obtained this grace from my Divine Son that those who propagate this devotion to my tears and dolors will be taken directly from this earthy life to eternal happiness, since all their sins will be forgiven and my Son will be their eternal consolation and joy."

I can tell you without any question that these graces are granted to anyone that is devoted to this prayer, the rosary. I myself have been saying the rosary with the frequency that I told you about earlier, for well over thirty years. I started saying it when I knew that I had to make changes in my life. I knew that if these changes weren't made, I would go to straight to hell when I died. I knew that I was a sinner... well, I still am, but not to the same degree as then, I hope and pray. I also knew that God would hear my prayers if I sent them to Him through His Son's Mother.

I remember a short prayer that I learned in first grade. It was taught to our class by our teacher whose name was Sister Jo Anne. She taught us this prayer that has always worked. I can't remember it not working if the request didn't upset God or affect my soul.

Learn it; you'll be glad you did. It's quite simple and goes like this:

You can't say you can't because you're His mother, you won't say you won't because you're my mother... so you will, won't you?

I have never been denied, even though I am a miserable and sinful creature. I wear a medal around my neck; actually, two: a cross and a "Miraculous Medal." I never take them off, ever, because I know that these two people represented by these religious symbols are the two who will always plead my case to God the Father.

Well, there I go, I've done it now, spilled the beans again. I guess that there is no reason to kill another tree for the answer to the question I asked earlier, other than some people will be looking for the answer because they don't have the patience to read the entire book; I better do it anyway. Prudence, one of the seven graces. Learn to practice all of them.

And that's very important. These graces are of no use and will not be given to you if you don't use them wisely and continually practice using them correctly. God is everything, including wisdom; He will not give the graces to those who will discard them. But those that use them wisely will receive them as long as they need them until the time of their physical death, no questions asked.

Funny thing just came to me: Einstein's theory of relativity. Part of it states that people interpret the same event differently. They can either see the same thing or not see the same thing. They look at an object, hear a statement, or observe an event and may have totally different interpretations of what that object is, statement meant or what just occurred in that event.

Most people consider him as one of the most brilliant men of the era. I see his picture on the walls of those who truly believe that he was and they consider him an idol. He had his moments... not all good, and I'm not comparing myself to Einstein by any means; I'm just making a point: People sometimes don't see or hear the same things, which is the way with graces. Some don't even realize they are receiving the Grace needed.

One last thing on graces before we move on. Because I am Christian and a practicing Catholic, I understand and believe that graces are granted freely to those who ask, provided they are in the state of sanctifying grace. This is a state wherein your soul is free from mortal sin. In order to be sure, you're in this state, as a Catholic, one must be absolved of their sins by an ordained priest; no, not your secret confession to God because you don't believe confession to a priest a necessity, but the actual sacrament itself.

Through this sacrament, you will always receive as the graces you actually need to survive this test, whether you ask for them or not—and that is guaranteed.

There is another sacrament that gets you the same graces: Holy Communion, the reception of Jesus in the form of bread. He's really there; this is a fact, as well.

If you take part in these two sacraments on a regular basis, you will get the graces to succeed and past this test.

Next chapter...

Chapter 13
Lucky Number 13

Well, I've been praying to God to let me know where to go next. We've spent a great deal of time in several of the books of the Old Testament and really didn't get very far. There's so much more contained in the Old Testament that you should read, that we need to look to the more recent past next.

The Old Testament has so much history contained within it text that it would be a shame if you didn't spend the time necessary to read the writings contained within. The historic time line contained in the Old Testament will lead you to the place we're going now. Numbers will give you an idea of how the Hebrew people were losing favor with God and just how long they were in the desert before they reached the Promised Land.

Samuel and Kings will give you the information on how the line of royalty and leadership was established with these people. The key figure is King David, the line from which the true king was born.

That's where we're going, to a manger in the City of Bethlehem to find the child wrapped in swaddling clothes. We are going to visit this child who we owe our salvation and eternal life to, the child who was the Son of God. But He didn't earn the title of the Son of God without paying an extraordinary price; He gave His physical life for all of us… yes, all of us.

But maybe first, you should meet David. David is an extremely important figure in the Bible who ruled as king of the Israelites for about forty years. He was the son of a man named Jesse who also had seven sons. Three of these sons were warriors and fought for King Saul's army. The king's army was at war with the Philistines.

This war appeared to be futile because the Philistines had a secret weapon by the name of Goliath. He was an enormous man by most accounts, depending on the version of the Bible you are reading. If you are reading the King James Version, he was six cubits and a span tall; that's nine feet nine inches tall. If you are reading the New American Version, he was six and a half feet tall.

I'm not certain I agree with the change that was made during the last purification of this text. Today, a man six and a half feet tall is not that big of a man... I'm six feet two inches; my sons are both six feet three inches, and I know plenty of men who are taller than we are, but that's my opinion and a man is entitled to his opinion... true that!

Well, at the risk of scrutiny yet again, I'm going to say it: Goliath was indeed nine feet nine inches tall. If you do as I asked you to do and read the Old Testament in its entirety, you will see what I am talking about. But you must read both versions for this to make sense. The New American Version does not include certain words that are clearer and extremely important in understanding the development of the human race walking around today. The editors of the new text have eliminated many words, but one word that they eliminated is a descriptive word about this Goliath of a man. They eliminated the word *giant*, for there were giants in those days.

In fact, the David and Goliath story is not the only place where the editors eliminated the use of this word. They took it out of the Book of Genesis and replaced it with the word *Nephilim*: I think we saw that already. This word is not as clear as *giant*. *Nephilim* does mean *giant*, but most people don't know the definition for this word.

In the New American Version, they also substituted the word giant with the word *Rephaim*, which is indeed translated to the word *giant*. The whole moral behind this story, the battle between the Israelites and the Philistines, is that the Israelites worshiped the true God and the Philistines worshiped false gods. This little shepherd boy David defeated their fiercest warrior... a giant!

This little shepherd boy was fearless because he believed that God would protect him from being killed in this fight. He was just a meek young boy whose people were at war against the fiercest enemy of them all. The Israelites could not destroy this giant Goliath, nor could they defeat this nation that threatened their very existence because of this man Goliath and those like him. But this young lad, David, who was armed with only a sling and five smooth stones killed the giant and beheaded him with his own sword just to make a point, what a great story.

This story is the connection, the reason for the generational line between David and Jesus. David was a shepherd who protected his herd from all the dangers of this world. This little shepherd boy was sent here to defeat the archenemy's champion, their giant.

Jesus was also the shepherd of a flock. He was sent here to defeat sin and corruption and their champion, their giant, Satan.

David then became a great king who reigned over the nation of Israel, the chosen people of God. Jesus is the greatest king who reigns over the entire universe and all the children of His Father, God. David won his kingship because he had the courage to fight the foe. He was not afraid to lose his physical life for the cause he was fighting for because it was a mission from God, a mission to defeat this enemy and free his people from their captivity. The deal in this matchup between David and Goliath was that whoever lost this battle, the losing "teams" were going to be the winning "teams'" slaves.

And so it was with Jesus; He fought the enemy, the giant, Satan. This mission was also a mission from God. He also won His kingship because He did not fear the loss of His physical life. We are His "team," and if He lost the fight, we would be the slaves to the other guy's "team." But because He won His battle with this enemy, we His "teammates" are free, and Satan is our slave. We control him and his "teammates" if we chose to do so.

Let's meet this man, Jesus, and let's find out how He won His battle and His kingship. There is not much in the New Testament about the childhood of this man, only a few mentions and only one mention of His birth. It's contained in the Gospel of Luke. I read several books on the "Lost Years" of His life, but find them to be just fiction, in my opinion. We'll stick with the facts, the facts within this holiest of documents... the Bible.

Jesus' birth was preceded by the announcement of His first cousin John, who would be His biggest supporter during His life. Let's start with that event and look at its importance, okay?

Without John the Baptist, we would never have had the most recognizable biblical book, chapter and verse. Come on, everybody knows this one: Remember the guy at the football games with the rainbow-colored hair holding the sign, the sign with "John 3:16"?

But how many of you have ever looked at the verse to see what it actually says? I'm going to tell you...

John the Baptist didn't write the Gospel of John as assumed by many, maybe most. However, the gospel does contain John's testimony about the Man, Jesus Christ. This is the second or third time that I referred to Jesus as the Man instead of God the Son and that's because He was a Man all of His life on this earth. We'll get to that shortly.

"For God so loved the world that He gave His Only Son, so that everyone who believes in Him might not perish but **might** have eternal life." (John 3:16)

Might... you gotta love some of the present-day Christians. They boldly proclaim that they found Jesus and they've been saved! But they continue to sin and haven't changed their evil ways at all, but they found Jesus. I didn't know He was lost! If I'd known He was lost, I would have been out looking for Him myself! (That's funny.)

Might... just because you believe in Jesus, doesn't get you the ticket in to the "Big Show." No, not the Super Bowl, the *really* big show; no, not the Ed Sullivan Show, either. I'm talking about the biggest show of them all—no, not the Barnum & Bailey Circus either, well, maybe the "Big Show" is the wrong term. But just believing in Jesus doesn't get you into heaven; it might, but it isn't a guaranteed pass through the gates.

Living a life similar to the lifestyle of this Man Jesus will get you through the gates. Living a lifestyle of love and generosity filled with concern for humanity is the ticket, centered on your brothers and sisters, your neighbors instead of yourself... that's really the ticket. You have to be concerned with your own safety and health, but you can't put your wants in front of their needs... that's truly the ticket!

John was born to parents by the names of Zechariah and Elizabeth. Zechariah was a priest of the religious division of Abijah, and his wife was the daughter of Aaron and both were righteous in the eyes of the Lord. Now let's look where the announcement of this bouncing baby boy occurred, shall we?

"But they had no children, because Elizabeth was barren and both were advanced in years. Once when he was serving as priest in his division's turn before God, according to the practice of the priestly service, he was chosen by lot to enter the sanctuary of the Lord to burn incense. Then, when the whole assembly of the people was praying outside at the hour of the incense offering, the angel of the Lord appeared to him, standing at the right of the altar of incense. Zechariah was troubled by what he saw, and fear came upon him. But the angel said to him. "Do not be afraid, Zechariah, because your prayer has been heard. Your wife Elizabeth will bear you a son, and you shall name him John. And you will have joy and gladness, and many will rejoice at his birth, for he will be great in the sight of the Lord. He will drink neither wine nor strong drink. He will be filled with the Holy Spirit even from his mother's womb, and he will turn many of the children of Israel to the Lord their God.

He will go before him in the spirit and power of Elijah to turn the hearts of fathers toward children and the disobedient to the understanding of the righteous, to prepare a people fit for the Lord." Then Zechariah said to the angel, "How shall I know this? For I am an old man, and my wife is advanced in years." And the angel said to him in reply, "I am Gabriel, who stands before God. I was sent to speak to you and to announce to you the good news. But now you will be speechless and unable to talk until the day these things take place, because you did not believe my words, which will be fulfilled at their proper time." (Luke 1:7–20)

And so, let's call him Zech. Zech was now unable to speak because he didn't believe in the word given to him by Gabriel directly from God Himself. Let's call him Gab, shall we? Gab is one of God's top archangels. He's not just an ordinary angel; he's an archangel. Archangels are special because they can, in fact, be in the presence of the Lord whenever they need an audience with the Chief. Archangels are the first line of defense governing and protecting against the infiltration of any unwanted trespassers into the presence or about the presence of God. They are, and always have been, His "bodyguards" so to speak. They have power and authority beyond any other angel because God has given them that power and authority.

I have never spoken with or seen Gab, but I have spoken with an archangel. He has visited me several times through visions and has helped me through many situations related to His power and authority. I have a tattoo on my right shoulder blade as a sign of honor and respect for this magnificent angelic creature. His name is Raphael. He is the angel of healing, wisdom, justice, and knowledge. He is a most spectacular vision, and I'm sure Gab is equally impressive.

I never doubt anything that Raphael has told me or revealed to me through any of these visions. Believe me, it was kind of scary the first time we met; I was in the jaws of death, but apparently, it wasn't my time to go Home. The healing I received was directly from God, delivered to me through Raphael, and for this, I am truly grateful. I am not scared to die because I now know that death is merely the end of the test and is the beginning of real life. I am anxious to see how I scored on the test, in the right time, because I know that I've made mistakes on this test, but the beautiful thing about this test is that you can go back and correct the errors you make—as long as you're still taking the test. It's an open-book test.

I have also gained an enormous amount of understanding, wisdom, and knowledge from my friend Raphael.

Gabriel, okay, let's call this archangel by His proper name: Gabriel—because He most certainly does deserve the respect of the use His proper name. His name means "God is my strength." He is one of only three who are actually named in the Bible; Michael, Gabriel, and Raphael.

Gabriel's next mention is shortly after this passage, and we're going to get to that very shortly, but we need to see why John's birth and his name were so important first.

Zech was not certain that Gabriel was on the up and up; maybe he was having a bad day, I'm not sure, but Gabriel announced that this boy was going to be born, and they, the proud parents, were going to name him John. In the Hebrew language, the name *John* is *Yochanan*, and by the strictest translation, it means "Yahweh is gracious." Gabriel also told Zech that this child would bring them great joy and would be filled with God's Holy Spirit. Now I ask you, if an archangel would appear to you and told you that you were going to have a son truly righteous in the eyes of the Lord, wouldn't you do exactly as you were told? I would, no questions, no doubt! But Zech had doubt, and for this doubt, he lost his speech until...

"Her neighbors and relatives heard that the Lord had shown His great mercy towards her, and they rejoiced with her. When they came on the eighth day to circumcise the child, they were going to call him Zechariah after his father, but his mother said in reply, "No, He will be called John." But they answered her, "There is no one among your relatives who has this name." So, they made signs, asking his father what he wished him to be called. He asked for a tablet and wrote, "John is his name," and all were amazed. Immediately his mouth was opened, his tongue freed and he spoke blessing God." (Luke 1:59–64)

And so, Yochanan, John, was circumcised and given his formal name of John and was to be a messenger from God. He was to be the man that was to announce the presence of the long-awaited Messiah. In fact, this human messenger John was one of the first witnesses of the trinity on this earth at the baptism of Jesus. John's primary mission was to proclaim the coming of the Lord in Human form, his cousin Jesus.

At this baptism, which John actually first refused to do, God the Father sent down His Holy Spirit unto Jesus and God proclaimed that Jesus was His Son, in whom He was well pleased. This was the first time in human history that God revealed to His people, the Hebrews, the Jews, the union of three Gods in one person and the truth of the Trinity. They saw it, but they didn't understand that event. However, this was the beginning of the enlightenment of mankind.

Today, still most do not understand this concept; it's one of the greatest mysteries of Christianity. But not so big of a mystery if you have faith and can see past the physical universe.

John also called the people of the times to repentance. Just like today, it was no different then. People were and still are sinners. John offered them a ritual of cleansing, which was an outward sign, a humbling of themselves in front of the multitude in proclamation and admittance of their sins. That's why John first refused Jesus the baptismal rite; Jesus never had any sin on His soul... there you go... I did it again... your second answer...

But John knew his place. He was merely the messenger sent by God. He was a humble man with two purposes in this physical life.

His first purpose was to announce the coming of the second Person of the Trinity, the long-awaited Messiah, and his second purpose was to introduce the third Person of the Trinity, the Holy Spirit, or Holy Ghost, as it was used for many years. The new term, Holy Spirit, was introduced when I was a young child because it is a "nicer" and less "threatening" name for the third Person of the Trinity.

John made it very clear that he was not the Messiah; he baptized with water in the Jordan River incidentally, while Jesus was going to baptize with the Holy Spirit. Let's see this now...

The Gospel of Mark doesn't get a lot of use for some unknown reason; I like the Gospel of Mark, so let's go to his gospel for this, shall we? It's also located in Matthew's and Luke's gospels.

"As it is written in Isaiah the prophet; "Behold, I am sending my messenger ahead of you; he will prepare your way. A voice of one crying out in the desert: 'Prepare the way of the Lord, make straight His path.'" John the Baptist appeared in the desert proclaiming a baptism of repentance for the forgiveness of sins. People of the whole Judean countryside and all the inhabitants of Jerusalem were going out to him and were being baptized by him in the Jordan River as they acknowledged their sins. John was clothed in camel's hair, with a leather belt around his waist. He fed on locusts and wild honey. And this is what he proclaimed: "One mightier than I is coming after me. I am not worthy to stoop and loosen the thongs of His sandals. I have baptized you with water; He will baptize you with the Holy Spirit." It happened in those days that Jesus came from Nazareth of Galilee and was baptized in the Jordan by John. On coming out of the water he saw the heavens being torn open and the Spirit, like a dove, descending upon Him. And a voice came from the heavens, "You are my beloved Son; with you I am well pleased." (Mark 1:2–11)

Thank you, John, for all your faith, and thank you, Lord, for giving us John the Baptist.

John was beheaded for his faith and belief in the laws of God. But John left this world free and clear from sin and is Home in heaven, where he belongs. Before he died, his cousin Jesus visited him in prison and comforted him, allowing him to give up his physical life without worry.

Let's meet the man, and He is the man!

Chapter 14
You Da Man

Before we go any further, I want there to be no misunderstanding: Jesus Christ is the Son of the living and true God!

I'm going to continue my mission, and we are going to "meet" this Man. We are going to learn how He won the battle against sin and how He ultimately earned the title "Son of God." The timing is perfect, and I truly thank God for the opportunity to write this chapter.

I made that last statement because when I originally wrote this chapter, it was September 1, 2004, the day after the release of the home version of *The Passion of the Christ*. My wife purchased it the morning afterward, and we watched it that very night. I was a little disappointed that subtitles were used throughout the movie; it makes the movie too difficult to follow. I have watched it several more times since and focused on the film itself. I would suggest that you might want to do the same because this movie contains everything that we should see and know to fully understand this Man's devotion to our Father God.

That being said, let's go to the announcement of the birth of Jesus.

We'll look to Luke for this because the story of the birth of Jesus is only told in this gospel, from the announcement, to the manger in Bethlehem, so there's where we're headed...

"In the sixth month, the angel Gabriel was sent from God to a town of Galilee called Nazareth, to a virgin betrothed to a man named Joseph, of the house of David, and the virgin's name was

Mary. And coming to her he said, "Hail favored one! The lord is with you." But she was greatly troubled at what he said and pondered what sort of greeting this might be. Then the angel said to her, "Do not be afraid, Mary, for you have found favor with God. Behold, you will conceive in your womb and bear a son, and you shall name Him Jesus. He will be great and be called Son of the Most-High, and the lord God will give Him the throne of David His father, and He will rule over the house of Jacob forever, and of His kingdom there will be no end." But Mary said to the angel, "How can this be, since I have no relations with a man?" and the angel said to her in reply, "The Holy Spirit will come upon you, and the power of the Most-High will overshadow you. Therefore, the child to be born will be called Holy, Son of God. And behold, Elizabeth, your relative, has also conceived a son at her old age, and this is the sixth month for her who was called barren; for nothing is impossible for God." Mary said, "Behold, I am the handmaid of the Lord. May it be done to me according to your word." Then the angel departed from her." (Luke 1:26–38)

This is a very difficult concept for most to believe. I'm not sure why people can't believe that this is possible, if God created all life, then why couldn't He do this simple little miracle?

In fact, her betrothed, Joseph, didn't believe it either. He was ready to issue a decree of divorce, and they we're even married yet! In those times, there were "marriage arrangements," and this marriage was one of the prearranged by the parents of the bride and groom.

Infidelity was a just cause for divorce in those times; well, it still is a just cause, but then, it was also considered a reason to be put to death by means of another barbaric method called stoning.

The following information is only contained in the Gospel of Matthew. I know that I said that we were going to look at the Gospel of Luke, and we will but all the Gospels vary in their information. I want to show you something else, it's in Matthew and explain to you why there are two other important matters to be clearly established and understood.

"Thus, the total number of generations from Abraham to David is fourteen generations; from David to the Babylonian exile, fourteen generations; from the Babylonian exile to the Messiah, fourteen generations. Now this is about how the birth of Jesus Christ came about. When His mother was betrothed to Joseph, but before they lived together, she was found with child through the Holy Spirit. Joseph her husband, since he was a righteous man, yet unwilling to expose her shame, decided to divorce her quietly. Such was his intention when, behold, the angel of the Lord appeared to his in a dream and said, "Joseph, son of David, do not be afraid to take Mary your wife into your home. For it is through the Holy Spirit that this child has been conceived in her. She will bear a son and you are to name him Jesus, because he will save his people from their sins." All this took place to fulfill what the Lord has said through the prophet: "Behold, the virgin shall be with child and bear a son, and they shall name Him Emmanuel," which means "God is with us." When Joseph awoke, he did as the angel of the Lord had commanded him and took his wife into his home. He had no relations with her until she bore a son, and named Him Jesus." (Matthew 1; 17–25)

First thing, let's talk about these "forty-two" generations between Abraham and Jesus. In previous chapters, we saw how the lineage and "generations" were traced from Adam to Abram and here we see how we get from Abram to Jesus. 14 + 14 + 14 = 42.

That would be forty-two for sure—true that!

I hope that most of you will understand what I am going to show you next:

When we talk about generations in the twenty-first century, we assume a time line to be of about twenty-five to thirty-two years between generations, true? My father and mother were about twenty-eight when I was born. The time line between their generation and my generation is twenty-eight years. Let's use that as a median number and do some math.

If we use twenty-eight as a median number; $42 \times 28 = 1176$. Abram would have lived in or around 1176 BCE, true?

Well, I think I thoroughly covered the time line from Adam to Abram, don't you agree? Let's see how the forty-two generations could establish the correct time line from Abraham to Jesus.

The name Abraham actually means from the tribe of Abram. I guess I should have mentioned that back in the chapter about circumcision. But I didn't... sorry, but I'm not changing it now.

Anyway these "forty-two" generations mean something a little different in this passage. They are—now follow me closely— measured from the grandfather to the grandson, and are counted as one, but in fact are two.

There are my grandparents, two different sets; they had children who, in turn, were my parents. When I was born, I started the new generation, but from which lineage am I?

Am I from my maternal grandparents' or from my paternal grandparents' line? I am third-generation male from my paternal line, but only second-generation male from my maternal line.

There is one generation male... me, that separates me from my maternal grandfather. I am the second-generation male from this lineage, so the two generations will equal one.

Now understand this: Jesus was born of the Holy Spirit; that's His "daddy," not Joseph. But Jesus is from the house of David, of which Joseph's paternal lineage can be traced; in fact, it is traced back to Abraham and then to Adam within the text of the Bible.

But based on the account of Matthew, Jesus was not of the Joseph/David lineage mathematically. He was born of His maternal linage according to Matthew.

Now, knowing that the truth is that Jesus was conceived of the Holy Spirit, we then must also accept the truth that He would have been second-generation male of His maternal line, right... true that?

Let's do some math again using twenty-eight as the median and eighty-four (42×2) as the number of generations, shall we?

179

First time we see Abram is in the year 2,453. Most assume that the Bible says that Abram and Abraham are one and the same, even though we now know the difference.

And so, $28 \times 84 = 2,354 + 99 = 2,453$ (the year of Abram's first appearance on this planet). What do you think about that?

But remember this fact as well; the male was dominant in those times and the Messiah was to come from David line. If Joseph had fathered Jesus, then perhaps Matthew would have used twenty-eight generations instead of fourteen... don't know, won't ask.

But the fact is that Joseph didn't father Jesus; the Holy Spirit of God did and this mathematically works and brings us right to Abraham.

Far-fetched, maybe, but again, it's all in the Bible. The funny thing is, however, all the time lines I've shown you, all do work perfectly based on math! How ironic! When I was a young child, and through my entire formal education, I was often referred to by many of my teachers as a mathematical genius because I've always been able to see the logic in math and how math sciences work... fortunately I still can.

Thank you, Lord!

No one knows for sure when these events really happened, and to this point, time travel is not possible to verify this further, so we must have some faith and trust in the assumption that Jesus was born in 0 AD as a fact.

Second, the other thing that I wanted to clear up is the issue of whether Jesus did or did not have siblings. He did; He had half-brothers, four who are named in the Bible. Most people disagree, but see for yourself: Joseph had no relations with her until she bore a son and named Him Jesus.

Joseph was Mary's husband, and in a normal marriage in those times, tradition was to have many children. They were a normal couple and complied with Jewish tradition and did in fact have other children after Jesus was born.

Now, I can't tell you how many because the Bible only names four sons, but Jesus also had sisters according to the text; I'll show you that later.

There is also one other thing I need to clear up before we go to Bethlehem. In and about the fourth chapter or so, I told you that God talks to me, as well as to anyone else who is willing to listen.

Throughout this book, I have often referred to a message as the "voice" in my head, and no, I'm not crazy, absolutely not…

However, because I pray the rosary daily and receive the graces promised by the Blessed Mother, God does talk to me, or in fact, will talk to you if you pray with regularity. He may deliver a message Himself, and when this happens, it will be His voice, a vision, an intensely clear thought or something similar, and trust me, I know when it's Him or His Son.

Please understand this: I am not one of the "chosen" few who God personally speaks to with all messages I receive, but God Himself always gets the answer to me, guaranteed. As He will for you, if you just believe and pray. But belief is not enough; you must show your belief in the form of devotion daily, hourly, every second of the day, via prayer. Prayer every second of the day is always trying your best to do God's will with every breath. Then you will also be in the counted group of people that will pass this test, and God will be a part of your life and will speak to you as He does with me. Start with the rosary daily… it's miraculous!

I was just told to clear that up; I don't know the why, but I did as I was instructed — perhaps someone reading this needed to know if what they are hearing is from God.

Let's now look to Bethlehem in the land of Judea where Jesus was born.

The date December 25 has been the accepted date of the birth of Jesus since around the second century. Hippolytus of Rome, a Presbyter, was an early member of the governing body of the early Christian Church and was the man responsible for introducing this date. There was plenty of disagreement on the date by the "Eastern" Church; they claimed it was in January. But in the fourth century, the East Church and the West Church agreed temporally on the now accepted date. Today, incidentally, the Greek Orthodox Church (Eastern) still observes the January date.

Some theologians still disagree that it happened in the winter months because of the biblical reference to the shepherds keeping watch over their flocks. Traditionally, the flocks in this area are kept in shelters during the months of November through March because of the "rainy" season. These theologians seem to feel that it wasn't possible for the shepherds to have the flocks in the field during this time of the year—poppycock!

These were sacrificial lambs that were to be fattened up for the Passover. They needed them to feed in the now flourishing pastures; it was the rainy season, and the pastures were filled with fresh "greens" for the sheep to eat. You don't think that they could tell if it was going to rain? They had the same chance of knowing what the weather was going to be that day, as we do... hey, looks like rain today. I mean, how often do the "weather" people actually get it right anyway? So, what would stop the shepherds from taking advantage of the fresh pastures? Nothing! The climate is mild, and so what if it rains, the sheep will get a bath... big deal. And what about the star, the one in the Gospel of Matthew? The star that leads the magi to the manger. Really quick:

"They were overjoyed at seeing the star, and on entering the house they saw the child with Mary his mother. They prostrated themselves and did Him homage. Then they offered their treasures and offered Him gifts of gold, frankincense, and myrrh." (Matthew 2:10, 11)

I never saw a star when it was raining; have you? Anyone with a reasonable amount of intelligence must believe that it was a clear night because of the star. But we live for controversy and always will; that's the trouble with us, we just can't accept the truth.

Are we so blind that we can't see the truth?

Do you want the truth?

Well, I'm going to show you the truth. We're going to go see the birth of this baby, Jesus. We're going to "meet" the Man... well, He's not a man yet, but He will be very shortly, and I'm going to tell you the absolute truth of why He is the Son of God Almighty.

"In those days a decree went out from Caesar Augustus that the whole world should be enrolled. This was the first enrollment, when Quirinius was governor of Syria. So, all went to be enrolled, each to his own town. And Joseph too went up from Galilee from the town of Nazareth to Judea, to the city of David called Bethlehem, because he was of the house and family of David, to be enrolled with Mary, his betrothed, who was with child. While they were there, the time came for her to have her child, and she gave birth to her firstborn son. She wrapped Him in swaddling clothing and laid Him in a manger, because there was no room for them in the inn. Now there were shepherds in that region living in the fields and keeping the night watch over the flock. The angel of the Lord appeared to them and the glory of the Lord shone around them, and they were struck with fear. The angel said to them, "Do not be afraid; for behold, I proclaim to you the good news of great joy that will be for all the people. For today in the city of David a savior has been born for you who is Messiah and Lord. And this will be a sign for you; you will find an infant wrapped in swaddling clothing and lying in a manger." And suddenly there was a multitude of the heavenly host with the angel, praising God and saying; "Glory to God in the highest and on Earth peace to those on whom His favor rests." When the angels went away from them to heaven, the shepherds said to one another, "Let us go, then, to Bethlehem to see this thing that has taken place, which the Lord has made known to us." So, they went in haste and found Mary and Joseph, and the infant lying in the manger. When they saw this, they made known the message that had been told them about this child. All who heard were amazed by what had been told them by the shepherds. And Mary kept all these things, reflecting on then in her heart. Then the shepherds returned, glorifying and praising God for all they had heard and seen, just as it had been told to them." (Luke 2:1–20)

And so, it was, the child Jesus, Emmanuel, was born in the city of David, no hotel, no midwife, no boiling water, not even new clothing to wrap this wonderful new son. And no, it wasn't like we imagined; it wasn't a little wooden stable in the back of this "inn" with the barnyard animals, straw on the ground, the three wise men, or the "little drummer boy," either. There was rejoicing by the shepherds, and the magi showed up to pay their respects and I'm sure that a few of the people that were in town were wondering was going on stopped in to wish the parents luck and congratulations on the birth of their son.

But this was in essence, a quiet event, and was a normal occurrence in those times, and that place in history, a child being born without prior arrangements for the expected date was normal. Maybe they didn't have medical insurance; or, worse yet, maybe they had O-llama Care.

Now that's funny... LOL... but that's how things were back then: plain, simple, and natural. However, He was not an average newborn son. He was a special boy, bound for greatness, heir to the throne of God. That's the reason God let this birth be known to the selected few, including His earthly parents. Mary and Joseph then had this fact reinforced by these visitors who were to be witnesses to the fulfillment of Scripture and the birth of Emmanuel.

Hey, did any of you happen to notice that Jesus was called the firstborn son? I would think that He must have been the first of others, you know, brothers and sisters, or why refer to Him as the firstborn son?

This is a very important point; we have always been told that Jesus was an only child by most religions and their leaders. But Jesus was not an only child. There is further evidence of this fact just around the corner, in about twelve years. But first, the circumcision...

"When eight days were completed for His circumcision, He was named Jesus, the name given Him by the Angel before He was conceived in the womb." (Luke 2:21)

Now Jesus is an official member of the Jewish faith and community. There is only one more thing to complete the ceremony and that is the presentation in the Temple.

This was a ritual that might be compared to the baptismal ceremonies of today. But they didn't bless the baby with water, have godparents and have a big party afterward; they simply presented the baby in the temple. They offered the sacrifice of either a pair of turtledoves or a pair of pigeons as a consecration to the Lord during this ritual.

The verses are contained in the Gospel of Luke as well, chapter 2, verses 22 to 39. The highpoint of this section is the man named Simeon. He was, according to Scripture, a righteous man filled with the Holy Spirit. He apparently asked God to let him live until he could see the Messiah, and apparently God granted his request. This man recognized Jesus immediately upon seeing Him entering the temple with His parents, Mary and Joseph.

Simeon took the child in his arms and proclaimed, "Now, Master, You may let Your servant go in peace, according to Your word, for my eyes have seen Your salvation, which You prepared in sight of all the peoples, a light for revelation to the Gentiles, and glory for Your people Israel."

Of course, this amazed Mary and Joseph, and then Simeon blessed them and made another comment when they were entering the temple. The comment was a prophecy of pain to come to Mary.

There is further documentation about Anna, a prophetess who gave thanks to God for allowing her to see this child before the ceremony was complete, further in this Gospel. Mary and Joseph left town and started their way home to Nazareth but were instructed by an Angel to flee to Egypt... which they did to avoid Herod's decree to kill all the male children under the age of 2. This information is in Matthew. We will not see or hear of Jesus again until He is a young man of twelve years of age.

Most of us might assume that Jesus took up the family business as a carpenter following in His earthly father's trade. Perhaps he did help "dad" with some of the tasks; and Joseph, being a righteous man, more than likely wanted to teach Jesus, his firstborn, his trade. However, nowhere in the Bible does it mention that Jesus was, in fact, a carpenter. Perhaps some would like to think that Jesus was a carpenter, but I can assure you of one thing: He didn't come here to make furniture.

Now is when I'm going to show you an event where anyone with a family can assume that Jesus had siblings…

According to the Gospel of Luke, the family went to Jerusalem yearly to participate in the festival customs of Passover. When the Passover was over, they left to journey back to Nazareth. Jesus remained behind in the temple to teach the elders about His real Pop. You see, Jesus already knew what His mission in this life was going to be, He was going to save mankind from the perils of sin and spiritual death; we'll get to that soon.

But I ask you this: How is it that any parents would or could leave their only child and assume that He was with the caravan, unless there were other children with them? Unless they had their hands full with the smaller children, then the assumption would be correct. Jesus was twelve years old and capable of walking on His own without having "mommy" or "daddy" holding His hand. But the smaller brothers weren't; the four of them named were younger, and the parents would then assume Jesus was with the caravan because they were busy tending to the other children. This has happened to every parent with children when they had other children and relatives with them on a family outing… true?

And what if there were a couple of baby sisters in the family at the same time? Maybe six other kids and their eldest brother Jesus, now then it is absolutely possible for these parents not to look for the eldest son until they were underway on this long journey home.

It's not out of the realm of reality for a family, especially in those days, to have seven children. And if they had seven children at this Passover festival, they were probably tired from having to care for the children because they were on "the road" and at this "carnival." Maybe they weren't paying much attention to the fact that Jesus wasn't around. Jesus was a perfect son; He gave them no reason to assume He wasn't with the caravan, perhaps with another member of the family. But after a day of not seeing their son, they then realized He wasn't with the group... perfectly feasible.

"Thinking that He was in the caravan, they journeyed for a day and looked for Him among their relatives and acquaintances, but not finding Him, they returned to Jerusalem to look for Him." (Luke 2:44, 45)

So how many times has this happened to you? At least once, I'm sure. You're at a family gathering and you're taking care of the kids, a half of a dozen or so; it's time to leave and you're trying to get everyone together, you don't realize that they're not all "accounted" for, but you really don't pay close attention because there's a lot of family members there and you know that your child is safe.

Maybe this is an unfair question to those with no, one, two, or even three kids; but those of you who have plenty of kids in the household know exactly what I'm talking about, don't you? Need further proof that Jesus had siblings...?

"Is He not the carpenter's son? Is not His mother named Mary and His brothers James, Joseph, Simon, and Judas? Are not His sisters all with us? Where did this man get all this?" (Matthew 13:55, 56)

This is a section in the Gospel of Matthew where some were questioning how this Jesus person gained such wisdom and knowledge. He was from a family that didn't have access to the education that the people assumed that this man Jesus must have had to be so "smart." It was also not uncommon not to mention the women by name; remember, the male was the dominant one of the species, and they alone mattered in those times.

They were also amazed that He could do such wondrous deeds because He was just "common folk." He wasn't royalty in their limited understanding of the true meaning of the word. Jesus was merely a common man, and that He was the entire time that He spent here with us teaching us the ways of His father in heaven.

Next, the mission assigned to Him by the Lord God Almighty. We're going to see how this "Man" earned His title the Son of God.

There's nothing else in the Bible about His life from the age of twelve to thirty, so we have no truthful evidence to look at; everything else that anyone can tell you about His life is theory not truth. We're sticking to the truth and nothing but the truth, so help me God!

And, of course, I know You will…

Chapter 15
The Man Who Saved Us

I don't know the history of Jesus' youth, and no one does for sure. We can assume that He had a normal childhood and grew to be a fine young man. During His life from the age of twelve until He reached thirty, Jesus did not publicly practice His ministry. He might have taken up His earthly father's trade or perhaps not; one thing is for certain, during this time, Jesus became very close to our Heavenly Father God Almighty.

Jesus was one of the men of this Earth that the Lord God chose to speak directly with every time there was communication.

I know from my own personal experiences that hearing His voice directly could be a confusing situation. Even though God Almighty has spoken directly to me on a few occasions, just the mere thought of God Himself speaking to me without the use of His messengers still terrifies me.

It's kind of like when your boss wants to see you, not that big of a deal, but when the owner or president of the company request an audience with you, you kind of cringe and get a little nervous. I'm sure you know what I mean.

I could only imagine how Jesus felt when He heard the voice of our Heavenly Father God Almighty for the first time. He was probably a little confused, terrified, and probably was nervous.

Of course, this is pure speculation; however, anyone who tries to explain with any certainty of how He felt or give the history of the missing years of Jesus' life is nothing more than hearsay. It's not really that important, I suppose, because He lived His life out of the public eye until the time came to do what He was sent here to do, save mankind.

Every man and woman are sent here to accomplish a task, and so it was with this Man; however, this man's task was the greatest task that God ever gave any man.

Some religions believe that Jesus was the Archangel Michael, but He was not. He was an individual soul that was part of God from the beginning of time. He was a soul that God knew would do His work to the point of completion because He was a part of Him, His Son. He certainly was not Michael. He was the one soul; the Son that from the beginning of time our God had chosen to become Heir to His throne. But this inheritance did not come to Him without a price.

Did Jesus know that He was to be the heir to the throne of God, and that this was the case? That's a question that's never going to be answered, and that question is definitely not important to us. I'm sure that I told you: We should never, ever question the will or authority of God. But God had this planned from the beginning of time. He knew what was going to happen with Adam and Eve. He didn't predetermine or prearrange that outcome, but He knew. He also knew from the beginning of time that Jesus was going to fulfill the task at hand, and He was to be part of the Holy Trinity.

Now, I keep saying the task at hand, and maybe some might be confused on what the task actually was and why that task resulted in Jesus' brutal death. I'm going to tell you, I'm going to show you, and you will get the true reason that the life of Jesus on this planet was so necessary... but not yet.

Let's get back to this Man and his relationship with God the Father...

We know that Jesus grew up under the guidance of Mary and Joseph who also knew that this child was special in the eyes of the Lord. They were His earthly guardians, and sure as God made little green apples, these two were informed about Him and the events to come prior to His birth.

God apparently chose these two because he knew that they would and could help Him find His way. So, because they were the perfect parents to raise this child, one sinless and one righteous in the eyes of God, this child learned the way to find God through them. That was their mission; not only to give birth to the child, but also to guide this child to the Father.

But it took quite a number of years of their guidance for Jesus to fully understand this task at hand and the mission that He was given. Remember, Jesus was a human being, just like the rest of us. He presumably may not have come to fully realize who in fact He was until about that age of thirty. But who was He? Was He the Son of God, or was he just a man? This is the question that keeps us all in the dark; the question that keeps us out of the light.

Mary and Joseph knew who this boy was; they were shown the light. So as Jesus' life continued and His relationship with His Father became stronger; He Himself became aware of the things to come, but His revelations were presumably piecemeal because of the lack of hard historic evidence.

The task…

First on God's list was to send the Messiah to the Jewish people. In those times, as well as these times, there were and are many so-called prophets. If you don't believe we have these so-called prophets here, do some channel surfing on the television on any given Sunday morning. You'll see them, with their thousand-dollar suits, their big diamond rings, their Rolex watches, and they're going to convince you to send them some money to help save your soul. Because if you send them some cash, they will pray for you, and you will be saved, a laugh a minute. While I'm waiting for my wife to get ready for Mass on Sunday mornings, I entertain myself by surfing and pausing to listen to their "truly inspired messages"; it's a hoot! My opinion: truly inspired by greed. There's even one reverent couple on the television with the last name Dollar, which is how we refer to our currency… true that.

Jesus was not greedy; He was a poor Man raised by a carpenter, and carpenters didn't make a lot of money… enough, I suppose, but not a lot. And Jesus didn't have a fine suit, nor did He have a diamond ring, or a Rolex. Jesus didn't ask anyone for money to save his or her soul.

And like these "holy people" of today, those times also had a full complement of people that preached the "truth" for the almighty coin.

They were all over the place, everywhere you looked; another preacher of the word was in your face. So, Jesus had His work cut out for Him. He had competition from everywhere—even His older cousin John.

John knew that he wasn't, and that his cousin Jesus was the Messiah. But the people believed that the message that John was delivering was so compelling that John must have been the man that God sent to free them. Those people wanted a man to lead them from the captivity of the Roman rule, and they expected this from the long-awaited Messiah.

Their concept of freedom was much different than the word that Jesus taught, which made His task much more difficult. People of the times were not very receptive to the idea of loving their enemy because they couldn't even find in their hearts the love for their neighbor Jesus was preaching about, similar to today. At least the other prophets were preaching doom, gloom, the fires of hell, the end of times and death to the unjust, but not this man.

This man was preaching nothing of the sort. Jesus was preaching love and kindness, and He was preaching the truth about the divine nature of the one God, His Father. The Jewish people didn't want this type of messiah; they wanted a leader who would command the troops and lead them to victory against their Roman enemies. When this Man Jesus started to preach love of your enemy, the leaders became a little annoyed to say the least. But this took a while before they became aware of the "threat" that this Man posed to their positions of reverence as the religious leaders.

By the time Jesus was thirty, He had become one with His Divine Father, one with Him in His heart, mind, and soul. He had at this point, some unusual gifts because of this relationship with God. So, let's start there: these gifts, and what He was going to do with them to work toward the completion of the task.

Jesus was a miracle worker. His first public miracle was the water into wine deal... everybody knows the story. He was at a wedding, and they ran out of wine. His mother Mary asked Him to help the couple out to spare them the embarrassment on their special day. Jesus was a little reluctant to "perform" the miracle, but because His mom... woman... asked Him to do it, He did. The story is contained in the Gospel of John, it's called "The Wedding at Cana." It is located in chapter 2 and starts at verse 1. Read it if you never have. It's only twelve verses, and the funny thing is how it ends: Jesus, His mother, "brothers" and His disciples left to go to Capernaum.

Jesus had already started to preach at this point in time and had His disciples in place, twelve of them. Oh yeah, the number 12. I told you I would tell you about that number; this is later and as good as a time as any.

Twelve is a number from the beginning of the Bible; right up until the end of the Bible. It's in Genesis and continues throughout the text right up until Revelation.

It's actually a very commonly used number, even by today's standards. You got your dozen doughnuts, your dozen rolls, your dozen eggs, your dozen ears of corn, and so on. But this number's origination in this text has really got a kind of pagan twist. Some scholars, even today, insist that this number reflects the astrological chart of twelve signs. They claim that the twelve disciples were selected because each of them bore a different sign, completing the personality variations in man. I think... no, I know that this is not true; you could say a little "birdie" just told me.

I'm an Aquarian, born on January 31, and so is my wife; her birthday is January 27. We share the same sign, but our personalities are totally different. That's one of the reasons our marriage is so successful; we're opposite, and like they say, opposites attract, and we do, but that's only one of the reasons that we have a successful marriage.

Astrology is an ancient religion, which actually has survived until today. The basis of many of these "new-age" religions is centered on this astrological system and astrological chart. Mankind developed these beliefs well before the time of Adam and Eve. They had nothing else to believe in because God had not yet shown His presence. And afterward, mankind could not find release from this well-rooted type of idolatry. Because of this, astrology is well rooted in all cultures, so convincing man to throw away this pagan-rooted religious belief has not yet been accomplished... and perhaps never will.

God is all knowing and knows that we morals would cling to this belief. He conceded this point because of "free will" and allowed this to become part of the mystery of interpretation of this Bible text; love our God. So anytime you see the number 12 in the text, remember this: God is allowing us to exercise our free will.

But the number 12 also refers to completion. So anytime you see the number twelve used, it should always be interpreted and refers to the total completion of His Church in the Bible.

Likewise, Jesus was twelve when he went to the temple for the Passover festival. But there are no other mentions of this child other than at the age of twelve; this number 12, his age, solidifies the completion of the Church.

This is the same case with the twelve tribes of Israel; man clung to the astrology and numerology, established prior to Adam and Eve, and adopted these into his ways of thinking in all aspects of the formation of this religious group.

Many biblical scholars believe that this number 12 refers to "governmental" completion because of these mentions in the Bible, but it is not. It is, however, an extension of astrology and numerology that man chose to use in his formation of religious groups because he chose to cling to the physicality of this plane.

There is no such a thing in the spiritual plane of existence. There, stars and numbers have no real meaning. That's why mankind has such a hard time dealing with the concept of three Gods in one. Man can't differentiate between the physical and spiritual planes because he lacks the faith necessary to do so, but not this Man Jesus.

Jesus chose twelve disciples because He needed to have the completion of the Church. What did you say? Yeah, you. I heard that thought in your mind: Twelve disciples and one man make thirteen. Is that what you were thinking? Good, I'm glad you're paying attention.

Jesus was directed by His Father to choose these twelve men. Jesus was obedient to the instruction of His Father always, and in this case, because of the betrayal of one of these disciples, twelve were left in total, the completion of the Church.

Understand one thing; this Bible has been written in terms of the physical plane for us so that we can indeed interpret its contents.

There is no need for "instructions" in the spiritual plane, but because we are separated from God by the "chasm" of the planes, we need as much help as possible. And so, that's why Jesus, the Messiah was necessary... no, absolutely *needed* for mankind.

Mankind rationalizes most events so that they make sense to him because of his lack of faith and trust in God. In this particular case, the case of Jesus being the Messiah, the men at the time did the same thing. They could not accept the fact that God would send a mere man to save them, a meek man who preached love and forgiveness of their fellow human being. There expectations were much different. But this man was not here to meet their expectations; He was here to meet the expectations of God the Father, and this he did.

God Almighty blessed this man from the beginning of time. God gave Him all these supernatural powers here on Earth, but these supernatural powers are available to all men, if they simply have faith.

"And the apostles said to the Lord, "Increase our faith." The Lord replied, "If you have the faith the size of a mustard seed, you would say to this mulberry tree, 'Be uprooted and planted in the sea,' and it would obey you." (Luke 17:5, 6)

Warning: Don't try this at home! This man was specially trained to do these miraculous tasks, but we are not. We don't have the faith to accomplish this task; start with something small; ask for understanding.

Jesus said this to His disciples after they were witness to a series of miracles. They were witness to the wine thing, the healings of many sick people, and even the raising of two dead people. They wanted some of this power—but for the wrong reasons.

Jesus had these amazing gifts from God because He was one with God and would eventually inherit the Kingdom of God... but not yet. He had to complete the mission. His mission here on Earth, the task... yep, I'm getting to it right now.

Throughout the New Testament, there are countless mentions of Jesus' lineage, His lineage back to Adam, this first man with God's gift of "life." The writers of the Bible seem to go out of their way to establish the fact that Jesus was from Adam's line, when in fact, all humans with souls can all be traced back to Adam and Eve. And we know the Adam and Eve story; they broke the first rule and committed the first sin against God. This first sin opened the floodgates for mankind to continue their sinful ways against God. God then sent several "inspired" men to Earth to act as guidance for mankind, but mankind was nonresponsive to their pleas to repent of their sins. So now, it was time for God to show us the love that He has for all of us. He sent this Man to redeem us, and a man he was... until He completed the task.

God asked this man to be brutally murdered by the "righteous" for payment of that first offense, the apple deal. God gave Adam and Eve one simple little commandment: Don't eat from that tree. They couldn't do it. So, God upped the ante; He wanted someone, Jesus to give the most precious of any of man's possessions as the fee for forgiveness: His life. After many thousands of years and countless offenses against His loving nature, God demanded a full ransom for all of the past sins. He asked this Man to give His life, and not only give His life, but subject himself to the most brutal type of death ever in the history of mankind, crucifixion by the Romans, which was indeed the most barbaric type of death ever performed.

You see, we all are uncertain of the outcome of this life. We don't know for sure that there is life after death, our faith drives us to that belief; same with Jesus the man and men are uncertain.

If you're still not convinced that He was truly a man at this point in His life, then why did He ask His Father to let the "cup" pass Him by in the garden the fateful night of His capture? Why was He afraid to die especially if He was God in the form a man? Perhaps He was showing us that all men have that moment of doubt and pain. So, that's when Jesus showed us that at this point, He was still a Man in all senses of the word, because He was.

But God needed to give this man some special talents so that He could get the attention of the right group of people, the people who would ultimately fear this man so much that they wanted to eliminate Him completely from their presence. This man was causing them trouble. They had the laws from Moses, from Abraham, and from the prophets; they didn't need this man to preach to the people. "Oh, it's all right not to follow those ancient laws, forget all that, love your enemies." They wanted a Messiah that would stand up and fight for them, a Messiah that would conquer their conquerors and finally free them from any nation's rule. But not this man Jesus. He preached the truth and the leaders didn't like it. They didn't want to believe that their God was a "wimp" and would send them someone who wouldn't fight for their freedom.

Jesus had to make an impression—an impression so great that His brutal death not only paid the price for our salvation, but also was so great of an impression that His legacy would carry on until the end of time. And because He was the chosen Man and His

Now that I have presented the fact that He was a man and defined the task, let's find out when and why He earned the crown and title of King... Son of God.

Chapter 16
Three Years on the Job

Jesus spent three years working on the mission at hand; it would have been of no use if He had not done some groundwork prior to the task. There were many preachers of the word of God then, just like now, but this man was different. He preached to the sinner; He ate with them, spent time in their homes, even stayed overnight, and this was objectionable to many of the religious leaders of the time.

He healed them of the physical illnesses and their deformities, not to mention the forgiveness of their sins. But how did He get this authority over this world's physical limitation? That was the question of the time.

Who was this man, and where did He come from? No one knew, with the exception of the chosen few: His mom, His earthly dad, His brothers, His sisters, His disciples, and most of them weren't 100 percent positive of who He was either.

What we do know about Him is that He really led a simple life, not concerning Himself with earthly possessions, merely focusing on the souls and eternal salvation of mankind. This was atypical of a preacher then as well as now. So, you see, this man was very different; He was a miracle worker that wasn't in it for the money, which totally confused all the people, including the religious leaders. It's even more confusing to us; we actually have such a statement on a record, to those of you that might not know what a record is, it's a flat piece of plastic that turns on a "turntable" and produces sound through your stereo system. The album, another word for record, came out in the early seventies and was entitled "Jesus Christ Superstar." There are several references asking why faith in God was so strong, God gave Him authority over this physical plane and allowed Him to do things that no other mortal has ever done and or even understood: raise the dead, multiply the fishes and loafs, and not to mention, forgive man of His sins against God. This was the straw that broke the camel's back. Who was this Man, they, the religious superiors, thought? "He must be from the Devil to preach against our laws."

Their laws demanded death from the sinner, but this Man never sinned, not once. That's the irony in this; these leaders demanded the death of a Man who never committed a sin, so they set this man up and fabricated the sin of blasphemy.

God knew that this was going to happen; He knew the hearts, minds, and souls of the Pharisees, priests, and scribes, the hearts of men. God knew that these men were going to want payment for this man's sin via the law that had been passed down through the generations from Moses; the law that demanded death to the sinner, especially the blasphemer. And because of this, God made the brutal death of this man, a death that only wicked men would earn, a requirement for the completion of His earthly life and the fulfillment of His inheritance of this kingdom in the physical plane.

Jesus the Man knew this fact. He knew what He was sent here to do, as all men know the outcome of life, death, but this man's death was going to make things right. When God told Moses that there were "rules" and the penalty for breaking the rules was death, God was referring to spiritual death, but man had and still has no concept of what this meant.

And for completion of the "task;" one man had to suffer the penalty that man had prescribed, by man's interpretation of God's word, and this man had to be put to death by the worst possible means, which included all the sinful ways of mankind. Then and only then would the ransom for man's sin be paid in full, and Jesus knew this, too.

Jesus told us this throughout His earthly life, but we still can't comprehend that this man would be and now is the king of this universal plane. Jesus passed His test, even though He did have a moment of doubt, even though His humanity was an issue, just like our humanity is always in question because we don't know for sure what's on the "other side." Jesus was here in this plane just like we are now. The only difference is that this man had direct contact with the Almighty and was given this mission firsthand, knew the outcome and had to use His free will to decide if He would follow His will or the will of the Father.

That's the true importance of receiving Holy Communion at Sunday Mass. I'm a Eucharistic minister. I help with the distribution of this most holy and sacred sacrament. This man was offering up His life and His free will to pay for our sins. Remember what He said in the garden: "If it be Your will, let this cup pass by Me by." He didn't say, "Hey Dad, are you kidding? I'm not doing that: be beaten, be humiliated, be paraded through the streets like a common criminal, and then be nailed to a cross that I have to carry up that hill after they beat Me close to death!" He didn't say that. "Not My will, but Your will be done," is what He said. He said OKAY and did the task even though He knew how much pain He was going to endure. He still agreed to do our Father's will and not His own.

So, it truly bothers me… no, it angers me, when I see people pop the "magic cookie" in their mouth and show no reverence whatsoever for this blessed gift that Jesus Christ, the King of this Universe, God's Son, gave to us in remembrance of the total sacrifice that He made to make thing right with His Father, our Father God.

Now don't get me wrong: Many people do respect this Sacrament, but some receive Communion just… because. And "because" isn't the reason. I would crawl on my hands and knees to the altar, over fire and broken glass if needed to partake in this blessed gift of life.

I thank the Lord God Almighty every time I receive this gift for giving us His Son, the man who did what no other man would ever want to do for another man, for all of us; He gave His life, dying in the most brutal way, subjecting Himself to murderous men who displayed every sinful offense known, the task.

did you come to Earth in "such a backward time, in such a strange land." I have the album somewhere and always wondered the same.

But it had to be that way because today the media would have rationalized His importance away. Because we would not have understood His mission either, so we would have found faults in this man authenticity and dismissed Him from our minds. These miracles that he performed would have been scrutinized, and we would have justified them as magic, similar to other famous magicians of our time, or we would have put this man in a mental institution to protect Him from endangering Himself. How compassionate we have become, don't you agree? But that's just my opinion; maybe we could have dealt with it. And we will have to deal with it, someday, the day of His return.

So, the timing on the event of Jesus' first coming was correctly placed because God chose the timing, and God is never wrong. God chose that time in history because there wasn't any media to influence the impression made by this man. God knew that mankind, through his sinful ways, would indeed assist in the fulfillment of the scripture that these people were so familiar with, and God knew that the truth would prevail.

But what was the truth? Was He the Son of God or the Son of Man? Both. Men are made to the image and likeness of God, so these terms are interchangeable. This is the hurdle that most people can't get over, then and even now. God knows that these terms are confusing, and yet, throughout the text, these terms, for Jesus, still exist; Jesus Himself used both terms.

But He didn't walk around all day long saying, "Hey, look at Me, I'm the Son of Man," or "God's My Daddy, and My Daddy can beat up your daddy." No, He was an extremely humble individual. He only referred to Himself as the Son of Man or the Son of God when the time was right to reach the correct people's ears, and He wasn't boastful about it.

Imagine if you were this man, how would you handle that responsibility? How would you handle the task of telling everyone that you were the Messiah? About twenty or so years ago, I started seeing WWJD everywhere I looked. Admittedly, I had to ask what this meant, and I found out that it meant: What Would Jesus Do?

There were key rings, bracelets, notebook covers, T-shirts, and so on. I was on the fence on this one because someone is making a serious profit on capitalizing on this showing of faith. However, many people are in fact publicly showing their faith by displaying their support of the life that Jesus lived; this is a good thing.

As was the life Jesus lived. I'm going out on a limb here, but it's starting to come to me. It really started right after His public baptism. Jesus had never sinned as a child and wasn't in need of this baptism, but because we are the sinners, He made this public display to show us that everyone, including Himself as a human being was capable of sin. He was a flesh and blood Man and He was here in the same day-to-day situations that we encounter ourselves.

Directly after this baptism, He went off into the desert alone, for the cleansing of His soul, more accurately, His communion with God His Father, and our Father. Jesus made no bones about this fact. He never once said that He was the only Son of God, but insisted that we are all sons and daughters of the same God. But the difference between us is that this Man acted only in a pleasing manner to God's will, He truly was the perfect son. None of us have a son or daughter that does what we ask always, but the Father God did in Jesus.

The desert was this man's testing ground. Forty days and forty nights without food, water, or shelter would either purify Him or kill Him as it would any person. Forty days of solitude, just Jesus, the desert, God, and the demon. Jesus needed to know Himself if this was on the up and up, so off to the wilderness He went to pray. This was the struggle this man had to endure in His own soul. This was the moment in His life that He gained the grace to fulfill His Father's will. This is the forty days in which He was given authority over physical death in this physical plane because He never did succumb to the demon's temptations.

The temptations that all of us succumb to daily—money, power, hunger, thirst, sins of the flesh, and the list goes on and on—each one of us has our own individual weaknesses, and this man's weakness at that particular time was doubt: the doubt that this was actually true. He didn't wake up one morning and say, "I think I'll go out today and be the Son of God, do a couple of miracles, impress all the people, and then die on a cross so everyone will remember me as the Messiah." No! He was just as uncertain of the validly that He was the chosen Messiah, at that point in time, as some of us are still uncertain today.

Face it, Jesus was looking for guidance. He was looking for the answers; he wanted the straight skinny, so off to the desert He went. He supported God even in the direct presence of Satan himself. He passed His test with flying colors, and now He knew for sure that He was chosen by God for this mission and task. The story is contained in the Gospel of Matthew, it is located starting on chapter 4, verses 1 through 11. It doesn't tell you what I just told you, but it's written between the lines. Read this passage, pray for the vision, believe that you are a child of our God and watch and see what happens to you. Show your faith… I do.

So now that Jesus got the "juice" from God, He was off to do the job. But He needed His disciples to help Him with the completion of His task. If He just died on the cross and didn't have anyone around after the fact to testify that He did rise from the dead, then it wouldn't have worked. And this rising from the dead thing… very important… we're getting to that in a little while.

But why these twelve, was it that astrology thing? I think not, I know not. I know that Jesus was looking for 12 sinners, common people just like you and me. He was looking for the men, men that if He gave the right instruction, would carry out the mission that He was about to put into action. He needed strong men; no, not physically strong, but men strong of will. He wanted men that could go on even in the face of ridicule of their peers. He needed men with just enough faith, but He needed men that could decide for themselves, if this was a worthy cause to pursue. Hence the search for the twelve, and twelve He found.

Let's get all their names; most people can name a couple. Everybody knows Peter and the doubting Thomas and of course we all know John and James... maybe, but most think that Mark and Luke were included in list of the first apostles; they weren't. The twelve are named in the following gospel, chapter, and verses. I can also remember them being named two places. First, we'll look at this one:

"When day came, He called His disciples to Himself, and from them He chose Twelve, whom He named apostles: Simon, whom He called Peter, and his brother Andrew, James, John, Philip, Bartholomew, Matthew, Thomas, James the son of Alphaeus, Simon who was called a Zealot, and Judas the son of James, and Judas Iscariot, who became a traitor." (Luke 6:13–16)

Now they are also in the following gospel, chapter, and verse. However, when you read this one, please take note that the names are slightly different.

"The names of the first twelve apostles are these: first, Simon called Peter, and his brother Andrew; James the son of Zebedee, and his brother John; Philip and Bartholomew, Thomas and Matthew the tax collector; James the son of Alphaeus, and Thaddeus; Simon the Cananean, and Judas Iscariot who betrayed Him." (Matthew 10:2–4)

Okay then, which were the first twelve? Ten for sure are the same, but what about Thaddeus and Simon the Cananean? I thought it was Simon who was called a Zealot, and Judas the son of James, but Matthew said, "Thaddeus and Simon the Cananean. Hmm... how can this be? Folks, I'm to show you another passage that should clear this up. I'm being told to look here. I will... "

205

"Jesus then said to those Jews who believed in Him, "If you remain in my word, you will truly be my disciples, and you will know the truth, and the truth will set you free."

(John 8:31, 32)

I'm a little confused… pardon me while I pray for a moment. Got it; thanks God!

There is some confusion on the subject of disciples versus apostles: a disciple is a learner and an apostle is a messenger. Many times, the two words are interchanged, and I'm sure I've done this myself in this work and in everyday conversations, but there is a notable difference. The disciples were students of Jesus, and the apostles were "graduated" students that were ready to go into the world to spread the word of God in a truthful manner.

Jesus was the teacher who was sent by God to give us the instructions that we all needed to complete our tasks here on Earth. He was sent to this plane of existence because we all lacked the understanding of exactly what we were supposed to do here to pass this test. We're all confused, but this man spoke the truth, the truth that would set us free, and once these disciples actually learned the truth, then and only then, were they ready to be called apostles.

But it seems that even with the teacher present, they still couldn't get past their humanity. Vanity, that's the culprit, the demon's favorite sin. Look at this…

"Then an argument broke out among them about which of them should be regarded as the greatest." (Luke 22:24)

This took place at the "Last Supper," the last night that the teacher was going to be on this Earth in human form, and still, they didn't get it. These twelve who were in attendance were supposedly the twelve who were the "graduated" students, and yet one betrayed Him, and another denied Him. Okay here's the answer: There were only twelve original apostles, but there were many disciples at the time that this, the New Testament was written. There were literally hundreds of them learning the words of the new way of thinking that Jesus inspired and taught. And when these were written, the "original" twelve were really one man's opinion in one gospel and another man's opinion in the other of their actual names. But the fact is that these two in question were in fact the same men. They were, however, named differently by the two writers.

Matthew's gospel would be the more accurate names that these men used, because he was one of the first twelve "original" apostles, but the truth be known, it doesn't matter because they all scattered when it came time to show they were true Apostles of Jesus, the time to complete the task. There were only a couple of these apostles in the Garden at the Mount of Olives, and after the soldiers of the Sanhedrin took Jesus away, there were none.

WWJD... I'll tell you what He would do: exactly what He did. He went before these people and spoke the truth. He wasn't afraid to lose His life for the truth because He knew that this life wasn't the end of His existence. It was the beginning of His reign in this new kingdom of this physical universe—His reign in the neutral universe that bridges the positive universe, God's kingdom of heaven, and the negative universe, Satan's kingdom of hell.

God is positive, love and kindness; Satan is negative, hate and sinful deeds. God is the truth, Satan is a liar, and this plane has both in common. That's what Jesus' mission was: to tell us that fact and then to complete the mission with the task; death in the physical nature of His humanity and transfiguration to fulfillment of the uncertainty that boggles our limited human minds, showing us that there is no death of our spiritual nature and gaining for us our rightful place in the kingdom of His Father, again united in the same spirit of God as the sons and daughters of God.

This truth that He spoke was the objectionable and controversial message that ultimately led to the completion of the task. Not to beat a dead horse, but mankind just doesn't get it. These people were so disappointed in the message of love and kindness that Jesus taught that they had no other choice than to kill this man.

They fabricated charges of blasphemy to justify His murder. Jewish law was written, and grievous sin merited death for the sin of blasphemy.

The leaders of the Jewish religion were so afraid that they would lose control and ultimately lose their positions of honor as the communities' revered religious leaders, and they most surely didn't want to lose their cushy jobs.

They decided death was to be this man's fate and the conniving SOBs brought this innocent Man to trial. Trial, that's a joke, too! This was a sanctioned murder, but that's the way God wanted it to go down. God wanted these people to see that they twisted His law into the self-serving law that they applied. When these laws were put into place, God was referring to the spiritual death of the soul, and He was going to be the judge, not man who unrightfully placed himself at God's level and turned this into a physical penalty and death of the body.

That's why Jesus had to rise from the dead. If this murder went unanswered by God, then they would have succeeded in their mission to eliminate the threat of this so-called Son of God. But more than that, Jesus' rising was conformation to the spiritual being and life after death. It was also a confirmation that physical death has no power over someone that truly believes in God and dedicates their entire physical existence in delivering the truth about the loving nature of our Father God. That's what Jesus did and His reward was the kingship of this universe. So, let's just see what happened that day, a Friday, in the assumed year 33 AD just outside the walls of Jerusalem, the trial, the beating, the humiliation, the pain, the sorrow very well depicted in the movie *The Passion of the Christ*. I've seen this vision so many times, more than I can count.

The moment of truth had come for this man. Was everything that He had been preaching for the last three years going to be fulfilled? Was He going to rise from the dead as told in the Scripture?

Was He the Son of God or was He just a mere Man who tricked us all into thinking that He was special in the eyes of the Lord?

Only a few people were in attendance at the crucifixion of this man and only a few witnessed this horrible and brutal death. He was nailed to the tree, He died within hours because of the beating and severe loss of blood from the torture He had to endure prior to His sentencing to death. The Earth did shake, the Earth did quake and Jesus did give up His Spirit to God Almighty.

Those in attendance questioned this man's validity and taunted Him, still looking for proof, come down from the cross, save yourself. But Jesus did not, He could have, but then the task would not have been completed to God's satisfaction and Jesus would not have earned His reward, Lord, God and Master of this world.

But what happened to Jesus after he gave up the spirit? Did He lie in the tomb Friday night, Saturday, and rise on Sunday morning? Where was His spirit for those three days? Did He in fact rise from the dead, or is this just a story told to us to convince us the He was the Son of God?

Faith, faith, faith, my dear friend, that's the question inside the question of faith. I know what happened to Jesus, and I'm going to tell you. This I cannot show you, for it is not written in the Bible, but it is burned into my soul. This is my mission and my task; this is what I was put here to do, and I absolutely will obey the will of God Almighty. Putting at risk the ridicule that I might be subjected to, I will complete this message delivery, for the driving force that is continually guiding my fingers, my mind, and my soul, will not allow me to stop until this is told. His will be done!

Chapter 17
Three Days in Hell?

When Adam committed the first sin, cursed was the ground because of his deed. Toil and labor for his entire life was his penalty for this disobedience to the Lord. When he died...

"Until you return to the ground, from which you were taken; for you are dirt, and to dirt you shall return." (Genesis 3:20)

And so it was, every man, woman, and child cursed to the ground as a result of Adam and Eve's disobedience to the Lord. Cursed to the universal plane of this Earth's existence, never to be in the presence of the Lord again, dirt they were and dirt they became, until the ransom was paid.

When Jesus breathed the last breath, and gave up His spirit, "Into your hands I commend my spirit," the ransom was paid in full.

God was truly pleased with this man's completion of His task. Even though God gave Him authority over the physical universe to show us the awesome power of God's love and generosity toward the souls that he created to share His eternal life and happiness, Jesus did not invoke this power given Him while He was on the cross. He surrendered His will to the will of God. But what happened next? Is the rumor true? Did He actually go into hell?

Rumor is that when people died before the death of Christ, they were commended to hell until Jesus died and redeemed their sins. This then opened the gates of heaven, and Jesus escorted these souls back into heaven. This rumor is somewhat true, but not completely accurate.

The truth in the rumor is that the gates of heaven were indeed closed until the ransom was paid. The inaccuracy of the rumor is that Jesus went into hell for three days to free the souls. Hell is reserved for the judged souls, and at this point in time, they were not judged. Hell did exist, but only the first group of rebellious souls were inhabitants of the place.

This judgment of the souls — the souls that were in "limbo" — was reserved for Jesus. This additional power of judgment was His reward for the completion of God's work. Jesus earned this because He spent His entire life on this Earth doing nothing but God's will, spreading the message of love throughout the country-side that He inhabited. He was a perfect example of what God expected from man, all men, but only this man was the one who met God's fullest expectations.

Limbo is another term used for the place that Jesus went for those three days; it's a little more accurate, but not completely accurate. Let me show you something — the transfiguration, which is located in the Gospel of Matthew:

"And He was transfigured before them; His face shone like the sun and his clothes became white as light. And behold, Moses and Elijah appeared to them, conversing with Him." (Matthew 17:2, 3)

Only three apostles were witness to this event and Jesus charged them, "Do not tell the vision to anyone until the Son of Man has been raised from the dead."

I'll tell you something right now: Jesus didn't want this information to be leaked out because this secret is part of the mystery of this universe. This universe is the bridge between the two other universes. It has both physical and spiritual dimensions, and it is unique in its own way.

When Jesus died, He left this physical plane and His spirit went to the spiritual plane within this universe—the spiritual plane that some mystics claim that they can transcend and breach; perhaps they can, but this man's spirit certainly did.

Did you ever hear the term *purgatory*? Of course, you have. Do you know where its location is? I do, and you should know it, too. It's located right under your nose, right here beside you, right here in this space that you occupy daily.

Some people don't believe in purgatory—and shame on them for the lack of commitment to reality. Spiritual sightings and hauntings are all the rage now and in the entire history of mankind. There must be some validity to this, don't you think?

There is a complete scientific field dedicated to the investigation and discovery of evidence to prove the existence of this spiritual plane. In fact, the friend I originally wrote the concept draft of this book with is one of the leading authorities in this field. Some scientific communities are, in fact, looking inside this sacred text of the Bible for "hints" to lead them to the evidence they need to convince us fully of the true facts about this universe that we live in. And just another little fact: NASA is using the Bible to fix time lines for programming of deep-space exploration crafts. Don't believe that? Look it up; it's true. If you have the Internet, you may have received the e-mail, if not, that information is on file in public records pertaining to space-exploration mission facts, and not that hard to find.

Purgatory, that's where Jesus went; he went within this universe's spiritual limbo, the place that all souls with sin were sent, to await their judgment until the ransom was paid in full.

The Catholic Church says that purgatory is the area that souls are sentenced to for purification. This is also somewhat true because while they carry out their sentences; they are still not permitted to be in heaven and are subject to the troubles, trials, and tribulations of this universe. But these souls are not in the same dimension and are not subjected to the same troubles, trials, and tribulations as we are in the physical dimension. They are, however, subjected to the same emotional pains that plague us throughout our physical lives. Only one question has been answered for these souls, and that is the question related to the uncertainty of the physical death.

Now these souls no longer have the need for the basic physical necessities of life that we here in this dimension require: food, water, shelter, clothing, and so on. They have passed this portion of the test and are awaiting their eternal reward; but they are still separated from God and His total love, and they are not completely done with the requirement to gain the passage back into heaven. They must pay their own individual ransoms for the sins of this life that they committed. But first, they must be judged and get their sentence.

The souls that were in purgatory when Jesus paid the ransom were souls from the beginning of this spiritual enhanced humanity, all the way back to the day that Adam first received his soul. They were awaiting the Messiah as well, the man who would deliver them from the bondage of their enslavement and their enslavement was in this place called purgatory.

When Jesus gave up His spirit to God, He had no sin to pay for; He was sinless throughout of His physical life, and He did good deeds for His fellow man without a motive or expectation of reward. He was the perfect human being; the fulfillment of man made in the image and likeness of God. He earned the title of "Son of God" by His everyday thoughts, words, and deeds here on Earth.

So, when He "passed" to the next dimension, the judgment and sentencing dimension, He was faultless: "let the one without sin throw the first stone... "

He was the best of the best, better than Moses, better than Elijah, better than all souls that preceded Him in this physical plane of existence. The witnessing of the "transfiguration" was merely an inspirational vision for the apostles' benefit, not the benefit of Jesus. Jesus already knew of this dimension and knew what was to be the outcome of His death on the cross.

And with the choosing of God's will and not His own, He received the greatest gift of all—the gift of kingship of not only this universe, but also the universe in which heaven exists.

No one can go to the Father unless they go to the Father though Jesus; that's where He was for those three days. He was releasing the souls that had paid the penalty for their sins, and He was judging the souls that were in need of condemnation as well. He was throwing the stone.

This universe is the bridge between the other two universal planes, and the dimension of the spiritual plane within this universe is the "boarding" dock. Once we die the physical death, we will enter this dimension and be judged as well as everyone else that ever breathed a single breath in this physical plane. Jesus will be there waiting for us, He is here now, and He will make fair judgment on our physical lives. He has not left us, He's not lost, we need not find Jesus, and we only need to follow His example.

"Then Jesus approached and said to them, "All power in Heaven and on Earth has been given to me. Go therefore, and make disciples of all nations, baptizing them in the name of the Father, and the Son, and of the Holy Spirit, teaching them to observe all that I have commanded you. And behold, I am with you always, until the end of the age." (Matthew 28:18–20)

He is here in this dimension as well. He has, because of His perfect life, kas become what we all strive to become. He is complete in the eyes of His Father God, and He can pass between either of these two universes, the universe of ours and of God the Father's, and the dimensions contained within both, because He has been given the power to do so. But some of us… no, many of us can't seem to believe this fact; we question the authority given to Jesus because we don't understand the basics of the setup of this testing ground.

It is all the "unknown" to us simple creatures of little faith. But know this: When Jesus went to this place of purgatory, He did judge those souls from the beginning. He also gave passage to the worthy and damned the unworthy to the third dimensional plane of hell, and those that were sent to hell are not going to be allowed back into either of these two universes or dimensions until the final judgment day.

Oh, that brings up another subject: day; it took Jesus about forty hours or so to do all of this judging. There were a lot of souls that had to be judged in that time, so how did He do it? I know that y'all want to know that, right?

Well, a day is like unto a thousand years and a thousand years unto a day; all power had been given to Jesus in heaven and on Earth and once anyone breaches this dimension, time will have no value. As it had no value when Jesus passed into that plane of existence.

Jesus put us into a very good position with the life He led and with the death He endured for our sakes; he truly did love all mankind equally, but that's not the end of the story. What good would it have been unless He showed us the real truth behind our physical death. Oh yes, much still would have been accomplished, even if He wouldn't had risen from the dead, but we faithless creatures would have dismissed this man's life in an instant. We would have called this man... well, just another one of those wannabe prophets and His life truly would have been forgotten. And because God did promise—and did deliver—the Messiah, God gave us yet one more sign of the eternal life we will earn for the obedience of His simple little rules.

Let's use that Matthew 22 again... because there's only two rules anyway. Jesus told us this in the simplest way. He said:

"You shall love the Lord, your God, with all your heart, with all your soul, and with all your mind. This is the greatest and first commandment. The second is like it: You shall love your neighbor as yourself. The whole law and the prophets depend on these two commandments." (Matthew 22:37–40)

And the sign that God gave us was the raising of the dead. Now, Jesus did raise the dead during His ministry of those three years, but most people were skeptical of the validity of the stories of these events. Face it, they didn't see, they didn't believe, and even if they saw, some still didn't believe. And that's why when Jesus was raised from the dead, only the people that truly believed that He was the Son of God were allowed to see Him in His purest form, the purest form that all of us that pass this test will someday be transformed into. Reunited with this physical body and this physical dimension without the need for the physical necessities to sustain this life form. Yes, certainly, we will be able to enjoy the physical-ness of this dimension, but we will not be dependent on it, because that is what God intended from the very beginning. He placed Adam and Eve in the Garden of Eden, a place where there was no want or need. That's the irony of the apple deal; they didn't need the apple to survive, they didn't need any food. They were made to the image and likeness of God Almighty and their sin was totally unacceptable because it was defiant and totally unnecessary — as unnecessary as the death of this Lamb of God, Jesus.

And that's really why Jesus asked Our Father to have the "cup" be passed. Jesus knew that He had lived the life that God expected from all of us. He loved God, and He loved His neighbors no matter what they were capable of in their defiant nature of in this physical plane of existence. But obedient He was, even until the end of His "tour of duty," giving His life for His comrades in arms, us. Jesus was here with us, He was one of us, and He ate, drank, slept, and was subjected to the same daily perils that we all must contend with daily, but sin, He didn't.

Thus was His reward; life everlasting, and a shared and equal "partnership" with God Almighty. Reunited with His transfigured human body, a body completely without need, yet capable of enjoying the pleasures of the physical bounty surrounding us here on Earth.

The beauty of this is that someday, all of us get to see this for ourselves, all of us will be given the chance to be transfigured into this type of spiritual/physical creature, provided we pass the test.

Also, there is absolutely no distinction between man and woman within that plane of existence. This concept is probably the most difficult for you to understand.

So, just a little recap, and then we'll move on...

Jesus died on that Friday afternoon. He died on the cross to make peace with God for the sins of man.

He left this physical plane of existence and when into the spiritual plane of existence within this universe; that place is purgatory.

Millions upon millions of people who had died at this point in time were awaiting the arrival of the Messiah. Their souls were trapped in purgatory — limbo — until His arrival.

Upon His arrival, because He was spotless and free of any sin whatsoever, God reopened the gates of heaven.

Jesus then was given authority to judge these souls. Jesus alone grants admittance or denial to heaven.

Once this initial judgment was complete, God gave Jesus the ultimate reward: the reuniting of His transformed physical body and completion of the promise of man made in the image and likeness of God Almighty.

Jesus then showed a select few what the true meaning of eternal life was by appearing to them in this perfect and complete image of what all of us, as sons and daughters of God, will become on the final day of Judgment.

Jesus didn't need to wait for the transformation of His body into the spiritual body; there is no sin to be judged by God Almighty and no reason to wait until the judgment day.

All that succeed in passing the test will be given the same power and authority in heaven and on Earth on the final judgment day.

We will all be part of God, and God will be part of us. Jesus was the first to experience this reward, and that is why the resurrection was so important, proof positive of God's promise of eternal and everlasting life, free of all the pain of this dimension.

Bold, isn't it? There's proof. Look:

"Jesus said unto her, "Stop holding on to me, for I have not yet ascended to the Father. But go to my brothers and tell them, 'I am going to my Father and your Father, to my God and your God." (John 20:17)

Jesus was talking to Mary of Magdala just after He was raised from the dead. He was telling her not to touch Him because His transformation was not yet complete. He had just "awoken" from the sleep of death, and His body was still being transformed into the spiritual/physical being...

"Not all flesh is the same, but there is one kind for human be-ings, another kind of flesh for animals, another kind of flesh for birds, and another for fish. There are heavenly bodies and earthly bodies, but the brightness of the heavenly is one kind and that of the earthly another." (Corinthians 15:39, 40)

This was written by Paul. We're going to meet Paul pretty soon and some of the other Apostles of the Lord Jesus Christ next. Paul was not one of the original "twelve," but Paul is a very important figure in the formation of the Christian Church, but first...

Chapter 18
Mice into Men

TGIF, for sure, but this Friday wasn't a good day for these twelve. One denied Him, one betrayed Him, and the others scattered like roaches when the lights come on. You know they're there, but where?

It's an accepted fact that Judas, the betrayer, hanged himself due to the grief and remorse that he felt in his soul. Judas was never a believer in this Man Jesus, but only followed Him because of financial gain. Judas was the "bookkeeper" for the group, and he held the purse for the community, Jesus, the twelve Apostles, and the other unnamed disciples; well, only once does the Bible mention a number for the followers: seventy-two.

"After this the Lord appointed seventy-two others whom He sent ahead of Him in pairs to every town and place he intended to visit." (Luke 10:1)

Judas was responsible for the monies that were collected and his responsibilities included distribution of these funds to the poor and needy. But Judas had other priorities; he was only interested in the money he could steal from the funds, kind of similar to the so-called ministers of today, not all, mind you, but some for sure. And after he saw what he had done to this innocent man, the demon claimed his soul, and he responded accordingly by conceding his perceived unforgivable sin.

Poor Judas! He only had to ask for forgiveness, and he would have been forgiven. The death of Christ was necessary; someone had to betray the Lord and that man was Judas. Judas was never free from sin; he was a thief and a scoundrel only interested in his own welfare.

Judas got his just reward and eternal death is his penalty, but he really didn't have to lose his soul if he had just asked for forgiveness.

And what about the other eleven? Where were they? Hiding behind locked doors, afraid that they would be the next to be captured by the Jews and then executed by the Roman forces in that same brutal manner that Jesus underwent. These men were not men, they were mice, disbelievers in all that they had witnessed for the past three years. Scared beyond belief, frightened by the thought of their own death. They were trembling and shaking because they still had no conviction or faith, but that wouldn't last long, their physical needs would overtake their fear, and on that Sunday, three days later, some had left the security of the locked chamber.

That same three days later, Jesus sent Mary of Magdala to tell them that He had risen—and yet they were skeptics and did not believe. Some still remained behind locked doors fearing for their safety.

This is human nature at its best... or at its worst. Well, somewhere in the middle, I suppose, but it surely is human nature. God knows that we are fragile and lack understanding of the unknown, so Jesus came to them in the spiritual/physical flesh.

Let's look and see:

"On the evening of that first day of the week, when the doors were locked, where the disciples were, for fear of the Jews, Jesus came and stood in their midst and said to them, Peace be with you." (John 20:19)

This was an amazing sight to these apostles and disciples within their "hideout." How did this man breach the security of the locked doors and penetrate this location… that's what they were thinking? But more so, who was this man, it couldn't have been the master, He was dead. They needed proof, and proof He gave them because they lacked faith in His words, "Peace be with you."

He showed them His hands and side, and they then realized that this was Jesus who obviously was alive and well. Ya think that after three years with this man, they would have recognized Him without His showing them the marks of the crucifixion? Ya think they would have recognized His face, run up to the man, dropped to their knees, and given Him the adoration that He indeed is entitled to? Nope, not these folks! They started to party. Let's see their reaction:

"The disciples rejoiced when they saw the Lord."

But this was their moment of truth, the moment when these men received the gift that made them famous. The gift that turned these frightened little mice into the revered men we have come to know. This was the moment that Jesus introduced them to the third person of the Holy Trinity, the Holy Spirit.

"Jesus said to them again, "Peace be with you. As the Father has sent me, so I send you." And when He had said this, He breathed on them and said to them, "Receive the Holy Spirit. Whose sins you forgive are forgiven them, and whose sins you retain are retained." (John 20:21–23)

By this time, Jesus had been totally transformed into the king and master of this universe and had all the power and glory of God because He was now again God in the second person… equal, one, and united to the Father in the Holy Spirit of the Living God. I'm praying right now; this is my moment of my truth. I've been writing this for about twenty years, and I've only written what has come to me through my soul and spiritual guidance. This message is being delivered moment by moment, and in this moment, prayer is needed. I know that God and His

Holy Spirit will not disappoint me and give me the next inspired part of this message.

And now the moment has come: Jesus died and went into the spiritual plane to claim His throne in this bridge universe between heaven and hell, our universe. God the Father is ruler over the universal planes of heaven, Earth, and hell; His throne is mighty and He is ruler of all.

The Holy Spirit is ruler and keeper of the lost dimension of hell, keeping it separated from the pure and righteous. His authority is over those that do not obey His authority and law. He is the God of the spiritual plane of existence and because we are all spiritual by nature, He prevents those unworthy spiritual beings from infiltrating His righteous plane of existence and this makes Him God of all as well.

Jesus had become the master and ruler of this dimension that bridges the two, and because of His humanity and His total obedience to the Father and the Holy Spirit, He also is God of all.

These three are God united in one living and true God because of Jesus' pain and suffering for the salvation of our souls. God chose to become man through this man, so He could unite these three separate—yet one—in the completion of His plan to reunited the oneness of God, contained within all the dimensional planes of existence. And so, Jesus now has the authority of God united as one with the other two, thank you, Lord!

Now equipped with all the power of God, Jesus breathed the Holy Spirit into these men, giving them the authority over the demonic plane of existence. He gave them the authority to forgive the sins of man, which was reserved for the authority of the Holy Spirit only until this point in time.

Yes, Jesus did forgive sin while He was in the human form, but Jesus was a very special man. He was conceived in the Holy Spirit, and because of this, He had this power and authority from the beginning of His human life. But when He again became totally united with God in three persons, He now had the rightful and blessed privilege to pass this power to these apostles and disciples that had not yet passed into the spiritual plane of existence. Man to this point was not yet supposed to have this power, but because of our humanity and sinful ways, we positively had to have mediation between God and man in this plane, and so it was granted.

So, these men were blessed into the Holy Spirit, the God of the spiritual and the God that could hold sin everlasting to your soul. There's a passage—actually, two—in the Bible that verifies the authority of the Holy Spirit over the demonic spiritual plane. I'll tell you where they are. Go look sometime. I'll explain later what these two passages actually mean, but right now, I can't stop this: Mark 3 and Matthew 12.

These cowardly mice were now powerful, spiritually guided men; they were men of God. No longer would they hide in the shadows watching Jesus perform the miracles of forgiveness. They were about to take the reins and drive Christianity into the world, but only because Jesus gave them the authority to do so, blessing them and giving them that authority to forgive man's sins. And along with this power came the authority of this physical plane. These men now could also heal the sick and disabled human beings and raise the dead of this Earth with true authority, which was also granted to them.

Yes, they did go out and heal the sick while Jesus was still in the human form, but they didn't have this total authority until Jesus allowed them to receive the Holy Spirit. With this authority, they could heal the most debilitating of all men's infirmities, sickness of his soul... thank you, Jesus. Come on everybody, say it: "Thank you, Jesus." By the way, try to make this part of your everyday life: Be proud to say, "thank you, Jesus," and do not be ashamed to proclaim your gratitude for what He has done for all of us.

Thank you, Jesus, for this blessing, this privilege of man's new authority over demonic damnation. These men were the first priests of the new Church. They were given the power of absolution of sin and also the authority to bind sin to our souls. These men now had the Holy Spirit within them; they were now truly men of God.

Today, we wonder what happened to this blessed and sacred privilege. We wonder why priests of these times do the devious and demented acts of the flesh. I'll tell you; it is because they are not one in the Holy Spirit of God. Those priests are not, but they will answer for their sins, and Jesus will be their judge. When they accepted this tremendous privilege and authority over sin, they were bound to uphold the purity that came along with this Holy vow of representation of the Lord Jesus Christ.

When Jesus breathed the Holy Spirit into these first priests, He was making them equal to Himself as God, in all of God's total authority over sins. And so, any one that accepts this vow of the priesthood is also bound to the pure representation of God, as Jesus did, totally and fully committed to the will of God, displaying all of His love and mercy for humanity. Thank you, Jesus!

Okay, I'm hearing that the Sacrament of Reconciliation, confession, should be the next on the agenda, and so it will be.

All the leaders of the Christian communities that are not of the Catholic denomination claim that confession is a personal and private matter between Jesus, God, and that individual person. They are wrong: Look for yourself. "Receive the Holy Spirit. Whose sins you forgive are forgiven them, and whose sins you retain are retained."

Jesus didn't say, "Oh, it's fine, just ask me for forgiveness, and I'll grant it to you. He didn't say, "Hey, no worries, no guilt, no remorse, ask me, I'll take care of it." That's what those other denominations would have you believe in the matter of absolution. Absolution is granted just by asking Jesus in private... not!

Jesus *did* say to these apostles and disciples that they, as acting priests in His New Church, were going to determine the severity of the sin and determine if it was a forgivable offense in accordance to the new law of love and mercy. This new law of mercy and forgiveness included the penitent's feeling of guilt and remorse for those sins against God, and without those feelings, people cannot be forgiven their sins. Additionally, some sort of penance must be done in order to show God that it is your intention to eliminate these thoughts, words, or deeds from your persona and your individual faults of the flesh. All sin is a sin of the flesh. Holy and righteous spiritual beings cannot commit sin; only mankind and demonic beings can commit sin. However, demonic beings have already been judged and sentenced to the ultimate penalty of death.

We, as humans, have an unequivocal opportunity to purge our souls of the stains of sin by this Sacrament of Confession; however, because we are basically ashamed to tell another "human" of our sins, we avoid this beautiful and grace-giving sacrament—we avoid it like the plague. I have a good friend, and I love this person as a person; he is a righteous and honest man. He goes to Mass every Sunday, every Holy Day, and every day during the Lenten season. He is generous and gives to many charitable organizations. He has many friends and is loved by this community. He is a very religious man in many people's eyes. He, in fact, will not receive Communion from anyone other than a Catholic priest, not even me, and I'm a close lifelong friend. Yet he has, to my knowledge, not been to confession since he was a very young man. He's three months older than I am. He also believes in the "self" confession, a heated discussion every time we speak of this matter.

He is not alone in his beliefs; I know many individuals of the Catholic religion who feel this way, but they are wrong, and I've had this heated discussion with some of these others on many an occasion. Their souls need the graces that come with the Sacrament of Confession, but yet, to this point, I've had no success.

Catholic doctrine says that if there is no serious sin on the soul, an "Act of Contrition" is all that is necessary to cleanse the soul. For those of you who don't know what that is, it's a prayer expressing sorrow and remorse for your sins. This is accurate; however, by not receiving the sacrament, you do not receive the graces of God's absolution or the graces necessary to avoid these sinful practices in the future.

But who are we to determine if the sin we committed was serious in the eyes of the Lord? Yes, I hear you; I know, when you were confirmed, you received the Holy Spirit though that Sacrament, but it's not the same thing. That sacrament is the acceptance of you as an individual member of the Christian Church, but you did not receive the privilege of forgiveness of sin at that ceremony. You received the graces and blessings of God and the protection of His Holy Spirit, protecting your soul from the demonic influence within this plane of existence. Are we clear? Not yet, okay…

We are here, but we are not alone; we are surrounded by good and evil. And yet, we are all made to the image and likeness of God. God is three persons in one: He is the Father, He is the Son, and He is the Holy Spirit. He loves us as if we were His only child, and we are all equal in His eyes. When we dedicate ourselves to Him, in this Sacrament of Confirmation, and the last "piece of the puzzle" is put into place, the receiving of the Holy Spirit, we are now accepting ourselves as a completed likeness of God Almighty.

Completed in the very essence, both physically and spiritually, and now capable of earning our place in the paradise known as heaven. However, we are not yet equal to God Almighty, in His eyes, because we have not completed our individual tasks and missions. We have not proven that we love Him in the same way that He loves us. We have not done His will and His will only in this physical plane. And because we are "trapped" in this physical plane, we need all the "help" we can get. We need some extra assistance to protect us, from being consumed by Satan… that's where the Holy Spirit shines, that's God protecting us from Satan and his dark forces.

But God did not say to us that we are equal when we received His Holy spirit, and we falsely assume that we can absolve ourselves from our sins because we now possess all the elements of God within our souls. This is our never-ending inner conflict, which always seems to drive each individual to the position of equality with God, which is another one of our original sins… all of us, gods in our own eyes.

We all need God Almighty to grant us His forgiveness and mercy and because only ordained priests of Jesus' Church have that true authority granted by Jesus to absolve sin, confession to an ordained priest is absolutely required—because Jesus, who is God Almighty, said so. He said so to these apostles and disciples at His very first meeting with them, after He received His throne and kingship, confirming Him the second person of God Almighty... clear now?

And now, I have a question for you: Did you read those two passages? I know; I told you to read two chapters. Sorry, I guess I should have been more specific on the locations and the exact passages I was thinking of, but it's good to read the Bible, and I hope you enjoyed these two chapters.

The two passages I was thinking about are the two that say this:

"Therefore, I say to you, every sin and blaspheme will be forgiven people, but blaspheme against the Spirit will not be forgiven. And whoever speaks a word against the Son of Man will be forgiven; but whoever speaks against the Holy Spirit will not be forgiven, either in this age or the age to come." (Matthew 12:31, 32)

"Amen, I say to you, all sins and all blasphemes that people utter will be forgiven them. But whoever blasphemes against the Holy Spirit will never have forgiveness, but is guilty of an everlasting sin. For they had said, "He has an unclean spirit." (Mark 3:28–30)

At first glance, these seem to say that all bets are off when it comes to the Holy Spirit; say what you will about Jesus, but don't say a bad word about the Holy Spirit.

Kind of reminds me of my kids: Don't say one negative word about their brother, because you'll open a can of whoop ass that you can't close; but that's not really what these passages say. They confirm without any doubt what I was just told to tell you: These say, if you abuse the power of forgiveness by not having your sins absolved in the correct and appropriate manner prescribed by the law of the one true Church of Jesus Christ, God Almighty, then forgiveness is not granted, and your spirit and soul will be "unclean" from now until the end of time.

I know that some religions don't require the absolution of the soul by a minister or priest, and I know that some of the ministers and priests are sinful, and I know that you are embarrassed and afraid to tell anyone else of your inner most secrets, but that does not change the guidelines to this test. And most will argue that what I said is not accurate, and some will even call me a fool. Let them, because I know that this is the truth.

Jesus is in this room with me right now. He is looking over my shoulder, guiding my heart, mind, and soul. Open your heart, your mind, and your soul. Invite Him into your life. He is willing… no, eager, to have you be one with Him in His unity, in God.

Thank you, Jesus!

Come on, say it; you'll feel the power of Him. You'll feel His love, your body will shake and quiver, and His grace and protection will encompass your entire being.

You will not be afraid, you will not be embarrassed; you will no longer be concerned with the trivialities of this existence, and you will want to live your life loving your neighbor as you love yourself. You will want to share all your weaknesses with that person, because they have the same weaknesses as you. These weaknesses are the weaknesses of humanity. They are the common thread that joins us all to each other. These weaknesses are what make us all neighbors…

Jesus will join you… in your room, in your car, in your office, in your home, or anywhere you want Him to; all you have to do is ask Him and He will.

We're going to go take a look at what happened next…

Chapter 19
And Then

"And so, I say to you, you are Peter, and upon this rock I will build my Church, and the gates of the netherworld shall not prevail against it. I will give you the keys to the kingdom of Heaven. Whatever you bind on Earth shall be bound in Heaven; and whatever you loose on Earth shall be loosed in Heaven." (Matthew 16:18–19)

Since Peter was the first to recognize Jesus as the true Messiah, Jesus declared in the presence of the other apostles and disciples that he would be His successor and be in charge of the foundation of the new order of associates. Now that Jesus was no longer available (I'm laughing right now; you could have given me different words, Lord), someone had to take charge of the work force and proceed with Jesus' mission. I'm still laughing; Jesus was there but couldn't lead these men because there was now a new mission statement. Jesus taught these men for three years; His earthly and human mission was completed: The gates of heaven were opened, and the sins of mankind had been repaid. Jesus was and still is in His glory, but no longer would He lead this group of apostles and disciples. Someone else would have to do this job.

An enormous task and responsibility, mind you, but a job that had to be done, nonetheless. What good would it be for Jesus to have died for our sins, open the gates of heaven, and free us from the grips of Satan, if no one would do the followup or let the rest of the poor unfortunate peers know what just happened?

So, who better than the guy that had the keys? No one. I know that if I had the keys, I'd be driving. Hey, I *do* have the keys and I *am* driving, but Peter was going to drive a different vehicle. His vehicle was real, and he was going places. Peter was a strong leader; he accepted the keys to the kingdom and began to preach with such conviction and love for God that his newfound position of authority has become the accepted standard in the restructured Church— laughing again… almost wrote *industry*.

I'll tell you what. It's 3:50 AM, and I was awoken this morning at around 2:10 by this overwhelming urge to get up and start writing. God knows that I love humor and laughing, so please bear with us this morning, because I'm having a blast, laughing at what I'm hearing. And I know why these "corporate" terms are popping into my head. It's pretty simple, and I'm going to share it with you.

Many of you may feel that the organized Church is a "business" out to make money, gain power, and have control over the populations of the Earth. Well, you are mistaken. Yep, the Christian Church has a pretty big bankroll, that's what most think and those Catholics have got lots of gold and property and they even got a city for their head guy. In the recent past, he even had this cool little car with a bulletproof dome, so he can sit on his throne while he's being paraded through the crowds. And this "business" is mostly cash; we all see the collection plates and baskets being passed around in these churches at services; lots of dough, ray, me… oh, I pity the fool who thinks like this!

Let's start at the beginning of the "business" some call the Catholic Church. The "business" that this handful of men and women were concerned with was the "business" of the salvation of your soul. The "business" that they truly were concerned with was telling us of what this Man Jesus did for us and that was their primary—and only—"business." The Catholic Church is not in the "business" of making money.

Let me put this into perspective for you. My wife and I have been in "business" for many years. Our "business" is our marriage, and that's our only "business." In our time in "business," we have gained many possessions through our wise and honest "business" senses, and I told you this: We are comfortable. Imagine if we could live for two thousand years on this Earth and continue with the same "business" practices that we employ now. We could, in fact, be multi-billionaires; we could have more money that we could ever want or need on this Earth...

The Church has been around for two thousand years, so get over the fact that they have a large bankroll to work with. They need this type of funding to help the needy of Earth. If you are reading this book, then you're in the top 10 percent of the richest humans on the face of the planet. Bet you didn't know that... well, maybe you did. But the fact is, that that's what the Catholic Church's monies are doing: They're helping in the education of the less fortunate, they're feeding the hungry, they're clothing the naked, and there's so many who need their help.

The executive directive given to Peter by Jesus was clear and precise. Let's look at John 21:15–17 for a moment: just three statements, okay?

"Feed my lambs."

"Tend my sheep."

"Feed my sheep."

These three directives basically are what any of the churches, the "real" churches, are doing with the dough, ray, me. Jesus didn't say to Peter (Simon, son of John... love that stuff...) to, "go out there, kid and make this company something I can be proud of, put us on the corporate pages of those fortune magazines." Yet I can't help wondering why people still question the "collection" at Sunday Mass and the supposed wealth of the Church.

Most churches tell us that the first part of our income should be donated to them—10 percent is the recommended amount—and we complain that this amount is entirely too much. But the federal government taxes us, the state government taxes us and the local government taxes us; and, yes, we complain about that too, but we do give to those wealthy "businesses," disguised as our governing body, without hesitation. They tell us that they are doing wonderful things with the money: $60 hammers, $200 toilet seats, $40,000 lunches—and don't forget those vacations they need three months out of the year—all at our expense.

You know, the pastor in my church just celebrated his fifty-eighth year in the priesthood. He's got an old car, he's got a limited amount of clothing, he's got less cash in his pocket than most of the people on welfare, his watch is a Timex—one of those old $15 Timex watches—he gets two weeks' vacation each year, and lives in a house across the street from the church.

The man who started the phrase "I approve this message" was a senator in the state where I lived. I've met the man several times at functions. He arrived in an escorted caravan, police, special agents, limo—the works. He always wore an expensive suit; his hair was always groomed and colored to mask his age. I have never seen him take any cash out of his pockets, but I'll bet you he had plenty. I never saw his watch, but I'll bet it isn't a $15 Timex; and I'm sure he didn't live in a small brick house. He was appointed by the voters to serve four terms in office, so he'd done this job for twenty-four years and passed away some years ago.

Here's my point and then back to the real point…

We accept the fact that governmental officials should have status and wealth. We, in most cases, pay our taxes. We support the political officials who wastefully spend our money and never actually recognize this government for the "scam" that it truly is. When one of them is accused of an "inappropriate" sexual deed, not the guy from my state, there were many others, we say, "oh, well, they're human," and dismiss the charges as if nothing had ever happened. We are all hypocrites.

It's true that we are all human and it is also true that we all have physical needs. But why do we criticize an organization that's primary goal is to really help the needy, whose representatives are poor in earthly possessions and then, support with exuberance an organization whose motives are not righteous in the eyes of the Lord? Whose motives are self-gratifying and are truly seeking the power and authority over the people that they are supposedly representing, scamming them for every dollar on the way?

The Church is not trying to gain power over us; it is trying to give us the power over ourselves. The church is not scamming us; it is merely asking for some financial support and has never done this via any imposed mandatory extractions from our paychecks.

You know, I stopped laughing about ten minutes ago because this is sad but true. And I apologize for nothing I've said because of its truth. But if I have offended anyone, for this I am sorry, but they do say the truth hurts…

Before I started writing this morning, I wrote two checks to my parish. One at the request of our pastor who had sent a letter yesterday to all members of the parish, reminding us that it was once again time to support the church with our yearly "dues" for the maintenance of the church building.

The other was my weekly contribution. I freely give this money because I know that this is a righteous and charitable donation to a righteous and charitable organization.

Here's the truth: Pick your fights, give your money freely to those in need of your help—not only the extra dough; give your funds that you'll need as well. God cannot and will never be outdone in generosity. There is no money in heaven, and you can't take any with you: it has no value there. But it has great value here; get the most value out of your money while you still can because the time is coming for us all when we will have none at all.

So, let's talk about Peter, Simon, son of John… love that stuff! He was the first pope. Up to today, there have been 266 popes since the time of Christ; that's not important, but it's just one of those things that I know. My wife calls me a source of useless information because I know a lot of trivial facts. I just thought I'd share that information with you. But Peter was the first pope.

The word *pope* is rooted in and from the Ecclesiastical Latin language. The word was originally *Papa*, from the Greek word *Papas*, a variant of *Pappas* in the classic Latin language. Now, who said that four years of Latin in high school wouldn't pay off some-day? Just a little footnote: My Latin teacher was a nun, a poor woman in terms of earthly possessions, but a wealthy woman in terms of spiritual-ness; loved her, we called her Pickles.

We also called her *Hermana*. Spell-check says I got this spelling wrong, but I suppose that it's because I have it programmed for English, and this is a Spanish word for *Sister*. She also taught Spanish at the high school that I attended. I had four years of that too—very helpful in these times. Thank you, Sister, and I'm sure that you're enjoying eternal bliss and your true reward of the real wealth of life, and you deserve it for putting up with me for those four years...

Peter had his work cut out for him. He had to organize this group of men and not only had to give them instruction, but he had to act like the leader instead of the follower. Much resistance is what he was going to encounter, even though God Himself, Jesus, just appointed this man as His first "vicar." The term *vicar* is a term is defined as the cleric in charge of the chapel, but here it is referring to the chief pastor of Jesus' Church, the pope.

Some theologians call Peter the first bishop of Rome... wait a minute... weren't these guys in Jerusalem? How did they get into Rome anyway? We're going to get to that, but the term *bishop* refers to the leader of an area of the Church. Nowadays, they call this a diocese, also from the Latin language. (Root word *doiecesis*... spell-check doesn't work on Latin, either, it seems.) But Peter wasn't the bishop, he was the pope, the head of the whole shebang; he had the keys to heaven—and you don't entrust that job to anyone but the head guy.

So, Peter organized the remaining apostles and disciples and provided them with direction of how and what to preach about the word of God. Their job now was to get the word out about this Man Jesus, who they knew factually, was the Messiah and Son of God. It was a tough job, but somebody had to do it, and Peter was the right choice.

Peter loved Jesus more than any of the others. Peter was the one who understood the importance of this job, and he was going to make it happen, and happen it did. He sent the others in all four directions, to the north, to the south, to the east, and to the west. They went to Africa, they went to India, they went to Turkey, they went to Greece, they went to Ethiopia, and they went to Rome; but Peter's base camp was in Jerusalem, at least when the missions started. Peter eventually did go to Rome where he was put to death for his faith…

Peter was actually a businessman before he became a disciple, so he had many of the personal skill needed to organize this group of individuals. He understood what to expect from each of these apostles and the new disciples they would be recruiting. But more than that, he had the faith and the deepest love and the commitment to the Son of God. He experienced firsthand the generosity of this Man who gave His life for the entire world and asked nothing in return. He saw charity and selflessness in this man, and this was going to be his mission, the directing of this group of men in this same charitable and selflessness message and mission.

But Peter's newfound business was the business of salvation of souls. His mission was to change the beliefs of mankind and the self-gratifying nature of the species. Love for your fellow man was his mission statement, helping them in every way humanly possible to gain the ultimate reward, everlasting life in the new kingdom of the Messiah, Jesus Christ.

What a tough guy this guy must have been! Never met the man, but I'm looking forward to that moment. I'd like to shake his hand and tell him how grateful I am for the passion and devotion he had in his endeavors on this seemingly impossible mission. And if I pass this test, and do get to meet him at the gates of heaven, I will be grateful. With a little more charity and love for humanity, maybe I just will pass this test, but I can only hope and pray for the day.

But Peter, Simon, son of John (still love that stuff!)… wasn't the only man pushing this newfound religion. St. Paul, Saul, born in Cilicia, now part of Turkey, was another man that was one of the chief advocates responsible for the foundation of the Christian following.

Saul was a Jewish man, devout in his religious practices, and was actually a persecutor and proponent of killing followers of the early Christian Church. He, at first, wanted to stop this group of men from spreading the message of Jesus.

Until one day, on the way to Damascus, Saul/Paul encountered the Risen Christ. Lots of different stories on the details of the meeting, but none are as important as the single fact that Paul did meet Jesus. One of the stories states that the sight of Jesus blinded Paul and, several days later, searching his heart for the truth, Paul converted into the new way of thinking and proclaimed his allegiance to Christ — don't know, didn't ask, actually don't care.

That's not important, but what is important is the fact that Paul had a different take on the situation. Paul believed that this new religion should not be limited to believers in Jewish law, particularly the law of circumcision. Paul insisted that a man need not be circumcised in order to be a Christian, but Peter didn't dig it. There was plenty of conflict between Peter and Paul on this "sore" subject... laughing out loud. To think, Peter — the man who trusted in Jesus the most — would hold his ground on such a trivial point as this. But Peter was a stubborn man... thank God for that.

So, it took this guy, St. Paul, to really get the ball rolling. He was a visionary, and he accepted any man, woman, or child who wanted to be part of this new and real religion, no matter what their beliefs or which religious practices, if any, they had in their lives. Paul spent a great deal of his later years in this life preaching to many nations and many people, primarily the Gentiles (non-Jews).

St. Paul spent about fifteen years on the road, preaching. He moved quickly from place to place, often being mistreated and imprisoned. He traveled though northwest Asia Minor, crossing Macedonia, then Greece. He is credited with bringing Christianity to Europe. But Paul made a lot of "good citizens" upset in Jerusalem, the Jewish leaders in particular. These guys thought they'd put an end to this "revolution" when they had the Romans crucify Jesus, but good old Paul was relighting that fire; so when he returned to Jerusalem, they threw him in the clink… prison. Paul protested because he was a Roman citizen by birth and insisted that he be sent to Rome for his trial. So, they did grant him his request. Let the Romans take care of this problem, too, was the consensus.

And then to Rome, where he was imprisoned awaiting trial. Now, Peter was still in Jerusalem when this happened and feeling the heat as well. Peter and Paul had had some differences in the beginning of Paul's ministry, but by this time in history, they had worked out their differences and were on the "same page."

This is when Peter decided to visit Rome to see if he could be of any assistance to Paul. But Peter didn't have any luck with this situation. Paul was in the clink, and Peter couldn't get him out.

Nero was the king of the Roman Empire at the time, and Nero didn't like this new religion at all. This new religion was in direct conflict of the pagan religion and paganism was the accepted religion of the region. This pagan religion placed Nero as a god, and he undoubtedly thought, *Who are these people, these so-called Christians, who brought this message into my world?* Nero was not a happy camper, so he decided to let Paul rot in prison. And so, he did. Paul died in Rome around the year 60 in a Roman prison, but not before he fulfilled his mission on this Earth.

Peter was in town at the time of Paul's death and found that Paul had done a wonderful job converting many of the Roman citizens into the new religion. But Nero was still not happy.

Peter continued the work Paul had started because this seemed to be a somewhat better place to spread the word and movement. Peter was somewhat successful in Jerusalem but had much better results in this land of paganism. These people were starving for the truth. They were the common "folks" and didn't accept the pagan religion because that particular religion did not treat all men equally. That religion was based on social status. The higher you were on the ladder in society, the more godlike you were on the religious totem pole. Sounds like corporate America, doesn't it? Yes, the newest religion in America: wealth. The love for the Almighty dollar, that's paganism at its best.

But anyway, Peter had about three good years in Rome until one day, Rome burned to the ground… remember this visual, Nero with the fiddle? I know this is not accurate, but I do know that Rome burned down for sure, according to historical records. Nero then falsely accused the Christian movement of setting the blaze. I suppose because Peter was the head guy, the pope, the bishop of Rome, Nero wanted his butt. How dare this guy burn my house and my town to the ground!

I can actually hear him saying it now: *Portare il marsupio per me, io sono dio… mi obbediscono.* The Italian to English translation: "Bring the bum to me, I'm god… obey me." And so, the Roman troops went and tracked down Peter and brought him to Nero.

Nero wasn't as compassionate as Pilate; he didn't try to persuade the crowd to let this man go free; he immediately sentenced him to death by way of the cross. Peter accepted this willingly, but requested he be crucified upside down, because he did not consider himself worthy enough to be crucified in the same manner as Jesus. Nero didn't care; he wanted this guy dead, and crucifixion upside down was better. The whole idea behind being crucified was the person not only would suffer great pain and agony, but they ultimately would suffocate from lack of oxygen due to the collapsing of the lungs from of the weight of the body. Upside down was better, it was faster. So Nero granted Peter's request wantonly.

It's a wonder this new religion even survived. Peter and Paul were the two main advocates of this movement. Peter, Simon, son of John, is responsible for some of what we can read in the New Testament. However, Paul is responsible for a large portion of the New Testament writings — with the exception of the Gospels, Acts, Hebrews, Jude, Peter 1 and 2, and Revelation, which are credited to other authors. Luke wrote the Gospel of Luke, Acts, and Hebrews… well, *maybe* Hebrews; no one is positively sure. Judas, son of James (or his other name, Thaddeus), wrote Jude. Peter wrote Peter 1 and 2; and Revelation was written by John, one of the original twelve Apostles. The rest of the New Testament writings are correspondence from Paul to groups of people that were being converted to the faith.

And what about the other original apostles?

Well, most of them were martyrs for the faith, with the exception of John and Judas. We already know Judas Iscariot hanged himself. Andrew, James, Philip, Bartholomew, Thomas, Matthew, James, son of Alphaeus, Thaddeus (Judas), son of James, and Simon: All were martyrs, killed in various fashions. These men were all martyred in foreign lands, with the exception of James, son of Alphaeus. He was stoned and bludgeoned to death in Jerusalem when he was about ninety years old. John, on the other hand, died of old age... natural causes. He died on the Isle of Patmos where he received the "Revelation of Jesus Christ," the last book of the Bible.

Revelation is the final chapter of the Bible; most of the content is happening here and now, in the twenty-first century. No, I'm not one of those guys with the sandwich sign on the street corners, shouting, "Repent, the last days are upon us." Only God the Father knows that date, and I truly don't want to ask for the information, because I won't ask for anything that might upset our wonderful and intimate relationship.

This information is for Him alone to know, and that's exactly how it should be. This is God's house; His plan and God alone will decide when it's coming to finality. Same with this book: God will decide when it's complete, not me. I'll keep writing until I no longer am driven to do so. And God will decide when this is over, which I believe will be very shortly, but for right now, it's not.

I believe it's important to show you the some of the history of this Church's development with God's help and His guidance, I... we will show you some of the important dates in the Christian Church so that you can see for yourselves how the Christian religion became the true religion of the only God Almighty... God the Father, God the Son and God the Holy Spirit.

I'm also going show you how this Christian faith has adopted and developed in a multitude of denominations based on the disregard of the rules as given. Again, man wants it his way and not God's way. But before I do, I'll pray...

It would be appreciated if you would help me out a little bit as well, pray with me now:

Dear Lord, guide us, your meek and loving servants. We believe that every step and every breath we take is a gift of your loving and merciful kindness. We believe that if we seek, we shall find, if we ask it will be answered, and if we knock, the door will be opened. Please, Lord, show us the way. Thank you, Lord. Thank you, Jesus. Thank you, Holy Spirit, together in one, the Most Holy and Blessed Trinity. Amen.

Chapter 20
The First Thousand Years...

It seems like we're getting ready to end this book, but before we do, we need visit some important dates in the history of Christianity. We may also need to answer some of the questions that to this point are unanswered and show you how this Church of Christ has changed, agreed?

Let's start with this question: When did Saturday, the Sabbath day, become Sunday?

In the times of the foundation of the early Christian Church, both days were observed and recognized by the early Christians as days of worship. Saturday was the traditional Sabbath in accordance traditional law but this new religion selected Sunday as its day of observation. There were two reasons for this; Jesus rose from the dead on the first day of the week, Sunday was the first, but then...

Along came the Romans... well, they were there, but until this point in time they didn't get involved in the religious practices of the Jews. They were pagans and their "top god" was Caesar, and of course, all the "little" gods of importance within the chain of command. That's an interesting religion, sorry to see it seemed to survive in today's religious as well as corporate community, but anyway, the Romans decided to destroy the Jewish temple.

I have to let you in on a little thing that just happened. I was just reading the above paragraph and realized that this is not what I thought I was typing. I'm actually *sure* that this is not what I was typing, but it's there, so let's go see what did happen in the city of Jerusalem and the temple. I guess that where God wants us to go, and who am I to argue with Him?

The war was on: Jews versus the Romans. The Jews had the home-field advantage and were fighting a good fight. They were tired of being under the control of the Roman Empire and had enough. This war went on for years and in September of the year 70 AD, Titus, another of those little Roman "gods" ordered the burning and destruction of the temple. Incidentally, Jesus told them that this was going to happen. "One stone will not be left standing," and so it happened.

The temple was destroyed, leaving this community without a place to worship. This guy, little god Titus, was very proud of what he had done. He actually brought remnants from the temple back to Rome as sort of a "medal" of his victory over these poor, beaten, and humiliated Jewish people. Now, the details of this event are well documented in the history books, and if you want to read more on the subject, feel free to look it up, but this is when the Sabbath and Sunday worship made its first distinct separation; this was the second reason.

There was no temple left for this community to worship at, and this led to the "in home" services. The early-day Masses started around this time.

Those that observed Jesus-Judaism are the people who first started this practice. Hey, you can thank them for the two-day weekends that eventually resulted from this new rite. The typical workweek in those times started on Sundays because it was and still is the first day of the week. The Jesus-Judaism people believed that there was just cause to Honor both God and His Son Jesus; they were correct. They not only observed the traditions of Sabbath but also designed and instituted the primitive Mass.

The original Mass was nothing more than a simple prayer service that was typically done just prior to and during supper… some call it dinner… it depends where you're from, but it's the main meal of the day. These observers of the Jesus-Judaism movement would read some of the stories in circulation; the earliest writings of the New Testament, not always the most accurate, but nonetheless, the writings that were available and at hand.

Then they recreated to the best of their knowledge the original "Blessing of Bread and Wine." But this was not an observed day of rest as it is today. And the blessing of the bread and wine was in a way much more sacrificial than it is today. The original observers of the sacrifice of the mass were recreating the Lord's instructions and truly believed that the ritual they were observing was a direct mandate from Jesus. Explanation...

Today, we go to Sunday service because of many reasons. Some actually are there for the purest of reasons, and that is to participate in the celebration of the Mass, which is the right reason. Others might be there for an infinite number of reasons: obligation, pressure from outside influences, a social event, fear, this one is common in older folks, and this list goes on and on. But the real reason is the reenactment of Holy Thursday night so we can remember and acknowledge the sacrifice Jesus made, which opened the gates to heaven for all by giving His mortal life on that Friday afternoon, which in fact was the first Mass.

The Eucharist is the focal point of the celebration. The Eucharist, along with the wine, is — and this is where it's gets difficult for most — the Body and Blood of Jesus Christ. The instruction, "Do this in memory of me," is also very significant.

Jesus gave the supreme sacrifice of His human form and human life to pay for our sins; He did this without questioning the will of His Father. When we receive this Blessed and Consecrated Host, we are professing to that belief. We are acknowledging that Jesus is our Savior and He is *present* in the Consecrated Host. His presence then becomes part of our being, and we are, for those few moments after the reception of this Blessed and Consecrated Host, united to God in all forms of His Trinity through Jesus Christ, our Savior. But time has taken away the effectiveness of this sacrifice for most of the participants today. Again, there are many reasons that people approach the altar to receive this holy and sacred sacrament; but without sounding too judgmental, too many approach the altar for the wrong reasons, which, in most cases, mirror the reason they went to Mass in the first place.

The original participants of this primitive form of worship did believe in this ritual as the ritual prescribed by Jesus to fulfill their own personal connection will the Son of God. Each one of them was there for the purest of reasons, and there were few if any outside influences that were responsible for their participation other than faith in this Man Jesus and their salvation.

Also, bear in mind that this movement was not the most popular movement of the times. People were being executed, thrown to the lions, and persecuted for the faith they were proclaiming. That's why it was done, sort of in the shadows and in the home. Only the saints of those times didn't hide their faith and beliefs and proclaimed their acknowledgement of this new religion in public. God bless them all, and He has rewarded them with immortality in the spirit.

And that's the prize for passing the test...

Let me just tell you one more thing about these early Christians and why I have the admiration I do for them. Imagine if you were to go to the Sunday service of your choice. I am Catholic by birth and actually by choice, and I am not opposed to other variations and denominations of this religious group. I know how they were developed, and I will share that with you shortly; but for right now, let's just imagine that when you arrived at the Church, there were men awaiting you who wanted nothing more than to inflict harm on your person. How many of you would actually go to service? How many? Do you think if this were the case, this procession of faith would pass the litmus test? Do you think it would survive? How long would it take for this to fade away?

And that was the case back then: People were being executed by various means for their faith. The burning of the temple was retaliation by the Romans because they thought that the early Christians had burned Rome several years prior, and they wanted revenge for this act of insubordination against their god, Nero.

But that's just the start of this story. Who were these people? Everything was going fine, and the Romans felt good about their control over these people, but now these rebels were muddying the waters with this new religion—and that was unacceptable. But needless to say, some of these early Christians were unshakable and resolute in their beliefs and would not give up their faith, no matter what the consequences, even death. And for that, I truly admire them.

This went on for centuries, the persecution. Here's a thought: It's still going on now. Not to the same degree as then, but it's similar in many ways.

That said, let's look at some other important dates in history of the Christian Church:

In 325 AD, the First Ecumenical Council meeting of Nicaea.

This place in history is highly significant and is the first time that all the leaders of this new religion are gathering for a conference. There's a total of 318 men attending this Council and their objective is clear. They want to establish doctrine for the observance of two important facets of the new religious practice.

First and foremost was the issue of the observance of the Easter Holiday. Here's a big word: *Quartodecimanism*. Latin in origin, it means "fourteenth" as it refers to the start of the Pass-over and its timing. But at this first Council, some discrepancy still remained within the community regarding the validity of this practice.

In fact, years from this time in history, the Catholic religion will ultimately divide because of this issue. They will become the Roman Catholics and the Greek Orthodox Catholics. The Greek Orthodox will adopt this practice and affix it permanently to their doctrine and religious observational calendar. But not yet...

Today, these men are going to hash out this dispute and come to a conclusion that will temporally satisfy the group, at least for the next hundred years or so. Well, who am I kidding? One side of the Council felt like they had lost and were not satisfied with the results. They would continue to dispute those results until their ultimate separation, and that's the truth. But today they seemingly, in the presence of their peers, will agree on the date being set.

It will be a Sunday, and it will be the first Sunday of the traditional Passover feast. It will be this Sunday because that's exactly when the Scripture of the New Testament — which, incidentally, is in the formation stages at this time in history — claims that this event happened. This is a milestone in the actual adaptation of Sundays becoming the formal and required day of service and celebration of the Mass.

That was the other issue they were there to work out, the format of an actual ceremony and prayers to be included in the Mass.

This Council was under the directive of Emperor Constantine. He became emperor in 324, the year before, and this Council was an effort to unite all the different Christian communities of the Empire of Rome. These territories included the region of Jerusalem, which was still under Roman control. This was the first time in history that a Christian emperor had ascended to the throne, and it seemed like the best time for this Council to resolve these ongoing disputes. So, Constantine convened the Council; I guess I should have told you that earlier, a little oversight.

Well, now that I'm thinking about this emperor, I might as well continue telling you some of the highlights of his life and how they affected this religion. His recognized name is Constantine the Great. He was born in the late third century and led many troops in his effort to gain the throne of Rome. His father was Caesar Constantine, and he was an emperor of the Roman Empire. But there were many challenges from others in his family tree for the seat of his father: nephews, cousins, and the sort. But Constantine the Great fought for many a year to conquer the territories and united all of them, back into one kingdom of Rome. He ultimately claimed his rightful throne but only after a vision from God to use the Cross of Christ as his symbol, which he carried into battle.

Prior to this vision from God, he was not in the least interested in the Christian faith, but because these symbols lead him to victory, he became a believer in this faith.

Constantine was now a Christian. So much so, that once he was the emperor of this territory that had dominion over Jerusalem. He uncovered the site of the crucifixion, burial, and resurrection of Jesus in Jerusalem and built the Church of the Holy Sepulcher. As a result of his policies, legislation, and the preference for the Christian community, he transformed a marginal pagan territory into a flourishing Christian magnet for pilgrims from the whole Roman Empire. He did all this before his death in 337 AD. He left behind three sons by the names of Constantius, Constantine (Jr.), and Constans.

Sorry, I need to get back to the Nicene Council and its purpose, but that was an important bit of history related to the Christian Church.

Next on the agenda was the liturgy of the Mass: the when, how, why, who, and order of observance of this Eucharistic Celebration, establishing some consistency in the ceremony. This would be a breakthrough for the religion, and these men under the guidance of their `pope were going to make changes to these mish-mash rituals and the date of observance. Now, with the Easter date established, it became an easy transition to proclaim Sundays as the official day of observance, but the question of how still existed—and let's not forget the who and the why.

The other major issue at this time in history was the total belief in the Trinity of God, if you can imagine that. Not all the men involved in this Council were totally convinced in the validity of the Holy Spirit and His connection to this one godhead.

That is quite evident in the first draft of the Nicene Creed, which came from this Council. For all those out there who go to a Catholic Mass, this is the prayer that the congregation proclaims directly after the homily. The prayer we recite today, which was recently changed in 2012, is similar to the prayer written at this Council; however, without writing the whole prayer, I'll just give you the difference in what we are proclaiming now as opposed to what was written in the original draft.

The original version did not give credit to the Holy Ghost in the first draft of the Nicene Creed, a mere mention, not the full paragraph we recite in today's version: "I believe in the Holy Spirit, the Lord and giver of life, who proceeds from the Father and together with the Son is worshipped and glorified... " No, no... that wasn't in it.

From a factual standpoint, this Council actually wasn't totally convinced of the divinity of Jesus Christ either. But the first draft of this Nicene Creed did give Jesus second seat in the House of God, but many of the attendants of the Council weren't totally convinced of that fact either.

The pope at that time, Pope Sylvester I, also didn't have what is called infallibility of doctrine at this time in history either, so he couldn't set the definitive and accepted Creed, and the day of worship as doctrine or the standards for this religion.

The issue of the pope's infallibility was not going to be granted for some time yet. We'll get to that, but at this Council, the only resolution that actually was determined was the issues of the Easter Holiday and the original draft of the Nicene Creed...

Lastly at this Council, the date of observance of Mass was to be Sundays. This was because of the establishment of the Easter Holiday being on Sunday; however, Sunday still wasn't totally accepted by all who were in attendance of this Council.

In 364 AD, at the Church Council of Ladicea, that was when Sunday became the official day of liturgical worship and the celebration of the Mass. Let me quote the actual defining statement for you: "Christians shall not Judaize and be idle on Saturday, but shall work on that day."

And this is the why: This Christian community didn't want to be associated and referred to as a Jesus-Judaism. They wanted to be a stand-alone religion because that question of the divinity of Jesus still existed, and now the ball would start to roll...

This would no longer be a question. Jesus was the Son of God, and together with the Holy Ghost, they made up the Trinity of the Almighty God — their God, our God.

But not officially until 381 AD...

Constantinople, formerly the Greek town of Byzantium, was conquered by none other than Constantine the Great before he died.

This Council is where the religion made its greatest strides and established once and for all the Trinity of God. They refined the Nicene Creed to a very similar version of the one we use today and proclaimed the three persons of God as God in one person, and this is the why. But what about the who and the how?

Who was going to be the person who would be the celebrant of this "Mass," and how would they do it? They couldn't let just anyone be responsible for the consecration of the Host, the body of Christ. Not just anyone could bless the wine and change it into the blood of Christ. Oh no, this person had to be truly learned and understand this miracle of the transformation of the bread and wine into the Body and Blood of Christ.

Houston, we have a problem... My wife says that a lot. I think it's funny, so I thought I'd say it, but the truth is that there was a still a problem with the order of prayers of the Mass, and how these prayers would lead to the consecration, so let's see how that was resolved and how long it actually took.

By 387 AD, Augustine of Hippo is converted to Christianity and writes "The Confessions" and "City of God." These works will become the bedrock throughout the Middle Ages and influence the decisions on many of the forthcoming doctrines of the Christian Church. Augustine is a saint, and rightfully so. Without his writings, the direction of the Church would not have been solidified. The "books" are actually still available, and I advise you to read them if you get a chance.

In 405 AD, the "Vulgate" version of the Bible is completed and becomes the standard for the next eleven hundred or so years — 1,113 to be precise. It was written in Latin and still contained many "books" that will be eventually discarded from the next version of the text. However, this was the first Christian version accepted by the pope, bishops, and other leaders of this newly founded faith. A starting point for the group, and a good one, finally.

By 432 AD, good old St. Patty — who was also responsible for that green beer, thank you, St. Patty — was sent to Ireland as a missionary to convert the Irish people to Christianity. Here's another little fact that's rolling around in my brain, that useless information...

St. Patrick was actually taken there as a teenager and was a slave. He was chosen for his mission because of this fact. Pope Celestine I determined, because of Patrick's familiarity with the countryside and the cruelness of the people in that land, that he would be the perfect candidate for the job. Given authority now by the pope, and freedom, he took on the mission, and well, as they say, "the rest is history."

In 451 AD, we had the Council of Chalcedon. This is a breakthrough for the doctrine and the basic belief of the religion. To this point in time, many were still not convinced that Jesus Christ was truly God and man, and that an existence such as this could never be the case for any individual. I guess we should talk about this for a moment. By this time, four hundred years had passed since the death of Jesus the Man.

That was a long time, and the road had been very rocky for this religious community. There was uncertainty on many points and the influences of mankind's interpretation of the facts were sketchy to say the least. Four hundred years of trying to convince the recruits to this faith that there were three persons in this single God was difficult... no, almost impossible, as it seems today. But this Council set in stone and confirmed the orthodox teachings that Jesus was truly God and Man in one person.

With this now established as solid doctrine and law, the religion only needed to solidify the existence of the third person, the Holy Ghost.

Now, even though the Council of Constantinople seemingly made its greatest strides in this area by including the Holy Spirit in the Nicene Creed, the people still didn't fully believe in this to be a fact. Too much influence from the "mother" of this Church, the Jewish doctrine and too much time had passed since the physical death of Jesus. But with this new confirmation in place, the Holy Ghost was now a viable and real candidate for His position in the Trinity, and so it was.

Big... no, a *huge* day in the Christian Church, the confirmation that these teachings were fact. Now that they were all seemingly united in this one belief and one Church, it should have been a walk in the park, but it wasn't. This was a crossroads. From this point on, the religion now began taking turns in many directions of distinct and separate divisions of the dominations of this Church.

These sects still accepted this Council's confirmation of the facts of the Trinity, but dates of events, laws concerning the flesh, and acceptance of authority were going to play a big role over the next thousand years and then some, resulting in a split of this now-united Church into the 2600 or so different and distinct variations of Christianity. So, yeah, *big* day.

So, at this point in time, and for a few years afterward, the Christian Church was what we today call the Catholic Church. The pope was the leader; the bishops were in charge of certain geographic areas, and the priests handled the day-to-day tasks of the religious needs of their communities.

A good arrangement and accepted by all of the members of the faith, until... well, until certain individuals landed a proverbial "fly in the ointment." They disagreed with the pope, and with the rules governing the system.

I guess no one is always fully convinced totally in unity of his or her community; humanity is needy in the fulfillment of its own ends. But, for the moment, this Church is united as one. But still the question exists; can man serve God and not model the Christ? Can they have ties to the flesh?

In 529 AD, St. Benedict of Nursia establishes his Monastic Order. The "Benedictine Rule" governing this group of recluses becomes extremely influential in the Western region of Rome. This order established how one should conduct oneself as a model of Christ. Poverty, dedication to prayer and assisting other individuals in finding the way into a life of attempted sinlessness.

Many divisions and branches of the faith were seeded from this monastic order. Friars, monks, nuns, and the like are all direct results of this man's establishment of this first monastic order. Go get 'em, St. Benedict, and so he did.

By 567 AD, the Second Council of Tours establishes the "twelve days" of Christmas. Christmas at this point had no distinct date of observance. There were conflicting points of view on the exact date of Jesus was actually born. They ranged from dates in August through April. The Council adopted December 25, which was the date that Titus (remember him?) established. He burned the temple in Jerusalem, but when he came back to Rome, he brought census records indicating that as Jesus' date of birth. This date, ironically, was the date that the Romans celebrated as the feast of the Sun God Mithra, the date that Hippolytus of Rome initiated in the second century, a date that the Christians were always trying to establish as the date of observance of critical events in their calendar; Christmas is officially the twenty-fifth of December.

In 590 AD, Gregory the First, known as "Gregory the Great," becomes pope. This man once and for all established the order in which Mass is conducted: prayers, sequence, and language to be used—Latin. This doctrine will hold firm until the language change in the mid-1960s. However, the prayers and the sequence remain solid as a rock and observed in that sequence even today with the except for a few little "housekeeping" observances.

As it turns out, "Great" was a very accurate description of this man.

His leadership significantly advanced the direction in which the papacy was headed. He is responsible for clarifying the pope's position within this Church, the responsibility of leadership to be specific, clarifying the fact that Jesus appointed Peter as the first leader and the meaning of succeeding Peter in carrying out the mission of Jesus.

In the beginning, and for several hundred years... well, a little over 550... there was turmoil; everyone wanted to be in charge of the "show," but Gregory took the bull by the horns and set this straight: The pope was in charge and has been ever since, at least in the Catholic faith.

He also had an enormous influence on the recruitment of many regions in Europe. However, not all were in agreement with this pope's rules and doctrine governing the Church; hence, the Roman Church continued to criticize—and various groups still would not fully comply with—this pope's orders.

Yet, at this point in time, they were still united as one Church, but the undertones and scuttlebutt of the religious communities were moving in the direction of separation. Man is sinful… it's the pride and vanity issue again.

I suppose they didn't like having one leader who set the rules for all the members of the community. I suppose that these people still wanted the freedom of governing their formats and observational dates within their religious calendar. Simply stated, they were rebellious and didn't want to be told how, or when, to worship God.

Sounds very similar to the reason that Lucifer rebelled in the first place against God and started the whole mess, now, doesn't it? Satan had a lot to do with the turmoil within that community, just like he does today.

Gregory the "Great" also sent Roman monks to many regions in Europe to solidify this newly proclaimed unity of the Catholic Church. Gregory was bound and determined to accomplish this unification, and actually to a point did succeed; the Catholic faith would live on, but historically speaking, in a few hundred more years or so, there would be many variations of this now united Church, and…

In 665 AD, the English Christian Church held the Synod of Whitby… yes, once again… to bring this community back under the one authority of the Roman Catholic Church. And, of course, the biggest sticking points again were the dates of observance of calendar events in the Christian Church. But time would change these little squabbles and would bring on bigger issues of doctrine and law. But, for the time being, these were small matters and, in fact were ultimately resolved to the satisfaction of most of the present-day Christian churches, except for a small percentage. The others are actually in agreement of the dates in their calendar of events, so today there are two different accepted dates for the major events.

But not at this time in history. There was still controversy and uncertainty with regard to the dates of observance. Seems like an insignificant point, but this matter is one of the points that seeded the separation of the Christian churches.

That little voice in my head is telling me this: The dates aren't important, the events are… the birth, the instructions and teachings, the death, the resurrection, and the ascension: These are significant and critical to the understanding of this blessed and sanctioned presence, of this Most Holy Man, the man who would earn favor in God's Kingdom and earn the title of Son of God. The man whose obedience to the Lord God Almighty would or could never be in question, but mankind still can't grasp this concept because of his sinful nature—more specifically, his vanity and pride. That's what was wrong then, is still wrong to this point in time, and will be wrong until the end of this measurement of existence in this universal plane. Solely because Satan is still present here and influencing man's soul via his suggestive and enticing path of disobedience. Without our total commitment to this truth, we are susceptible to the ways of this physical plane. This causes us all to choose the "easy" way and to follow, whole-heartedly, after our own ends and means.

This is most displeasing to the Lord God Almighty, and we need to realize that fact. It's all well and good that we're seeing some of the history of the development of this human race and the religion of Christianity; however, we really need to focus on what is beyond this plane of existence and the ultimate outcome of our presence here. We need to focus on obedience to God… couldn't stop that… actually, I just read it and I'm glad I didn't.

In 732 AD, the Battle of Tours… come on, all you history buffs out there, you must know about this one. The Moslems and the French… well, I'll give the rest of you some of the facts. This is called the Muslim Invasion of Europe. The Muslims wanted nothing more than to stop Christianity in its tracks. They, under the leadership of one man, Abd-ar Rahman stormed Europe; he was dead set and determined to accomplish this task. Abd-ar Rahman led some four hundred thousand troops and basically pillaged Europe, killing anyone who got in their way, but this dude was mostly concerned with the killing of Christians.

Well, this was soon to change. When the Muslims arrived at Tours, France, they ran into a man by the name of Charles Martel. Charles employed a technique known as the "phalanx" style of combat: foot soldiers with swords, shields, axes, javelins, and daggers. And given their familiarity with the terrain, Martel's team had the home-field advantage and was extremely successful in defending the area from the attempted invasion.

Now, some historians say that this battle only took two days, while others claim it took seven days; that's not important. What is important is that because of this technique used by the French, they captured and killed Abd-ar Rahman, ending the Muslims' advances into Europe. Upon hearing of the death of their leader, the troops quietly retreated back into Russia without any further incident... at least, for now.

This was during the medieval times in history and more of this conflict was in the picture for the Christians, the "holy war." I'm not sure that there is such a thing, but that's what they called it. Just another one of mankind's faults... the want for power. If you can't convince them, conquer them: That was the tone then. Well, now, too. It's pitiful, the way we think, don't you agree? What happened to loving your neighbor? Did that rule go out the window? Anyway...

In 800 AD, Pope Leo III crowned Charlemagne emperor on Christmas Day, December 25. Charlemagne, also known as "Charles the Great," got his reputation from conquering Europe. It was a thirty-year campaign, and by the time it was all over, he was the undisputed champ— er, *ruler*, of Western Europe. What spurred this on was the inheritance of the kingdom of the Franks, France. In 768, he and his brother Carloman received joint ownership via this inheritance. But in 771, Carloman died and left the kingdom as a sole property to his brother, Charlemagne.

There was a lot of turmoil at this time, and Charlemagne launched this campaign to bring order back to his native land, but power overcame him and he was no longer happy with being king of this small territory; he wanted more. He wanted Switzerland, Belgium, the Netherlands, half of today's Italy, Germany, and parts of Austria and Spain, and he got them all.

Now, Pope Leo III wanted this territory, as well, but not for ownership, for conversion of the land into total Christianity, so the plan was to appoint him as king in St. Peter's Basilica on Christmas day.

Yep, it happened. The pope, on Christmas day in the year 800, crowned Charlemagne while he knelt in prayer. Charlemagne was actually surprised and is said to have stated that he wouldn't have come into the Church that day if he had known the pope's plan.

But now that the pope had done this, Charlemagne would be a cooperative soul. He learned to read Latin and some Greek and did his best to become a good Christian. And with his papal blessing, he actually did improve the standards of the people under his reign. He set up their original money standards and encouraged free commerce and trade. He also worked very diligently on the improvement of education and spread of Christianity. The pope had succeeded in his plan.

In 863 AD, Cyril and Methodius, two brothers from Greece became evangelists and moved to convert the Serbs. Cyril developed the Cyrillic alphabet, which still remains the basis for the Slavonic used in the liturgy of the Russian Church. These brothers taught the fundamental of the Eastern Orthodox Church to the Serbs, which in a few years—125 to be exact—would be accepted as the standards of the Russian people; this happened in 988 AD.

When Vladimir, Prince of Kiev, fully examined the regions of Russia and declared Orthodoxy as the accepted religious practice and unified the Russian people; this caused major trouble for the once-totally united Catholic Church. So, in …

Chapter 21

The Second Thousand Years...

1054 AD, it really hit the fan...

This conflict was brewing for many centuries, and it's almost hard to believe, but the major conflicts were about the dates of event observances, dating back to the beginning of the Jesus-Judaism conflicts. This wasn't the only conflict, but it certainly was one of the major troubles. Of course, these people were also and still are not convinced that the pope should be setting doctrine and law for their religious sect.

But this year was the first distinct separation of the Christian Church, the icebreaker, so to speak. From this point on, all bets were off. We're going to get to some of the others, but those break-aways aren't going to happen for some time.

However, this was the turning point for Christianity. And because of this, countless variations of this faith would ultimately emerge, all based on the disagreement with law, the disagreement with doctrine and the disagreement with leadership.

All of which were going to be seeded by the humanity within us; the need to satisfy our own needs of... well, the flesh, in this physical plane.

Now don't get me wrong: Jesus Christ will judge all men. Only He knows their hearts and souls, only He knows if their intentions are righteous, and only He will determine whether these religious variations of the Christian churches observed His teachings and followed His instructions correctly.

I, on the other hand, choose to follow the practices of the Roman Catholic denomination, and hope that I do my best to model the Lord Jesus Christ... because it doesn't matter, and this I am sure of, the particular denomination is the most insignificant piece of this puzzle. The modeling of the man is what it's all about! He is the Way and the Truth. Following His example will get us back to the Father.

This division of the churches occurred on July 6, 1054. Not only were the dates of observing important events a critical factor, but there were other issues. One issue, for example, was the issue of marriage of the clergy.

The year prior, 1053, Michael Cerularius, patriarch of Constantinople, circulated a treatise criticizing the practice of marriage in the Western Church. Pope Leo was the pope at the time, and he forbade the clergy to marry.

Note: This marriage issue is and has always been an issue with the Catholic faith. Sometimes you have it, sometime you don't. It must be apparent that I am not 100 percent convinced in the current position that the Catholics maintain in this century, but, needless to say, that's not my call. Even though I might disagree with this position, it doesn't weaken my faith or encourage me to choose another denomination because of this current requirement of clerical abstinence.

Another issue was the bread type to be used for the Eucharist. Cerularius disagreed with the choice... unleavened, a very small point, but one that was in question.

And, of course, there was the issue of the word "Filoque" used in the Nicene Creed. The word means "proceeds," the Creed states that the Holy Spirit proceeds from the Father and the Son. Cerularius disagreed with the use of this word.

Well, to make a long story short, Leo died before this separation of the churches. But before he died, he sent Cardinal Humbert to "work out" these issues with Cerularius. While negotiating the terms, Humbert, an unyielding man, was extremely rude to Cerularius, rude to the point that Cerularius refused to continue the negotiations. So, Humbert marched into the church and had a bull placed on the altar, excommunicating Cerularius once and for all.

The church was the Church of St. Sophia. This act of excommunication wasn't as ceremonious as one would expect from the Catholic religion. Humbert just marched into the church and did the excommunication without preparation. Afterward, Humbert made a "grand exit," shaking the dust off his feet and calling to God for Judgment on July 6, 1054.

The bull was a symbol of condemnation and there was no chance of reconciliation between the two viewpoints. Not to be outdone by the cardinal, Cerularius declared the separation of the Eastern and Western Orthodox churches and founded this new branch of Christianity — the first of many to come — on July 6, 1054.

In 1093 AD, Anselm was instated and proclaimed the archbishop of Canterbury. This man was a devoted monk and observed all the restrictions of celibacy, poverty, and holiness. He was a brilliant theologian and had written on the subject of "Why Did God become Man?" Entitled *Cur Deus Homo*, this writing explored the atonement for sin and is still available for your reading pleasure; read it if you get the opportunity.

By 1095 AD, the Crusades… this is one of my favorite times in the history of mankind. Men were men, and these men fought for the unification of the Church, killing one another in the name of God, because "God willed it." Oh, what a great time in the history of mankind!

If you haven't noticed, that was sarcasm. The Crusades were one of the worst times in the history of the Church. The origin of the Crusades is directly traceable to the political and moral conditions of Western Christendom in the era.

Europe was divided into a large number of states or, more accurately, territories, and those territories were absorbed in tedious and pitiful disputes. The emperor supposedly was the temporal head of the Christian communities in those territories; however, he was wasting his strength in the quarrel related to Investitures.

Now popes of this period, starting with Leo IX and Gregory VII, were also being threatened with the loss of power over the Christian community.

In particular, the Byzantine Empire and the Mohammedan tribes were developing contradictory and unacceptable policies and traditions. The Eastern Church had already split from the group of original Christian Church, and the threat of more separation from the "Christian church" was in the wind.

Pope Urban II, being the influential pope that he was, decided and convinced the people to take up arms and fight to preserve the faith, the Church. He wanted to "capture" the Holy Land and once and for all convert these people into Christianity.

His other objective was to secure these other territories that were causing this uproar in this Church. Now, of course, the emperors of the period had close ties with the popes and what the pope said was law, in their eyes. So naturally, when the pope said he wanted this "war," the people were willing to go to war; and because the emperors throughout this period willingly followed the pope's directive, there was no argument. Hence the Holy War, which proved to be a disaster over the next several hundred years; of course, it should have been because...

THERE IS NO SUCH THING AS A HOLY WAR! The only Holy War ever fought was in heaven, by the followers of Lucifer and the righteous angelic warriors. God and only God can sanction and declare a Holy War; that was the one.

In 1115 AD, St. Bernard founds the monastery at Clairvaux. St. Bernard was given the title of "Doctor of the Church" because of his tireless endeavors to reunite the Church. The monastery he established would become a major center for spiritual and political influence throughout the region. His writings and philosophies on the nature of the Catholic faith are the reason he earned this tremendous honor and title of the "doctor." He wanted nothing more than to heal this now-cancerous epidemic spreading through the Church due to the lack of spirituality and the political motivations of the leaders of this group. Stemming from this...

By 1149 AD, the Universities of Paris and Oxford are founded. Those universities become the incubators for reformation and became the precursors for the modern education systems and patterns.

In 1173 AD, Peter from Waldes, eventually named Peter Waldo, founded the Waldensians, another division of the Church. This is a reform movement emphasizing poverty, preaching, and the Bible. He and his followers were condemned for their beliefs and were persecuted then and until this day.

There are two reasons for this persecution, and they are in direct conflict with the beliefs of the Catholic Church.

First reason is the denial of the existence of purgatory. This group laid claim that there was and is no such place of existence in the spiritual "world." They believe that, upon death, an individual is immediately judged and sent to either heaven or hell.

The second reason for the persecution and ultimate split of faith is the more important of the two disagreements. This group absolutely believes that "Indulgences" are not acceptable to God.

Indulgences are the prayers we offer for the remission of "temporal punishment" for any sin. Now, these two actually go hand in hand. Let me explain...

Temporal punishment is the time we are going to spend in purgatory after the completion of the "test." If we are fortunate enough to pass the test, there will be a period of "payment" for our offenses to God. We make literally millions upon millions of mistakes on the way. These mistakes—even though they may have been forgiven—must be reconciled in the eyes of God.

That is then "our" temporal punishment, our time to serve begins. But, not to fear: If you get this far, you're in as soon as you pay your debt to God for the sinful ways of your life.

Another one of the major stumbling blocks for this Waldensian approach was their belief that indulgences offered for the dead were of no value whatsoever. Let me, again, clue you in...

We are sinners—each and every one of us. Our goal should be nothing more than to limit our offenses to God. No one in this plane can live a sinless life because of the influence of Satan. Satan is doing his best to win this game he has started. He wants our souls, and he wants nothing more than for us to have the same "death" that he is ultimately going to experience.

On the other hand, God wants nothing more than for us to make our way through this test and get back into His Home… our Home, heaven. In order for us to accomplish this task, we must pay to the Lord what is due to the Lord, but the Lord is not asking the impossible. Simply stated, He's asking for us to show Him "some love." This love is the prayers we offer to Him, acknowledging our weaknesses and offensive ways. This love can be offered for ourselves as well as our "neighbors." Remember that "do unto others" deal… well, indulgences are in the mix.

We cannot only offer prayers—indulgences—for ourselves, but others as well. Naturally, the prayers that one offers for another, without consideration of one's own personal benefit, are the truest act of kindness we can display, provided they are genuine, and without expectation of reward.

Indulgences can be offered to God every minute of every day. From the moment we awaken in the morning, until the moment we lay our heads on the pillow, we can offer everything we do to God. We can offer our work, we can offer our play, and we can offer our prayers, as well.

There are several definitions of the word *indulgences*, but for our purpose, it would have to be "recognition of sin and recompense for our involvement in this practice that all of us perform daily."

That said, I must object to this religious sect. Live and let live, I suppose, but they are wrong on this point. Let's move on.

In 1206 AD, St. Francis of Assisi, patron saint of the animals—how appropriate—renounces his inheritance of the family business, and the wealth associated with that business, and begins a life of poverty.

I've read a book or two on this man's life. St. Francis was a prime example of a person whose objective was to model the life of Jesus. He lived the simple life, renouncing the possessions of this Earth, but wealthy in love for all the Lord's creatures.

He was born and then baptized Giovanni Bernardone, but his father changed his name to Francesco when he was a youth, because his father was involved in a tremendous amount of business with France. Now I ask you, is that the right reason to change your son's name? Well, his daddy, Pietro Bernardone, did for that reason, so now this is Francesco Bernardone.

Francesco grew up in a wealthy family, but seemingly had no use for the family business. He'd rather drink and have fun with his friends, play all day — almost said, "Bang on my drums all day," but that wouldn't be quite accurate. Francesco was a musician, but I seem to recall that he played the violin. At least, I think so. Doesn't matter. What's important is that he was a "party animal," and, to a certain point in his life, had no use for work of any kind.

Pressure from his father caused him to retreat into the woods, and from there, he changed his attitude toward this physical life. There is a lot of uncertainty about the exact date when Francesco became Francis — somewhere in the early years of his retreat from society; however, one thing is for sure: St. Francis of Assisi would be the name he would be most recognized by throughout history.

He was responsible for the establishment of the Franciscan Order. This is an order of monks who live in poverty and basically live in reflection of the image of Jesus and the total renunciation of physical possessions. Now, this was initially considered a new religious order, and ultimately would be accepted by the pope as a "type" of priest. This man, Francis, fought to make this happen and encountered much resistance while establishing this Order.

Today, this order still survives and is under the original rules that Francis established during his life. These were called the Friars Minor rules. This man was truly a saint, and please, read about his life and the reward that was granted him for his faithfulness.

I'm most certain that He is now enjoying the eternal reward we all are eligible to receive. Toward the end of his physical life, he was blessed with "stigmata," the visible signs of the wounds of Christ. There are not many humans that received this sacred gift from the Lord, but Francesco Bernardone was one of the few.

Again, please, if you get the opportunity, read about this amazing example of what we should all strive to be in this plane.

Now, don't get me wrong: Francis totally gave up everything. Not many can do that, but the way he looked at life and the importance of others is what we can imitate and model. Hopefully we can find the love for our fellow human beings that this man displayed, which will assist us in our own test in this plane.

In 1215 AD, the Fourth Lateran Council met and reaffirmed Roman Catholic doctrine strengthening the authority of the pope. Pope Innocent III was pope at the time and guided this Council. Innumerable canons were put in place during this Council, some of which dealt with confession, and formation of religious orders; here are those examples and the basic descriptions of what they covered.

Canon 13 forbade the formation of any new religious order; no more separation from the Church and no more variation of doctrine. Disobedience resulted in immediate excommunication.

Canon 21, the Omnis Utriusque Sexes, dealt with confession, mandating the sacrament once a year for all those of age to cognitively decide between right and wrong. This is sometimes misread and assumed to be interpreted as the "first confession." However, the doctrine is applied to all Catholics within the community; whether is your first confession or your thousandth, once a year is the minimum requirement.

The Catholic religion was at this point in time was seemingly coming apart. This council's whole purpose was to reaffirm doctrine and Canon Law so that there was no misunderstanding about the guidelines on how one would conduct themselves if they were to be a Catholic. There were about a hundred of these "canons" put into effect as a result of this Fourth Lateran Council. If you're interested, they're easy to find; look 'em up.

By 1273 AD, St. Thomas Aquinas had completed his work on "Summa Theoligica." This work is considered a masterpiece of the Middle Ages and is still used as a teaching guide in seminaries throughout the world. Thomas himself was considered one of the foremost philosophers and theologians ever in the history of the Christian faith; I agree with that assessment of his life.

Thomas was responsible for many different works that are currently used in the Catholic and Christian religions. Prayers in particular were his forte, and he was truly prophetic in his insight into Christian theology.

He died shortly after the completion of this "masterpiece," in the year 1274, but his works will live forever.

In 1321 AD, Dante's *Divine Comedy* was introduced into the literary world. Some say that it is the greatest of Christian literature and some disagree; I disagree.

The greatest literary work is the Bible; perhaps Dante's work may be one of the better works to emerge from that period; but the greatest? I think not. In fact, I've read the piece, and I'm not convinced that there is much accuracy to the "stages" contained in his views of heaven, hell, and purgatory.

I think he based the "maps" of these places — heaven, hell, and purgatory — on Jesus' statement that "there are many rooms in my Father's house"… that is true. But Dante then manifested his illusions of these universal planes and placed them into the fragile minds of humanity. But perhaps I'm wrong; I've been wrong a time or two and am not ashamed to admit being wrong. No one is perfect, but everyone's opinion must be considered.

However, I would say it's worth the read, especially if you're reading this, because there are really some similarities in what he wrote and what I am being inspired to write. You can then form your own opinion and believe — or not believe — that his work should deserve to be considered as the number-one greatest literary work of Christianity; I'll tell you why I disagree…

This is what I believe his book did inspire and seed: the separation of the Catholic community into a multitude of new Christian communities at an accelerated pace. From this time, Christianity was looking at an entirely new game: new opinions. All those that had a differing opinion of the secrets contained in these planes of existence, and what would lead you to those levels of existence began to crop up like weeds. No longer would one man's (Jesus') opinion be the foundation of the Church, humanity was now going to embrace Dante's opinion and run with it, causing the Catholic faith to be set into a whirlwind of the new denominations, which would surface thought the next several centuries...

Yes, his work — my opinion, mind you — was really the beginning of the end of solidarity in the Catholic religion. I do not want any changes or new denominations to be a result of this work.

I merely want to bring back into the fold any lost souls I can, and help them understand how we got to this place in "time."

And time has changed the way we look at this once pure and unified religion. There are now a multitude of sects, cults, and denominations in our current era, and I believe they were mainly fueled by this "work" of Dante. There was a small smolder going, but this "work" was like adding gasoline to that little fire. And from that inferno — sorry, couldn't help myself! — would come the destruction caused by all fires. But fire is sometimes necessary for rebirth and change. Sometimes the change is good, sometimes the change is not so good.

I believe that this change was "not so good." There was no need for anyone to analyze Catholicism any further or "invent" any new divisions of the original basic religion. These people were looking for the truth, but they were looking in the wrong places. They should have been looking where the truth is contained, in the masterpiece we all overlook: the Bible. But from that time, 1321, and through the next 650-plus years, many reformations would take place. Many new assumed truths would emerge, and many new revolutionists would take their leave of this formerly unified Church.

Sure, the Eastern and Western churches were split, but they shared the same basic beliefs, differing only on minor issues. This work, *The Divine Comedy*, was the beginning of all the changes yet to come and the start of all the issues. These issues were going to be more than minor differences in dates of events or leadership; they were to be significant changes.

The first significant change happened in 1517 AD.

Martin Luther posted his "ninety-five theses," a simple invitation for debate among scholars that ultimately would become the "hinge of history."

These "theses" are ninety-five statements of Martin Luther's opinion of the Church, and the attack on the practices and beliefs of the Catholic Church; and it focused mainly on the authority of the pope. This was the heaviest blow that truly started the Reformation of the Christian churches.

Luther actually nailed his theses to the door of the Wittenberg Church. The document contained attacks on papal abuses and the sale of indulgences by church officials, because at that time, man's greed overwhelmed his path to righteousness. Yes, this was a time when money talked and bullshit walked. Sorry, had to say it...

Luther was, in my opinion, correct in some aspects of his theses. However, he went a bit too far in his condemnation of the pope's authority. The basics surrounding this "theses" are the belief that the Gospel — and belief in the Gospel — was all a person needed to be one with God in His Trinity. Luther put aside the need for any spiritual intervention from another human. He believed that priests were not a necessary tool for confession or absolution from sin. He believed that a pope and bishops were also unnecessary positions within the Church.

Now, this confuses me immensely, because the Gospel specifically states that Jesus gave authority to His apostles to either forgive sin or hold sin bound; remember, we saw that in the chapter "Mice to Men." So, if his thesis is correct, what happened to that verse in the gospel? Also, didn't Jesus appoint Peter, Simon, to be the Rock on which He built His Church? And shouldn't this Rock lead the sheep throughout the life of this said Church? That's in there, too!

So, the entire Reformation of the Church, the Lutherans, the Baptists, the Protestants, the Born-agains, and all the rest, a total of about 2,600, were a direct result of Martin Luther's Ninety-Five Theses, along with Dante's *Divine Comedy*.

The biggest issue I have with these two is that the individual gets to determine if he or she is on the right path to pass the test. We are very fragile, and sometimes we rationalize our sinfulness away. We have a tendency to dismiss the guilt that we should indeed have for the offense of our sin. I don't want to sugarcoat anything here, but those "spiritual guides" need to be there to help us realize the wrongful ways of our life. I wholeheartedly disagree with these two changes in the approach to the Christian faith.

And, I suppose, through the centuries these religious sects also realized that there was a need for some spiritual intervention because they do have ministers. But their "flocks" are subject to that minister's own moralistic values. There is no "rock" on which these denominations are built, only theses and maps.

Take, for example... 1534 AD.

Henry VIII appointed himself head of the Church of England because he disagreed with the pope on the issue of the number of wives a man could have. Henry had six... five too many, but Henry didn't want to hear that he was going to be damned to hell for his lustful ways. No, Henry just proclaimed himself as the one who could make that decision. This is another fault with these religious sects that were generated from the Great Martin Luther's theses.

Henry insisted that all the subjects sign a document proclaiming him as the head of his new church. This is when St. Thomas More, who was a religious counselor to Henry, refused to sign. Henry had him executed in 1535 because of his refusal. Thomas became a martyr and a saint that day because of this, and was officially canonized in 1935. But when someone gives his or her life for the faith, they are immediately given this title in heaven.

In 1536 AD, John Calvin published *The Institutes of the Christian Religion*, and Calvinism is born, an offshoot of the Lutheran religion.

Calvinism is the insistence on the literal translation of the Christian Scriptures. If anything was not contained explicitly in the Scriptures, it was immediately rejected; but if it was, it was followed unwaveringly... so they say!

Calvin decided to establish this Church and divide it into four levels. The first of these Calvinism churches was in Geneva, and the organization is as follows:

> Pastors
>
> Teachers
>
> Elders
>
> Deacons

Calvin, unlike Luther, understood from the start that there was a need for organization and authority in his newly founded church. But he also agreed with Luther that there was no need for a single authority figurehead, which was the mistake in his organizational chart that added to the ultimate confusion.

From a structural and formational standpoint, this is not the way the Christian church was originally designed to work. I keep hearing, "feed my sheep"; there are many shepherds, but no Good Shepherd, no rock, no foundation. No one to lead the group causes the group to stray, just like a flock without a shepherd.

Conceptually, the Calvinism religion was with merit, obedience to the Scripture. However, by this point in time — and in fact, from the beginning of time — literal interpretation is subjective to an individual's own reason and motivation. That is the reason for the "Rock," the Good Shepherd, the pope... praise be to you, Jesus, and thanks for looking over my shoulder today!

God doesn't care which religion you chose to practice, He only cares about you wanting to save your soul, and to do this, you must obey His commandments. You must actively — with all your heart, mind, and soul — strive to accomplish your salvation. He sent Jesus, His Son, to paint the picture on how we were to act in order to accomplish this task. However, because mankind "forgets," there must be someone to remind them what their real goals are in this life.

There is only one more place we need to see before the end of this book. The next several hundred years of history are the years when humanity becomes civilized. Many more of these variations of the Christian faith are going to occur…

In 1870 AD, Pope Pius IX proclaims the doctrine of papal infallibility; Jesus was infallible and so are His successors… the popes.

The pope is the "vicar" of Christ. That means that he is the living and breathing human Christ in this plane of existence. It also means that he is the earthly representative of Jesus Himself.

Infallibility of the pope specifically pertains to doctrine of the Catholic Church. The Christian community that you belong to is insignificant in the eyes of God, if — and only if — you follow the laws of Christ and His earthly and present-day vicar.

Finally, the current pope, Pope Francis I, who is in command of the Christian faith at this present time, will be a saint. He is truly righteous in the eyes of God. His beliefs in how we, as humans, are to conduct ourselves are without any question in accordance with His house and house rules.

Chapter 22

We're Done...

But first, the summary: Romans 13:8–10.

"Let no debt remain outstanding, except the continuing debt to love one another, for whoever loves others has fulfilled the law. The commandments, "You shall not commit adultery," "You shall not murder," "You shall not steal," "You shall not covet," and whatever other command there may be, are summed up in this one command: "Love your neighbor as yourself." Love does no harm to a neighbor. Therefore, love is the fulfillment of the law."

This book is now complete. This was for your benefit and actually mine, as well. I've learned so much on this journey of life and thank God from the bottom of my heart for allowing me to write this book for you.

I pray for you all and hope that all of you will succeed in this test.

Thank you and have a holy and blessed day.

The Answers

The only two sinless humans:

Jesus Christ

Mary the Mother of God

Literal truth defined:

We can most certainly take all the words of the Bible as the literal truth. Some individuals do, in fact, do this. Example: an eye for an eye and a tooth for a tooth. Some interpret this as meaning revenge to those who hurt you. Read on, and you will see that this is not the case; however, some stop at the point that satisfies their personal needs and interpret what they wish to be true.

But the literal interpretation of the Bible is based on each person's moral fiber and their desire to either pass or fail this test. The Bible is written so that the literal truth of every word is contained for each and every individual in existence. Each person must find the truth for him- or herself and not have someone else define the truth for them — and that is the literal truth.

www.ingramcontent.com/pod-product-compliance
Lightning Source LLC
Chambersburg PA
CBHW060906120626
46553CB00001B/221